KU-732-514

'Ultimately, it is through the winding process of self-repair that we get to share in the character's journey of self-understanding in this altogether human novel' *Irish Times*, Best New Translated Novels 2020

'A surreal employment odyssey ... Recommended for anyone missing time in the office' *Monocle*

'Delightful and disturbing in equal measure ... Mesmeric, funny, wry, delightful – this is a novel to help the millennials find their own paths through the world they've inherited' *Lunate*

'It feels pretty timely, as we consider the workplace and the purpose of work in our lives at a time of cultural and societal upheaval ... We move through absurdist tableaux and moments of deadpan, existential drama, but it's Tsumura's incisive eye on the small, everyday office stresses so many will find deeply relatable that kept me captivated. The neo-liberal work-life fantasy is obliterated so beautifully' *Dazed*

'Translated in a droll and understated style by Polly Barton, part of the novel's appeal lies in the narrator's distinct worldview and her deadpan humor that allows the surreal, metaphysical connections in the novel to bubble beneath the surface of her seemingly dull, day-to-day existence' *Japan Times*

'A wise, comical and exceptionally relatable novel on finding meaning and purpose in our work lives' Zeba Talkhani, author of *My Past is a Foreign Country*

'Quietly hilarious and deeply attuned to the uncanny rhythms and deadpan absurdity of the daily grind, Kikuko Tsumara's postmodern existential workplace saga both skewers and celebrates our deeply human need to function in society and keep surviving in an oftentimes senseless-seeming world'
Sharlene Teo, author of *Ponti*

'Read it before you burn out'
Asahi Shimbun Weekly AERA

'The fantastical flavour of this book is one of its charms ... This is a masterpiece of a book about the working world' Kentaro Tomoda, *Bunshun Toshokan*

'Spending time in the author's unique world, which seems so bizarre and random but is in fact artfully designed, I found myself healed and restored'
Kazufumi Watanabe, *Asahi Shimbun*

'Tsumura's novel is a pleasing, quietly enjoyable slice of fiction with a message for those who give themselves entirely to work, no matter how rewarding it may be' A Life In Books

'Completely different to anything I've read before ... there is an almost dreamlike feeling to the story'
Life With All the Books

KIKUKO TSUMURA was born in Osaka, Japan, where she still lives today. In her first job out of college, Tsumura experienced workplace harassment and quit after ten months to retrain and find another position, an experience that inspired her to write stories about young workers. She has won numerous Japanese literary awards including the Akutagawa Prize and the Noma Literary New Face Prize, and her first short story translated into English, 'The Water Tower and the Turtle', won a PEN/Robert J. Dau Short Story Prize for Emerging Writers. The Japanese Ministry of Education, Culture, Sports, Science and Technology recognised Tsumura's work with a New Artist award in 2016. *There's No Such Thing as an Easy Job* is her first novel to be translated into English.

POLLY BARTON is a translator of Japanese literature and non-fiction, based in the UK. Stories she has translated have appeared in *Words Without Borders*, *Granta* and the *White Review*. Full-length translations include *Spring Garden* by Tomoka Shibasaki and *Where the Wild Ladies Are* by Aoko Matsuda. After being awarded the 2019 Fitzcarraldo Editions Essay Prize, she published the non-fiction work *Fifty Sounds* in April 2021.

There's No Such Thing As An Easy Job

KIKUKO TSUMURA

Translated from the Japanese by
Polly Barton

BLOOMSBURY PUBLISHING
LONDON · OXFORD · NEW YORK · NEW DELHI · SYDNEY

BLOOMSBURY PUBLISHING
Bloomsbury Publishing Plc
50 Bedford Square, London, WC1B 3DP, UK
29 Earlsfort Terrace, Dublin 2, Ireland

BLOOMSBURY, BLOOMSBURY PUBLISHING and the
Diana logo are trademarks of Bloomsbury Publishing Plc

Konoyoni Tayasui Shigoto Wa Nai written by Kikuko Tsumura.
Copyright © 2015 by Kikuko Tsumura. All rights reserved.
Originally published in Japan by Nikkei Publishing Inc. (renamed Nikkei
Business Publications, Inc. from April 1, 2020), Tokyo
This English language edition published by arrangement with Nikkei
Publishing Inc. (renamed Nikkei Business Publications, Inc. from April 1, 2020),
Tokyo c/o Tuttle-Mori Agency, Inc., Tokyo
First published in Great Britain 2020
Copyright © Kikuko Tsumura, 2020
Translation © Polly Barton, 2020

Kikuko Tsumura has asserted her right under the Copyright, Designs and
Patents Act, 1988, to be identified as Author of this work

All rights reserved. No part of this publication may be reproduced or
transmitted in any form or by any means, electronic or mechanical, including
photocopying, recording, or any information storage or retrieval system,
without prior permission in writing from the publishers

This book has been selected to receive financial assistance from English PEN's
PEN Translates programme, supported by Arts Council England. English
PEN exists to promote literature and our understanding of it, to uphold writers'
freedoms around the world, to campaign against the persecution and imprison-
ment of writers for stating their views, and to promote the friendly co-operation
of writers and the free exchange of ideas: www.englishpen.org.

A catalogue record for this book is available from the British Library

ISBN: TPB: 978-1-5266-2224-2; eBook: 978-1-5266-2223-5;
PB: 978-1-5266-2225-9

6 8 10 9 7 5

Typeset by Integra Software Services Pvt. Ltd
Printed and bound in Great Britain by CPI Group (UK) Ltd, Croydon CR0 4YY

To find out more about our authors and books visit www.bloomsbury.com and
sign up for our newsletters

CONTENTS

The Surveillance Job

Both screens showed the same person. The footage
on the left-hand screen dated from 22:00 the previous night, and the footage on the right-hand screen
from 20:00 the night before that. In both, the person
was wearing the exact same fleece jacket, so without
the little date stamp in the corner there'd be no way
of knowing that there was a day separating the two
images. And in both, the person – or the target of
surveillance, I should say – was doing pretty much the
same thing: sitting on an office chair, staring at a laptop
screen with arms folded across his chest. Just when I
would think he'd given up on the idea of ever moving
again, he'd reach out for the keyboard without warning
and hammer away furiously for thirty seconds before
sinking back into repose, or pull out his dictionary and
consult it with a look of profound weariness, or open
up his browser and sit scrolling with grim focus for
the next hour. In the older footage, on the right-hand
screen, he'd eaten a meal about two hours ago: fried
eggs and ham, accompanied by rice cooked with hijiki
and spinach miso soup. In the one on the left, from

yesterday, he hadn't yet ventured from his computer. I was sitting there watching him, just as frozen to the spot as he was. The text editor window was open, but so far, I'd not written a single word of my report.

Observing the target eating his dinner earlier, I'd decided to go and get something to eat too, but a long time had elapsed since then and I'd done nothing about it. Somehow reluctant to get up, I'd been sitting in the exact same position for at least an hour and a half. Just as my hunger pangs were getting too strong to ignore and I lifted my bum from the seat with a mind to go to the shop, I sensed movement in the right-hand screen. The target, who until now had been sitting in an identical posture to his double in the left-hand screen, practically leapt out of his chair and hurried in the direction of the front door. Thinking it must be a visitor of some kind, I switched the right-hand monitor over to show the image from the camera in the entrance hall. I watched as the target bowed repeatedly to a woman in uniform, who looked like she was from some kind of courier service, then as he promptly closed the door and marched out of frame, carrying a box. The box was cube-shaped, neither very large nor very small, the sort of size perfect for carrying in both hands. The target often received deliveries of books or DVDs, but judging by the box, this was something different.

I switched the screen back to the footage of his desk, figuring he was about to return to his computer, but there was no sign of him there. Next, I checked the kitchen camera where I found him setting the box down on the corner of the smallish dining table and going at it eagerly with a pair of scissors.

I squinted at the image on the screen. Of course I didn't really believe for a second that the target was about to receive another delivery of contraband, but each time he was handed a parcel at the door, I found myself growing tense nonetheless. The target opened the box, flung the bubble wrap on the floor and pulled out a bag. I held my breath and zoomed in to see it better: Mrs XX's Oven-Fresh Cookies. Ignoring the strips of bubble wrap strewn across the floor, the target retrieved a large plate from the drying rack by the sink and began to arrange the cookies on top of it, classifying them into piles according to shape. He looked very content. It seemed the cookies came in five different varieties, including square, round and leaf-shaped types. Just one variety was dark brown in colour, which I assumed must be the chocolate-flavoured ones – these the target heaped up at a little distance from the others. Then he selected a cookie and bit into it.

Unlike the target on the right-hand screen, who was approaching the zenith of human happiness, the target on the left-hand monitor continued to stare at his computer screen, arms folded across his chest. His head lolled heavily for a second, then a moment later he righted himself. He must have dropped off earlier.

'I *told* you not to do that! It makes it too hard to tell,' I hissed at him. The basic rule we'd been given was

3

not to fast-forward the footage, the only exception to this being when the target was sleeping. So, theoretically speaking, I could have fast-forwarded the section where he dropped off. But when the target's sleeping posture was the exact same as his waking one, there was literally no way of knowing when he'd gone to sleep – which meant having to sit through bits that I could, by rights, have skipped. I wished he'd stop doing it, basically.

'Are you alright in there?'

Hearing my griping, Mrs Ōizumi – who worked in the next booth along – peered through the gap in the partitioning screen between us.

I nodded, making a series of non-committal noises. 'Mm, uh-hmm.'

'Okay, well, I'm off home then. I'll see you tomorrow,' she said, coiling a scarf around her neck. Then she left the room with a slightly harried expression. Mrs Ōizumi was a mother and a homemaker. She came into work after dropping her primary school daughter at an after-school club and left around the time the club finished.

20:35 – Target receives a 25 cm x 25 cm cardboard box from a delivery company containing packaging material (bubble wrap) and confectionery.

I typed this into the text editor, sighed, then opened up the desk drawer and took out a bottle of eye drops.

Before starting this job, I rarely had any use for eye drops, but now I found myself getting through an awful lot. Not just that, but I'd developed a taste for the slightly more expensive variety. I'd soon figured out that the best way of accommodating this extravagance was to buy up the luxurious, 198-yen-a-pop bottles in large quantities whenever I saw them on sale. As luck would have it, we were allowed eye drops as expenses for this job, up to a maximum of 1,000 yen per week. Our meals, however, we had to pay for ourselves. Recently, I'd started pondering the fact that, up front, a bottle of eye drops was actually cheaper than a yakisoba roll. But then there was the chance that if I went overboard with the eye drops, I might have dry eye syndrome by the time I left this job; so if I factored in long-term as well as upfront costs, it was possible that a yakisoba roll was actually more reasonable over a certain number of years. But then there were all the additives and preservatives in the yakisoba roll to think about – I couldn't rule out that they might actually take an even greater and more costly toll on my health than dry eye syndrome would. So it was impossible to say at this stage which would work out more economical in the end.

I know, I know. This was the train of thought of a person with far too much time on their hands. But guess what: with this job, I did have too much time on my hands. It was weird because I worked such long hours, and yet, even while working, I was basically doing nothing. I'd come to the conclusion that there were very few jobs in the world that ate up as much time and as little brainpower as watching over the life of a novelist who lived alone and worked from home.

I applied the eye drops, but even that didn't really pep me up in the desired way, so I paused the monitors and lurched unsteadily to my feet. It wasn't real-time surveillance I was engaged in because all the footage was pre-recorded, so I was allowed to stop and start when I liked. The only stipulation was that I had to check all of the footage from the hours when the target was at home. In other words, the longer that the target was in the house for, the more work there was for me. This particular target went to bed around 6 a.m. and woke at 2 p.m., which was on the long side as far as sleep patterns went, but to counterbalance that, he spent a hell of a lot of time at home. I had to check all that footage at its original speed, meaning I spent the best part of the day in this booth of mine. Once you were used to the job, you were allowed to check two days' worth of footage simultaneously, but even so, the amount of time a self-employed person spent at home was not to be underestimated. I lived right across the street from the office, so my commute was a breeze, but when you weren't allowed to go home, the issue of how close your house was to your work-place became more or less moot. The benefit was that because I barely encountered anyone while working, I didn't need to give my appearance much thought, so sometimes, I'd throw a coat over my pyjamas and head to work like that. And on days when I had the time, I would pop back home and eat dinner before returning to the office.

This whole situation had come to be because I'd sat down one day in front of my recruiter and informed her that I wanted a job as close as possible to my house – ideally, something along the lines of sitting all day in a chair, overseeing the extraction of collagen for use in skincare products. I didn't really think she'd be able to oblige, but I figured I had nothing to lose by asking. I'd quit my previous job after I developed burnout syndrome, and had gone back to living with my parents in order to recuperate. After a while, my unemployment insurance ran out and I figured I'd better start looking for another job. I'd left my last job because it sucked up every scrap of energy I had until there was not a shred left, but at the same time, I sensed that hanging around doing nothing forever probably wasn't the answer either. In short, I felt pretty confused about whether I wanted to go back to work or not, and that was why I'd come out with that line to the recruiter, which sounded like I thought the whole thing was a joke. As soon as it was out of my mouth, I figured it was going to get me in trouble. But instead, Mrs Masakado shot me a knowing glance that seemed totally out of place with her otherwise meek manner.

'I've got just the thing for you!'

I swear I saw her glasses glint, like they do when cartoon characters come out with these kinds of lines. Then she handed me the description for this job. There was no denying that it was exactly the type of thing I was looking for. Yet, as fate would have it, it turned out to have its own specialised set of hardships.

Yamae Yamamoto, the guy I'd been assigned to watch over, earned his living as a writer. Unbeknown to him, he had been entrusted with some kind of smuggled goods by an acquaintance. I knew that as contraband went, this was hot stuff, but they wouldn't tell an underling like me exactly what it was. I'd been informed that the contraband was hidden away in a DVD case, but that Yamae Yamamoto's film collection was so ridiculously extensive that they were unable to locate the case in question during the unofficial shakedown they'd given the place while the target was out. Instead, they'd installed a bunch of cameras in there, and now we were watching out for when his acquaintance would come by to collect it, or else for when, by some miracle, Yamae Yamamoto decided to sort through his DVD collection and come across the contraband himself. There was a possibility that given the size of Yamae Yamamoto's collection, he may well have lost track of which of his DVDs were borrowed. Also, since the individual who'd handed over the contraband had so far managed to evade arrest – thanks to Yamae Yamamoto's oblivious guardianship – it was also conceivable that he or she might think to entrust him with another load. That was what I'd been told by my supervisor, Mr Someya. Hence my having to be on high alert whenever a delivery came.

At the beginning, I was under the impression that monitoring the evidently harmless Yamae Yamamoto had to be a relatively cushy assignment as far as this line of work went. In actual fact, though, not only did Yamae Yamamoto spend a huge amount of time in the house, but he got tons of deliveries – and his DVD-watching habits were highly erratic. Just when you were thinking he had settled in happily to watch *Toy Story 2*, he'd suddenly change over and start watching the third-place play-off for the 2006 German World Cup. For that reason, Mr Someya sometimes stepped in to help me out. Mr Someya was a slight man in his fifties, with a gentle manner of speaking. He was always, always at work, no matter the hour of day, and sometimes I caught sight of him in the kitchen sitting perfectly still, a cup of his kelp tea in one hand, which made me think that I really shouldn't be calling on him for too much help. It wasn't just his health I was worried about, either. I'd heard that during his thirty years working here, he had watched over fish so big they made Yamae Yamamoto seem like a krill's little toenail, and so a fear of distracting him from his other, more important projects was another major reason for not relying on him too much. Plus, I'd heard credible-sounding rumours to the effect that, if I was to catch this Yamae Yamamoto guy finding the contraband, or spot his acquaintance coming to collect it, I'd receive a huge bonus. And, needless to say, money was of utmost importance to me right now. I had no idea when I might burn out next.

I walked down the clean, clinical-looking corridor, its fluorescent lights disconcertingly bright, until I reached the stairs at the far end and descended to the basement shop. The building didn't have a basement, exactly – it was just the shop which was underground, like it had been created in some kind of sinkhole. As might be expected in a place whose entire raison d'être was to check surveillance footage around the clock, the lights in the building stayed on throughout the night. They weren't the regular fluorescent lights you found in shops, either, but light fixtures used in the 'white night' nations. Spend a lot of time here, and you soon started to feel your sense of night and day melting away.

But the lighting in the basement shop, which was about the size of an average single bedroom, was disconcertingly dim, even in the daytime. It was like the building contained two different zones: the shop, and everywhere else. Actually, given the choice, I'd have preferred to be working in the shop, I thought conspiratorially as I placed my yakisoba roll and a plastic bottle of maté down on the counter. Both of these items were needless expenses. Okay, granted, in order to make a yakisoba roll, I'd have to first stir-fry the noodles with cabbage and then find a roll to stuff them in, so the expense was, perhaps, justified. But the maté I could easily have made at home if I only had the leaves, so forking out for a plastic bottle of the stuff brought with it a sense of defeat.

'I'll take these.' Even my voice had a glum ring to it.

'That's 290 yen, please!' said the shop lady. She sounded surprisingly businesslike for 9 p.m. on a Thursday night. Whenever I went into the shop, it was always this same woman working there. Just like with Mr Someya, I had my doubts about whether she ever actually went home.

I returned to my workspace carrying the clear plastic bag containing the yakisoba roll, whose only marking was its eat-before date, and the bottle of maté. All the bakery products sold in the shop came wrapped in plain plastic like this, which gave no indication of who made them, and all of them were pretty good. I wondered if there was a company whose job it was to supply these kinds of small, independent shops with baked goods.

I decided to watch for two more hours, then go home. Once I get home, I told myself, I'll order some maté leaves online. I didn't have time to go out and buy them. Although, given how much time I spent in this building, it wasn't clear whether I'd be able to take delivery at home. Maybe I could just get them delivered here? I'd have to ask Mr Someya about it.

11

'Ah, I'm afraid I can't give you permission for that. We just don't have enough hands right now.' As he shook his head, Mr Someya jogged the ruler resting on top of the report up and down. He used the ruler when reading through the daily surveillance reports, holding it under the individual characters to make sure he didn't miss anything. I'd done the same thing when I had a part-time job as a proofreader while at university. Noting how thoroughly he read the reports, I began to regret how little I wrote for mine. But the fact was, Yamae Yamamoto barely ever moved. What was I supposed to say?

'I'll make sure that I collect the package myself. It won't affect anybody else.'

'It'd be fine if it was just you, but if I give you permission then I'll have to give it to everybody, and you'll end up being the post lady. An unpaid post lady.'

'I don't mind. I've only just joined, so it seems fair. Call it an initiation rite.'

'You say that now, but do you realise that'd be over fifty people's stuff you'd be in charge of sorting, if they all started ordering? That'd be a serious impediment to your regular work.'

'Are there really over fifty people working here?'

Granted, it was a three-storey building, large enough to conceivably accommodate that number of employees, but the only people I ever saw were Mr Someya, Mrs Ōizumi and the woman from the shop, so I found it hard to swallow this as reality.

'Yep.' Mr Someya nodded, glancing down at his report, then looked back at me and said quietly, 'So I'm sorry, but we're going to have to keep the office a no-delivery zone.'

He coughed and went back to checking the report. Unable to offer up a more forceful objection, I left the room. The building didn't have any large open-plan spaces like a regular company. Instead, it was divided up into lots of little rooms, perhaps to help people concentrate on their targets. I'd heard that your room got larger as you ascended the pecking order, but being in my second week and still on probation, I was sharing a room with Mrs Ōizumi.

I made my way back to my room along the empty corridor, disconsolate in the glare of its lights. I hit play to see Yamae Yamamoto, apparently done with his work, turning on his TV and starting to watch a programme he had recorded: *NCIS*. The female special agent wasn't the Mossad one, so I guessed it must be either the first or the second series. I'd only ever watched post-Mossad Officer *NCIS*, so I squinted at Yamae Yamamoto's screen for a while, trying to fathom what was happening, but without sound it was supremely hard to make head or tail of it. The people who'd wired Yamae Yamamoto's flat had fitted it with a mic system, but it had turned out to be defective.

As I was sitting brooding over the fact that I couldn't mail order my tea, and how I didn't know whether it was season one or two of *NCIS* that my target was watching, Yamae Yamamoto paused the episode and galloped towards the door, leaving me alone in my grief. Unlike the cookie occasion, this time he brought the paper bag he'd been handed straight back to his desk and took out a small square box from inside, which he began to examine with evident fascination. The box had a big sticker on the side: Maté. Reflexively, I found myself baring my teeth and glowering, until I could feel the expression on my face had become one of ultimate distaste. Of all the items in the world, he had to go and order just the thing I wanted and couldn't have. I felt like calling him up and screaming down the phone at him, *Hand that maté over right now!* Not that I knew his phone number, of course.

Turning over the box in his hands, Yamae Yamamoto examined its fine print in detail. It was like footage beamed in from a zoo: monkey handles maté! Maybe this was the first time he'd ever seen the real thing. Once he'd read all there was to read on the box, he placed it a little distance away from him and admired it from afar. *Doing that isn't going to multiply its contents, you know,* I told him. *It won't get you a cup of tea, either.*

As I sat there making pathetic little jibes about everything that Yamae Yamamoto was doing, I remembered that there was, in fact, the possibility that the maté box contained a fresh load of contraband, and switched to scrutinising it with narrowed eyes. Yamae Yamamoto took the box to his desk, connected to the Wi-Fi and opened up his browser. Into the search engine that popped up as his home page, he entered the words 'Maté tea'. *Do some bloody work, man.* But Yamae Yamamoto ignored me, moving down the list of maté-related sites, opening one after another, craning his neck, leaning in to peer at them, bookmarking certain pages. I felt sure this wasn't related to my surveillance operation, but I zoomed in on the page he was absorbed in anyway to find an article about how Uruguayans drink over two kilos of maté every month. Wow, I found myself exhaling, admiringly. That was a hell of a lot of maté to get through in a month.

Yamae Yamamoto went on researching maté for the best part of an hour. *It's because you do this kind of thing that you're making such poor progress with your work,* I counselled him in my head, but then I stopped and remembered my own habits. After getting home from work, it wasn't unheard of for me to while away the precious window of time afforded me looking endlessly at things of no consequence on the internet. I pulled the block memo over towards me and wrote myself the following message:

Remember how silly you find the target's time-wasting, and don't do it yourself.

I tore off the note and put it in my pocket.

In fact, considering what Yamae Yamamoto did for a living, I couldn't say out of hand that spending an hour gathering knowledge about maté was a total waste of his time. I didn't know how much of a big deal he was as a novelist, but every time I zoomed in on his screen, he appeared to be writing about something entirely different. If yesterday he was writing about a favourite restaurant of his, today he'd be writing about colonialism. The words he looked up in the dictionary were varied too, from 'collocative' to 'superaffluence'. The only thing I felt confident in asserting about Yamae Yamamoto was that he had no idea that he was in possession of some highly illegal substance. From the way he seemed to make little headway with his work, and the melancholy expression that came over his face when he looked at his direct debit payments, to his distinct lack of progress through the names on his 'List of People to Contact', he certainly seemed to have his fair share of worries – but I'd never seen him do anything to suggest concern that there might be some smoking-hot contraband secreted somewhere in his flat.

As I said, Yamae Yamamoto went to bed at six in the morning and woke up at two in the afternoon. That meant he was awake for sixteen hours a day. Because he didn't have an office, his waking hours were more or less equal to the hours he spent at home, with the exception of a two-hour window between 18:00 and 20:00 when he was usually out. It appeared that during this time, he would go for a walk or buy groceries. It was Mrs Ōizumi's job to monitor the footage from the surveillance cameras positioned along his preferred route and inside his supermarket of choice, and she told me that there were never any furtive meetings with people or other suspicious happenings. He just walked and deliberated about what to buy.

In fact, I'd heard from Mrs Ōizumi that it was perfectly normal for him to spend over an hour in the supermarket. She told me about a recent occasion when he spent thirty minutes standing in the preserved goods section, weighing up which jar of sweet-and-sour marinated mushrooms to buy. He was torn between a relatively smaller jar of more expensive, domestically grown mushrooms and a bigger jar of the cheaper, Chinese-made kind. He'd decide on one, and put it in his basket, only to return it to the shelf again. His indecision was clearly so agonising, Mrs Ōizumi told me, that she was itching to go in and just buy a jar for him. From what I could gather, Mrs Ōizumi wasn't all that well off herself, so that was saying something. She was working here in order to raise fees for her daughter's cram school, and before this job, she had been fired from seven other part-time positions. This was the only one she'd managed to keep for any reasonable length of time.

Seven was kind of amazing, I thought as I gazed at the screens, when I heard her voice behind me. 'Bye, see you tomorrow.'

'Oh, bye,' I said, spinning my chair around – and instead of asking her about the jobs that she'd been sacked from, I started to say, 'By the way, I found out

that we're not allowed to have our post sent here, I
had no idea,' in a tone which I hoped conveyed that I
was able to do so at my previous work, and which also
suggested I needed to have a very important document
delivered.

'Are you wanting to order something online?' Mrs
Ōizumi said, without batting an eyelid.

'Well, actually, yes, as it happens.'

'Yeah. The girl doing this job before you wanted
to order anime DVDs, but she was at work such long
hours that she couldn't get them delivered to her
home.'

'What happened with her, then?'

'Oh, I think she's taking a break. She'll be back at
some point, I imagine.' As she said this, Mrs Ōizumi
glanced at the clock on the wall. 'But I'm sure part of
the trouble was the fact that it was DVDs. I mean, the
person in the next room along once had a cheesecake
delivered all the way from Hokkaido to eat on the job,
and Mr Someya orders in fluorescent ink that he uses.'

'But how can they do that if they're not allowed to
get post delivered?'

'The woman in the shop orders it in for them,' Mrs
Ōizumi turned to glance at the clock again, as if she
was eager to get away. 'But it's limited to one brand
per item, and only the things that she judges people
really need. See you tomorrow!'

She raised a hand and waved, then left the room at
a clip. It was really hard to work out if she was a kind

person or a brusque one. I guessed that at heart she was kind, but when she sensed a potential obstacle in her way, she became brusque. Which, when I really thought about it, just made her a normal member of the human race.

I paused the video, left the room and hurried to the shop, still doubting that what Mrs Ōizumi said could possibly be true. But anyway, if it was time for Mrs Ōizumi to be leaving, then it was more or less time for my dinner. Just as it was yesterday and earlier at lunch today, the shop was dimly lit. Now, though, as I looked carefully around, I saw a cluster of fluorescent inks in the corner of the stationery section, and a sign hanging by the rack with tights and men's socks that read 'Cheesecake 50% Off! Nearing Best Before Date'. All of the pencils had pictures of constellations on them, like the kind you'd buy as souvenirs from a planetarium, and all the tissues were of a particular brand advertised as being 'kind on the nose'. There were big bundles of blank DVDs and a load of 2B mechanical pencils. The money envelopes for weddings and funerals were not the standard-issue red and white designs, but the more expensive kind with fancy paper ribbons in several different colours. Hidden away, right in the corner of the shop, was a pile of about ten copies of a book entitled *Meditation to Relax the Mind*. Admittedly, there were a few different brands of consumable staples like bread and onigiri and drinks, but it did indeed seem like everything else they only came in one type.

'I never noticed you sold books before.'

'Yes. When those have all sold out, we'll get another title in,' the shop lady replied briskly. She was definitely friendly, but something about her manner suggested that underneath all the friendliness lay a vast lake of obstinacy.

'If possible, I'd like you to order in some maté tea. Not the ready-made stuff, I mean, but the leaves.'

'Okay.' In no time at all, she'd pulled out her tablet and was opening up a mail-order site. 'Which would you like?'

After deliberating for a long time, I selected the third-cheapest kind from the lengthy list of maté teas on offer. Using her tablet now as a writing surface, the shop lady took out a piece of paper and jotted a note for herself. 'I'll put in the request to my boss for you.'

'Oh, you mean it isn't you who decides?'

'No, unfortunately not!'

'Ah, I see, right.' Feeling strangely awed by the system they had in place, I made to leave, but then changed my mind. Now I was down here I might as well buy something, I thought, and picked up a roll filled with sweet bean jam and margarine, and a bottle of maté.

'That'll be 300 yen!'

Sheesh, I thought as I handed over the money, 150 yen for a sweet bean jam and margarine roll. Mounting the stairs, I wondered if maybe the shop wasn't a little bit too profit-oriented. I sat down at my desk and ate

the roll, which didn't disappoint. Even worth paying
that bit more for, arguably. On both the right and left
screens, Yamae Yamamoto seemed in worse shape than
usual. He had reclined his office chair as far back as it
would go, eyes still fixed on his screen. He was only
managing to write about a line an hour. After the roll I
was doing considerably better, but now I started to feel
a bit concerned for him.

The long hours, the sitting still all the time, the intense
boredom – once I got started on this job's bad points
I could have gone on forever, but of course it had its
perks too. For example, the amount of time I had to
spend talking to my colleagues was extremely min-
imal. Then there was the fact that Mr Someya was
the only superior around, so all his subordinates were
at the same level, which made working relationships a
lot easier. Also, Mr Someya wasn't at all high-handed,
and as long as you carried out the surveillance work
properly and wrote him decent reports, you could get
away without being pulled up for anything. Going by
his permanently exhausted expression, and the way a
fresh can of plum-flavoured kelp tea appeared on the
shelf in the staff kitchen every three days, it seemed
highly possible he simply didn't have the strength left
in him for anger. Knowing full well it was wrong of

me, I stole a bit of his kelp tea one day, just to try it out, and it was so tasty that I could understand the impulse to drink it all the time. I was just concerned about what it must be doing to his sodium levels. Having said that, though, I'd never once seen any evidence of Mr Someya eating actual meals, so it seemed possible that he drank the tea as a kind of food substitute. An alarming thought. It would certainly explain his slender build, but I prayed it wasn't true.

At my previous workplace I often had trouble deciding what I wanted to eat for lunch, but that problem vanished not long after starting this job, which was another plus point. The solution was simple: I realised that when I didn't know what to eat, I could just replicate whatever Yamae Yamamoto was eating. Of course, because the scope of my culinary activity was limited to visiting the convenience store and popping back home for a short while, I couldn't always fix exactly the same things Yamae Yamamoto did with all his leisure time, but at the very least, his meals served as an inspiration for me. If he rustled up a winter hotpot with pork strips, tofu and kimchi, then I could create a poor man's version by buying some fried tofu and pork-stuffed cabbage rolls from the selection they kept warming in a pot of broth in front of the convenience store counter, and stirring in some kimchi.

I also noticed that as I went on watching Yamae Yamamoto, I'd started to covet all the useful-looking devices he owned, like the long magnetic strip he kept on his kitchen wall for organising knives, and the thin bird-shaped silicon tool for getting the dust out from between the cracks in his keyboard, and the clothes dryers that had so many clips for small items of clothing. Once, on a whim, I zoomed in on the clothes dryer and counted the number of clips it had: fifty. Despite living alone, Yamae Yamamoto changed both of the two pairs of socks he wore – one on top of the other – each day, not to mention his underwear, so clothes pegs were always in short supply.

I'd hunted down all the items of his I had my eye on online and bookmarked the pages. I hadn't got as far as buying them, though, because the only time I could be at home to collect online deliveries was in the middle of the night. Admittedly, I was living at my parents' house so I suppose I could have just asked them, but I already felt embarrassed about the fact that I'd moved back home, and asking them to act as my collection service on top of that seemed too pathetic to bear.

This curious predicament I found myself in – of having my consumerist desires fanned by the person I was surveilling, yet being unable to satisfy them – caused me a considerable amount of stress. It was like I spent all day watching a TV channel where Yamae Yamamoto was not only the sole character in all the main programmes, but the star of all the adverts too. I wanted to watch over other people from time to time. According to Mrs Ōizumi, switching targets with colleagues was permitted once you were an old hand at the job, but as a rookie who hadn't even made it through a month on the job, I hadn't yet earned the right to so much as contemplate the possibility.

I wouldn't say that I thought the job a good one, but I had eventually got used to spending all of my time in the building. For my late-night meal today, I sandwiched some ham and cheese bought from a nearby supermarket into one of the bagels they sold in the basement shop and heated it up in the micro-wave in the staff kitchen. The yakisoba rolls I usually went for were perfectly tasty, so it wasn't often I was struck by the impulse to eat something that required so much legwork to put together, but after watch-ing Yamae Yamamoto knock up a similar creation for a late-night snack and being overtaken with envy, I managed to rouse the energy. To me it tasted abso-lutely great, but Yamae Yamamoto didn't seem all that enraptured. Maybe it was something he rustled up a lot and he was used to the taste by now, or else he was just down because his work wasn't going as well as it could be.

I tried putting the question to Mrs Ōizumi.

'Do you ever find yourself starting to imitate the people you're watching?'

'Oh yes, all the time,' she nodded. 'The target I had a while back, the one before last, was twenty years younger than me with a full-time job, and although she didn't have much money, she was very stylish. I started paying attention to what she bought and getting all these ideas about fashion and clever ways to wear accessories, and after a while I started trying them out myself, you know. In no time at all my daughter was saying how classy I'd gone and got.'

'Oh, wow ... '

'Mr Someya's been doing this job for ages, but he says it still happens to him sometimes too.'

'Really? What kind of thing?'

'Oh, he doesn't let me in on the details.'

Mrs Ōizumi went on to say that all Yamae Yamamoto ever cooked was hotpots, so he didn't provide her with any new dinner ideas, then she asked me how to calculate the area of a parallelogram. It turned out her daughter had been asking.

Somewhat disconcerted by the easiness of the question, I said, 'Isn't it just the length of the base times the height?'

'Right, of course ... ' she replied. 'I don't really come across parallelograms much in my everyday life, that's the thing.' Then she went off home.

Feeling envious of her for being able to leave just like that, I returned my gaze to the on-screen Yamae Yamamotos, both of whom were having work troubles. Mrs Ōizumi was a part-timer at this company, whereas I was a contractual worker on probationary period. Once the probationary period finished, then – if I was judged suitable – I could be promoted to the status of official company employee, which meant a permanent contract. Personally, I'd have preferred to be a part-time worker paid by the hour, even if it meant less money. But Mrs Masakado hadn't mentioned the option of working part-time, so maybe the company was only hiring full-time workers. I started wondering if it would be possible to ask them to make me a part-time worker at this stage. Who would be the person to ask? I guessed it'd have to be Mr Someya.

One of the Yamae Yamamotos seemed to have given up on his work and began to look at some kind of flyer. I zoomed in to see information about the special offers on at a nearby supermarket – the same one that Mrs Ōizumi monitored. Remembering it was open until midnight, I ran my eyes across the flyer as Yamae Yamamoto scrolled down it. We passed through every-day supplies like kitchen roll, to snacks, then vegetables, on to meat and then my eyes landed on the offer for 1 kg German wurst. A photo next to it showed what I could only assume was a kilogram of white sausages. A bubble informed me they cost '498 YEN!!!!!!' That seemed like ridiculously good value. Yamae Yamamoto appeared to feel the same, because he showed no sign of removing his gaze from that section of the flyer. I fixed my eyes on the time displayed on my taskbar. I'll go home in two hours, I decided, and on the way home, I'll buy the 498 YEN!!!!!! sausages. Just try and stop me.

The following morning, I made the short journey from my house to the office in a state of abject misery. I couldn't believe I'd been so stupid. Although when I stopped to consider my past record, I was forced to admit that such stupid mistakes were not exactly an exceptional occurrence. But still! Why hadn't I just looked to see when the offer was valid until? Why hadn't it struck me yesterday, as I gazed at Yamae Yamamoto gazing at flyers, that this was in fact the Yamae Yamamoto of the day before yesterday, and the special offer he was ogling was due to expire that same day? If I'd stopped for just one second to think about it, I could have worked it out, but I was so absorbed by the prospect of wurst that it hadn't even occurred to me. Dashing out to the supermarket in order to arrive just before it closed at midnight had been a totally wasted trip. Admittedly the supermarket was only about five minutes' walk from the office, so it wasn't an actual disaster or anything, but during my final two hours of work, my sense of anticipation towards those sausages had reached crazy heights, so when the shop assistant informed me that the special offer had ended and all the sausages were sold out, I'd fallen into a state of mild shock. 'I got three whole kilos of them,' some woman saw fit to butt in and tell me. 'They won't all fit in my fridge,' she added before turning her back on us, chortling merrily as she walked away. I understood in that moment how murderers feel. I also felt very strongly that I didn't want to go to work the following day. I wanted to laze around at home, wallowing in self-pity. Or ram that woman hard with a shopping trolley and run out of the shop.

Yet morning dawns, even on nights filled with thoughts as dark as yesterday's. With a face like the sole of a worn-down shoe – in fact, much like the face I had sported in the final stages of my old job – I crossed the street in front of my house and returned once more to the surveillance office. Of course, nobody likes it when their home and workplace are too far apart, but too near isn't great either. You end up going straight into work without having the chance to shake off any of that just-woken-up daze. My hours were from ten onwards, which might sound like a leisurely start, but when you're getting home after eleven every night, it soon stops feeling that way.

I turned on the screens and booted up the computer, loading the new footage from yesterday onto the left screen, and the footage of Yamae Yamamoto after his shopping expedition the day before yesterday onto the right. Post-retail Yamae Yamamoto was always as full of life as if he had been reborn. He didn't really buy sufficient amounts to suggest a love of shopping per se, so I guessed his new-found vigour was the product of being temporarily freed from the hardship of sitting in one spot for hours on end. I was also sitting still for hours on end, but unlike Yamae Yamamoto, who could exercise his own discretion when it came to the use of his time, the only excursion I was allowed was a trip to buy my lunch. Ergo: Yamae Yamamoto had more freedom of movement than I did.

On the left screen, Yamae Yamamoto of yesterday was struggling with his work, his arms folded across his chest as usual. Post-retail Yamae Yamamoto on the right-hand screen fixed himself a simple meal of soba noodles topped with finely cut spring onions, strips of fried tofu and shredded kombu, then hurried back to his desk and turned on his TV and DVD recorder. Immediately, the opening titles for a stand-up comedy special flashed on his screen. A noise escaped my lips inadvertently. I'd been thinking that this very programme must be coming up soon, and now it turned out that it had been on just the other day. I'd missed it. Why hadn't anybody told me? I thought mournfully. Living this kind of life, I had no way of finding out otherwise.

It turned out that watching a stand-up with no sound was a masterclass in frustration. I squinted and screwed up my face, trying to work out what they were saying, but there was no way of knowing. I couldn't even judge how they were going down with the audience. Yamae Yamamoto was pointing his finger at the screen and laughing. He seemed to be having a jolly old time. When he'd watched three acts, he checked how much time there was remaining, paused the programme, then went into the kitchen. I felt highly doubtful that he was about to get the contraband out or receive a new load at that precise moment, but rules were rules, so I switched the screen over to the footage from the kitchen, where I found him smiling as he retrieved some white cylindrical objects from the fridge. It was the wurst – the damned wurst that had been denied me. He quickly removed the packaging, took out two and cut them into bite-sized chunks with a knife. Then he put a pan on top of the stove and began to fry them.

I heard the air leave my body with a sound like a steaming kettle. The target was watching the programme I'd failed to record, cooking the wurst I'd failed to buy. The sausages were done in no time, and Yamae Yamamoto squeezed some ketchup into a little dish and sprinkled curry powder on top of it. This, apparently, was what he was going to dip them in.

I paused the image from the day before yesterday, leaned all my weight on the armrests of the office chair and let my head loll back. What a wretched life I led! And yes, I knew. Of course I knew that there were innumerable things in this world incomparably much harder and more terrible than what I was going through right then. But just for that moment, I wanted permission to crank my unhappiness gauge to the max. I'd dial it back down, I promised to dial it back down right away. By the day after tomorrow at the latest.

I'd found my previous job worthwhile, but had felt chronically betrayed in regards to both the nature and the quantity of the work involved, and it got to a point where I simply couldn't stand it any more.

Then, a while after quitting and moving back in with my parents, and my unemployment insurance running out, I had to find work again. However bad my situation might have been, all the time I'd been watching Yamae Yamamoto, a part of me had been comforted by the thought that, insofar as I wasn't having my life spied on by a third party, my lot was better than his. Now the realisation struck me that that wasn't the case.

I paused the left-hand screen too, and hauled myself to my feet in the way I imagined a bear in hibernation might do when it finally emerges from its den. I tottered out of the room and made my way to the shop. I fancied a tart drink. Something sparkling made with sour plum and black vinegar would have been ideal, but I knew I had little hope of finding such a thing. And yet I'd gone without speaking for so long that I felt myself in danger of forgetting to breathe, and as a kind of release, I ended up ardently explaining the nature of my desires to the woman in the shop.

'Well, I can make something like that for you,' she said brightly, and promptly disappeared into the back of the shop.

Common sense dictated that I should be fearful of what this woman was going to produce for me, but Yamae Yamamoto had done me in so thoroughly that I felt like I was inured to sustaining any more significant damage.

The woman eventually came out holding a regular-sized paper cup, the kind you'd get from a water dispenser, and handed it to me. The liquid inside was a pale golden colour, alive with the fizzing of a million tiny bubbles. From what I could tell, it was more or less exactly what I'd requested. I could smell sour plum, too.

'How much is it?'

'It'll be, erm, 400 yen.'

Woah! That was expensive. Also, the 'erm' must signify that she had decided the price right then and there. But when I put my lips to the rim of the cup, I felt very powerfully that this was exactly the drink I needed to revive me in body and spirit, so I set the cup down on an empty shelf and handed over the cash. I stood there, trying and failing to remember what had been on that now empty spot, as I downed half of the drink she'd prepared for me. Vinegar, carbonated acid, sugar. I am basically doping myself, I thought.

'The meditation book has sold out, so we're taking suggestions for a new title,' the shop lady said, as she pointed to the empty space.

'I'm not really the person to ask,' I replied. 'Ever since I burned out at my last job, I haven't been able to read.'

It sounded like a hopeless exaggeration, but it was more or less the truth. If I read more than one side of A4 a day, I was overwhelmed by a feeling of such despondency that I was unable to function. At the same time, my brain would fire up and I'd be on full alert. It was a really tiresome combination.

'It's first come, first served!'

Slowly I registered the fact that the shop lady was not listening to what I was saying at all.

'I'll have a think,' I said as a sensation of powerlessness rose up in me, and I made my way out of the shop.

Totally oblivious to my feelings, she called out after me, 'Yes, have a think and let me know!'

She sounded so amenable that it was hard not to draw some sense of comfort from her words, but I reminded myself that this was the same person who hadn't yet ordered in my maté and who had decided the price of my sour plum drink on the spot.

I ended up finishing off the drink before I was even back in my seat. I was feeling somewhat rejuvenated, it was true, but I now had to return to steeping my eyes in the sight of Yamae Yamamoto, who was far more fortunate than me. It struck me that it would be better to be watching over the lives of some fortunate people whose situation was very different to mine, like a just-married couple, or a family with a newborn infant, or a lottery winner. Better still, if the people in question weren't Japanese. Some Inuit newly-weds would be perfect, or perhaps a Patagonian family with a week-old baby. Unfortunately, the targets of surveillance were mostly people living not just in Japan, but within a pretty close radius of this office.

In comparison to those kinds of people, Yamae Yamamoto, who was just about bumbling along as a freelancer, felt a lot closer to my situation of being worn down and defeated by a job I loved. That was why I understood so needlessly well the appeal of the items that met with Yamae Yamamoto's approval, and why I ended up feeling this miserable at being deprived the opportunity to own them myself.

On the left-hand screen, Yamae Yamamoto was still sitting in front of his computer looking glum. The Yamae Yamamoto on the right, now eating wurst and laughing at stand-up, eventually had to go back to work too, and soon enough he assumed a state practically indistinguishable from the left-hand version. For a moment, I was ready to feel sympathy for the duo, but then I remembered that the one on the right at least had a belly full of sausages and I shook my head at him.

In a desperate attempt to throw off the exhaustion that was the product of working so late, Machio drained the last of his beer. He was drinking at such a pace that his tankard had disappeared in just three gulps. Sitting there in the corner of the kushiyaki restaurant, he murmured to himself, 'Damn, I'm tired.' Totally oblivious to his predicament, the young waitress took the customers' orders gruffly, then returned to deep-frying the kushiyaki skewers with a blank look on her face. Strands of her fringe, bleached to the colour of a brown envelope, peeked down beneath the edge of her bandanna. Tonight, I'll go for eringi mushrooms wrapped in bacon, ginkgo nuts and quail eggs, Machio thought to himself.

No, you've got it all wrong, I thought. In the chapter before last, Machio had come down with food poisoning after consuming too many ginkgo nuts, thus writing off his entire weekend. In terms of the timeline of the novel, that was probably only the previous weekend, so there seemed no way that Machio would forget about the perils of ginkgo nuts so quickly. Besides, hadn't Machio remarked to himself as he was leaving the office that he was getting off work a bit earlier than usual? If that was the case it didn't seem likely he'd have sufficient tiredness to 'desperately throw off'. And wouldn't the first sentence be better as 'the week's work' rather than 'working so late'?

I zoomed out from Yamae Yamamoto's computer and inclined my head to get a better look at him. Sitting there writing all this stuff that didn't quite match up, Yamae Yamamoto seemed in a better humour than usual and was proceeding at a decent pace, so I guessed he could do without my pedantic suggestions. Still, I had to wonder: was this really what it was like being an author? Could you just write whatever you wanted, regardless of how little sense it made? Or was it a case of going at it like crazy when the muse was with you, then going back afterwards and making careful adjustments? But now, Machio in Yamae Yamamoto's novel was observing the woman sitting next to him who had ordered nothing but ginkgo nut skewers – four of the things. Surely, with ginkgo nuts featuring so heavily in this passage, he needed to change the chapter before last to avoid repeating himself. Couldn't he change it to oysters, or something like that?

Oysters! Yes, oysters were surely the answer! I was overcome by the urge to tell Yamae Yamamoto this solution that I'd hit on, but it was company policy not to give out the contact details of the targets to those surveilling them. The people doing the watching were not allowed, under any circumstances, to exert pressure on the target, unless it was directly related to the surveillance objective. If anything untoward ever happened, anything which would necessitate getting in touch, we were supposed to consult Mr Someya – although all he'd do in that situation would be to refer the matter further up the chain as he didn't know the targets' addresses or phone numbers either. One time, immediately after one of the targets left for a family holiday to Tokyo DisneySea, an employee here noticed a minor electric leakage from the target's TV. Fifteen minutes after passing this information on to Mr Someya, a fireman and electrician were discreetly dispatched to the target's house to fix the problem. To this day, the target still didn't know how close his house had come to burning to the ground.

'I can't deny that there was a part of me that thought, just let it burn! That'll teach you for having such a perfect life,' the employee in question told me, when I ran into him in the kitchen. We had got into conversation by exchanging gripes about the shop. When I told him about my maté saga, he told me that the shop woman had also refused to get in the anime DVDs he'd requested. I'd seen his name around but it was an unusual kanji, and I had no idea how to read it, so at this point I decided in my head to call him Anime Guy.

'The TV guy had three kids, and he was just so, like, dictatorial with them. At mealtimes, he'd tell his kids "Hurry up and eat, you dumb little shit." There's no way I'd say that to my kids, if I had any. But then I'm not married. Actually, I can't even find a girlfriend, and I'm stuck doing this super-nothingy job. I sort of worry about myself sometimes.'

Anime Guy was plump, wore glasses and looked to be about five years younger than me. I asked him which anime DVDs he'd asked the woman in the shop to order in.

'*Dark Crystal*,' he replied, 'and another one which you won't have heard of.'

I hadn't even heard of the first one, so I figured there was no point pressing him for the name of the second.

According to Anime Guy, who'd been working here for three years, you mostly got assigned targets of the same gender and roughly the same age as you. But sometimes, you'd get landed with targets who you found really unbearable to watch. 'You know how there were always one or two people in your class at school who you really couldn't stand? Well, it's like that,' he said. The guy whose TV outlet had started shooting sparks had been one of those for him, and Anime Guy had dreaded coming into work while he was on his case. Apparently, these kinds of mismatches were really common, and the staff had started a union so that if you were paired with someone you really couldn't stand, then it was possible to negotiate a swap. 'You should join, when you become a proper employee,' he advised me.

When I confided in Anime Guy about the sausages, he told me, with a strangely proud note to his voice, that I didn't even know the half of it yet. 'Don't tell anyone this,' he said, before continuing, 'but if you do this job for long enough, you'll see married couples doing it on camera, and domestic scenes so dreadful that you feel bad just watching.' A bit of bickering was okay, he said, but when they were tearing each other's hair out about money or custody or care, then it got hard to watch. He lowered his eyes and drained the rest of his Real Gold energy drink. I felt a sudden burst of gratitude towards Yamae Yamamoto for having such a monotonous lifestyle, and at the same time, registered to myself the risks of staying on in this job.

Anime Guy seemed like he could go on speaking, but I got in there first.

'Do you mind if I ask how you read your name?'

'It's Masakari,' he said.

At least I've cleared that one up, I thought, and headed back to my booth, but the inconsistencies in Yamae Yamamoto's writing were bothering me so much that I wasn't in any mood to concentrate. Although, strictly speaking, I was just watching out for any suspicious movements, so there wasn't really any need to concentrate. I couldn't decide whether the fact that he seemed in such good humour when the work he was doing was so bad was annoying, or actually quite cute, or if it served him right for his past misdemeanours, or what.

For about a week now, Yamae Yamamoto had been working on this Machio story, which appeared to be a novel. That wasn't the only project he was involved in; during other time bands, he worked on other pieces too. I got the impression that he was less a novelist and more a jack of all writerly trades, but still being unable to read more than one A4 sheet's worth of text per day, I couldn't be too sure. It occurred to me that I'd been assigned this particular target to watch over because they knew I couldn't get unnecessarily preoccupied by his penmanship, although that was possibly just me overthinking the situation.

On the left-hand screen, Yamae Yamamoto had started to doze off, arms folded across his chest, so I timidly hit fast-forward. Having watched him long enough, I'd learned to differentiate between when he was just resting with his eyes shut and when he had actually dropped off. When he was just resting, his body inclined to the left, but when he fell asleep, his head drooped over to the right. On the other screen, he stood up and made for the kitchen. By the looks of things, work wasn't going well and he was off to make a cup of tea.

It wasn't yet half an hour since I'd come back from the kitchen myself, but I'd begun to fidget nonetheless and was vaguely planning a visit to the shop when Mrs Ōizumi came in. She was carrying a shopping bag bulging with groceries, as she shivered and commented repeatedly on the cold. Mrs Ōizumi often stopped at the shops on her way here. When I asked her what she did with her meat and fish and so on, she informed me that she kept them in the fridge in the staff kitchen.

'They've got a new book in the shop,' she said, poking her head around the partition to look at me so I'd turn to face her.

'What kind of book?'

She started rummaging in her bag, cocking her head and saying, 'That's funny, I thought … '

Thinking that she must not have heard me, I returned to my work.

After a while, I heard her say, 'Ah, here it is!' and there was a knock on the partition wall. I stood up and peered through to where she was standing.

'This, look!' She gestured to a thin paperback she was holding. 'My daughter started remarking on how bad my vocabulary is, so I thought I'd start reading more, you know, to improve. But I didn't know the name of a single novelist, so I bought this in the shop.'

She held out a book titled *The Baboon Dance*. The author was Yamae Yamamoto. The protagonist, informed the back cover, inherits a baboon from an illegal zoo and begins to allow the baboon to do menial tasks for him like collect the post, pay the electricity and water bills, and do the washing. Before he knows it, the baboon is gradually taking over his life. The final sentence of the blurb read, 'But is the baboon's devotion the real thing, or is it all a sinister ploy … ?' What the hell do I care, I thought. So the shop had decided to stock this book, had they? Who on earth had requested it?

And then as I returned the book to Mrs Ōizumi through the crack, I thought, if you wanted to improve your vocabulary, surely there were goodness knows how many better choices than this one.

'Can you really not think of a single other author?'

'Um … Natsume Sōseki?' Mrs Ōizumi replied, reclaiming her copy of *The Baboon Dance*.

Not long after, I heard her voice coming through the partition: 'Aw, what a cutie!' It seemed that as she checked the course of Yamae Yamamoto's shopping trip, she was also reading his book. For sure, there was no rule stating that we couldn't read the target's artistic output, but my skin threatened to shrivel up in discomfort at the prospect. Mrs Ōizumi, though, seemed far less fazed.

On the left-hand screen, Yamae Yamamoto shivered and opened his eyes with a jolt. He held his hand to his head for a couple of minutes, then started tapping away at the keyboard. Curious about what kind of thing a person writes when they've just woken up, I zoomed in to find the words: *Argh, I can't be bothered to work.*

Well, yeah, that figured. From beyond the partition, I could hear the sound of Mrs Ōizumi rummaging around in her bag again. Eventually I saw her rushing in the direction of the kitchen, yoghurt pot in hand.

Over time, my cravings for things became more and more synced up with Yamae Yamamoto's habits, until I ceased looking for things of my own accord. I wasn't a particularly materialistic person to begin with, and Yamae Yamamoto didn't buy that much, but it seemed that he put a great deal of thought into whatever purchases he did make, which was perhaps the result of his lack of funds. In that sense he made a very good role model for me. As it turned out, the basement shop stocked the straps he wore below his knees to improve blood flow when sitting still for long periods of time, as well as the liquid rollerball pens he favoured with fast-drying ink, so I bought them both. It was from Yamae Yamamoto's forays into internet news that I discovered they'd decided to make a tenth season of a particular American detective drama. And when Yamae Yamamoto was watching Kevin Großkreutz's goal over and over in a match he'd recorded, I rejoiced along with him.

Little by little, I was coming to feel like I was living alongside Yamae Yamamoto, sharing in his joy and his sadness, his pleasure and his pain. No, that's probably going too far – but definitely his joy and pleasure, at least. And if not his sadness, then certainly his boredom. Yamae Yamamoto got even sleepier than usual whenever it rained, dropping off in his chair constantly, and after a while I found myself starting to nap along with him. The times when the target was sleeping were my sole opportunity to fast-forward, and I was missing these opportunities because I was sleeping too. I still had a lot to learn in this job. Mrs Ōizumi would give me regular progress reports on *The Baboon Dance*. It seemed like she was only getting through about two pages a day. Her daughter, on the other hand, had finished reading it. Her verdict? 'Nothing special.'

Just as I was starting to think I'd have no problem watching this guy for another year – which I guess was another way of saying, just as I was starting to get properly used to the job – Yamae Yamamoto's behaviour took a turn for the unusual.

At a certain point in time, he began glancing in the direction of the cameras. Since the beginning, the camera in his workspace had been concealed in a cupboard diagonally behind him, while the one in the kitchen was secreted inside the cabinet above the sink. Suddenly of late, he had taken to turning around while at his computer, and glancing up while he was cooking. It seemed like he was particularly bothered by what was behind him when he was working.

However much of a sense of camaraderie I'd come to feel with my target, it still freaked me out when our eyes met through the screen. Had he cottoned on to the fact that he was being watched? But if he had, wouldn't he be searching about for the cameras? Instead, his vigilance seemed more aimless in character. Someone could have spilled the beans, I thought. Yet as far as I was aware, the contact that Yamae Yamamoto had with the outside world was limited to work-related transactions and the profoundly inconsequential interchanges he had with his friends. The only people to visit his house were couriers. Nobody called him, either. Occasionally he used his phone to arrange meals with friends, but all such upcoming arrangements were still at least a month away.

I gradually got more and more unnerved by the way that one moment, the target would be fully absorbed in his work, and the next, would be looking straight at me. I even started to conjecture that maybe he'd known that he was being watched the whole time and had just been going along with it. Maybe now he had decided that the time had finally come to let me know he was on to us.

As a first step, I consulted Mrs Ōizumi.

'He probably just has a stiff neck,' she advised me. Her daughter may have found it nothing special, but Mrs Ōizumi was apparently really enjoying *The Baboon Dance*, and told me she'd started looking forward to coming into work every day to read it. Of course, I couldn't reject out of hand the suggestion that all of this backward glancing was down to Yamae Yamamoto having neck problems, but identifying the possibility didn't do anything to alleviate my concerns, so I decided to take them to Mr Someya.

'Hmm,' he said, as he marked up someone's report with a fluorescent green highlighter. 'I wonder if it's that programme? You know, last Thursday there was that ghost stories special on TV, and one was about an axe-wielding maniac who moves thirty centimetres closer every time you turn around.' He sounded pretty unconcerned. I was aware that Yamae Yamamoto had been watching that programme avidly and had noted it down in my report as part of his general behaviour, but hadn't given it much additional thought.

'What's the deal with him?'

'Some man was convinced his wife was being unfaithful, so he killed his entire family and then himself, only for it to transpire that he'd been wrong about the cheating. He was so consumed by regret in his afterlife, that he decided to target anyone who set out to make other people's lives a misery.'

'Surely that makes no sense?'

'Not really, no. But, you know, ghost logic and all that.'

Mr Someya told me that the ghost's incremental approach had no significance over and above his intention to induce a crawling sense of fear and thereby make his victims suffer as much as possible. In other words, it was the product of sheer malice. But according to the guest medium they had on the show, the fact that the ghost's behaviour ensued from an 'incorrigible misunderstanding' meant there was nothing to be done to fix it. Mr Someya then told me he hadn't seen the programme himself, but after reading my report, he'd checked out its contents on online blogs. Wow, I thought, such professionalism! But then I reminded myself that he was a professional, at least at this job, so there wasn't really any cause for surprise.

Mr Someya went on to suggest that the upward glances Yamae Yamamoto was directing in the kitchen might be explained by the old coffee maker kept in the cabinet up there. The camera in the shelf above the sink had been installed by drilling a small hole in the bottom of the cabinet, and slipping the camera inside an apparently unopened box of plates. Yamae Yamamoto hadn't opened the cabinet once these past three months, but if he did start to take an interest now and went to sort through its contents, we could be in trouble. We'd received a rough inventory of what was in the cabinet from the person who fitted the camera, and there was, apparently, a coffee maker listed on there. But why would Yamae Yamamoto be interested in a coffee maker?

'He wrote an article about them recently, no?'

'Yeah, so he did. But he's usually a tea drinker.'

Not long ago, I'd found committed tea drinker Yamae Yamamoto writing promotional material for a fair trade coffee brand, where he falsely proclaimed allegiance to the coffee party. Since that time, perhaps lured by the persuasive power of his own lies, he had started dripping his own coffee using paper filters, but it didn't seem to be going very well. So now Mr Someya mentioned it, it did seem plausible that at this point in time, he'd be remembering that he owned a coffee maker and cooking up a plan to use it.

'Damn … We can't go around there and retrieve the cameras yet, either. I guess we'll have to set up a coffee maker competition or something and have him apply.'

Muttering about what a hassle this all was, Mr Someya quickly jotted down on a memo pad the words: *Prize Draw. Supermarket?*

'Is there anything I can do to help?' I said, remembering briefly what it felt like to make some form of proactive suggestion. This wasn't something I'd experienced since quitting my old job.

'No, no, you just get back to work,' he replied flatly, and so I went back to my seat, nursing a faint sense of disappointment. From time to time, it'd be nice to do things other than just watch surveillance footage.

Even after hearing a rational explanation of Yamae Yamamoto's behaviour from Mr Someya, I still found it hard to swallow entirely, and just watching him made me quite jumpy. As ever, Yamae Yamamoto looked behind him at intervals of ten-something minutes. *There aren't any ghosts, and you're about to get a brand-new coffee maker*, I wanted to tell him, but I wasn't allowed.

Change was afoot again. At some juncture, Yamae Yamamoto developed a passion for clearing out his flat. This time the cause was obvious: he'd recently written a couple of commissions on the subject of decluttering. It just goes to show, I thought, how easily influenced he was as a person. His flat was on the large side for someone living alone, so although somewhat cluttered, it had never looked like a total tip. Now, though, it was starting to get gradually neater. It seemed like he had finally learned how to throw things away. In fact, as time went on, it appeared he had come to find the act positively pleasurable. Today, as he glibly chucked away a box full of dictionaries, he looked most content.

Speaking of contentment, it appeared that the coffee maker we had sent him was going down very well, too.

In the end, we'd borrowed the name of the mail-order site that Yamae Yamamoto always used and sent him an email announcing that we were recruiting volunteers to review the performance of a coffee maker: 'Every applicant who responds by such-and-such a date will be accepted as a reviewer. Successful applicants will be asked to make use of the coffee maker for a week and write an 800-word feedback report. All applicants who submit reports will be allowed to keep the machine,' said the email, whose contents Mr Someya and I had concocted together. By setting a word limit, we were appealing to Yamae Yamamoto's professionalism as a man of letters – or that was the intention, at least. This new tack came about when the survey installed at the supermarket, promising a giveaway of 10,000 coffee makers, failed to elicit any interest from him whatsoever. When it was clear his first initiative had failed, Mr Someya had consulted me to see what kind of set-up would be most likely to hook the target. All I'd done in my job up until that point was keep watch somewhat aimlessly, so I'd felt pleased to be asked for my opinion. When Mr Someya stopped by to tell me that Yamae Yamamoto had applied to be a reviewer, and thanked me for my help, I felt like what I was doing actually mattered. I had never imagined that such a feeling was even possible in a job like this.

'You know, the reason we ask one person to keep watching a single target is so they can get to know them really well,' Mr Someya told me. It was a rare event for him to volunteer information like this. 'It's not just about watching them and getting enough evidence to nail their coffins shut. You also need to empathise with them, to have insight into their way of life.'

'Oh,' I nodded, and it finally hit me that on some deep level, Mr Someya really loved this job.

When Yamae Yamamoto began taking evident enjoyment in throwing things away, I started to sense danger. I wrote about my fears in my report – and Mr Someya agreed that there was indeed cause for concern. Which is why now – as I watched Yamae Yamamoto carrying a rubbish bag full to bursting with various household articles outside, then, cup of coffee in his hand and pensive look on his face, opening the door to the walk-in closet containing his ludicrous quantities of DVDs – I immediately placed a call to Mr Someya.

The footage was from early that morning, before Yamae Yamamoto went to bed. I told Mr Someya that it seemed perfectly possible, given Yamae Yamamoto's relatively impatient personality, that he'd start sorting through his DVDs as soon as he woke up. Immediately, Mr Someya switched my screen over so that, for the first time ever, it was showing real-time footage from Yamae Yamamoto's flat. As expected, real-time Yamae Yamamoto was standing there in the same fleece dressing gown he'd sported before bed, staring idly at the mountain of DVDs towering before him. A number of them – I guessed they were the first few dozen he'd put in the closet – were arranged neatly in plastic drawers, but it seemed that at a certain point in time he'd decided to do away with the hassle, and the rest were simply laid flat and stacked right up to the ceiling. He had so many DVDs that the thought of trying to count them made me come over a bit weak. If this was a car boot sale and Yamae Yamamoto was selling, I'd definitely just be asking him, 'How much for the lot?'

Inside one of the DVDs sitting in his closet was the contraband that his acquaintance had entrusted him with. I'd seen inside the closet before, towards the beginning of my time here, but looking at it again now, I felt that I understood the choice made by those who were responsible for the shakedown. Faced with the task of opening up all of these cases and checking the contents, I too would have installed a bunch of cameras and gone on home.

So, which of these DVDs was the impostor? Sometimes I came dangerously close to forgetting to ask myself that question, but of course, figuring that out was a key part of my job. Which of these would be an unlikely purchase for Yamae Yamamoto to make? Back in the beginning, Mr Someya instructed me to save a screenshot of the closet locally so I could familiarise myself with the titles when I had some spare time, but I'd never got around to doing that. At a glance, one could see his collection ran the gamut: old faithfuls like *Die Hard*, obscure Soviet-era masterpieces, tons of Adam Sandler romcoms, box sets of old detective series and even DVDs of documentary footage showcasing the beautiful Japanese countryside. Basically, he watched everything. Or rather, there were several genres of films that he owned, but didn't watch: erotic dramas, splatter horror, pop concerts. My guess was that they were online impulse purchases, from when he was feeling mentally weak after a hard day's work.

Now, Yamae Yamamoto calmly reached out a hand and plucked a copy of *Lady in the Water* – with a sticker that read *JUST 100 YEN!* – from the top of one of the DVD stacks. He deliberated for about a minute, then put it back again, this time on a stack to the right-hand side of the closet. So that's a keeper, is it? I thought. Then his eyes fell on the DVD that had been lying underneath it, *Memento*. He looked at it for a little while, then placed it at his feet. Watching him sorting, I quickly grasped his basic principle: the DVDs placed on the pile to the side were those he was planning to keep, while the ones at his feet were those he was planning to let go of.

Surely he wouldn't get rid of something that someone else had lent him? Surely he had more sense than that? If so, it would follow that as he was sorting, one DVD would emerge that would belong in a third category – namely, return to lender – and that would then be the DVD with the contraband inside. At least, that would be the majority take on the matter, but however much time elapsed, the third pile failed to materialise. He still had five stacks to get through, so there was no cause for panic yet, but when I considered the very real possibility that Yamae Yamamoto had forgotten which of the DVDs had been lent to him, I started to feel quite hopeless. I supposed this was the time when I should have been utilising the knowledge I'd garnered, through daily observation of the target, to help me identify which was the suspect DVD – but it felt pretty unfair that I should be expected to figure something out about someone that he didn't himself know.

Fully immersed in the task at hand, Yamae Yamamoto made steady headway through the mountain. There was still no sign of him remembering the borrowed DVD and putting it to one side. When I saw there was just one stack remaining, I called Mr Someya and explained that it seemed as if Yamae Yamamoto really had forgotten ever being loaned a DVD.

When there were just seven DVDs left to be vetted, Mr Someya entered the room, speaking on his mobile. I heard him ordering the person on the other end to station themselves nearby immediately.

'No, we still don't know if he's going to throw them out or sell them off. Yes, yes, of course it'd be much easier if it was the former.'

Saying that, Mr Someya moved to stand behind my chair. When I suggested that given how many DVDs there were in the discard pile, he was more than likely planning to box them up and sell them off to a used bookshop, Mr Someya relayed this information to the person on the other end of the line.

Now Yamae Yamamoto emerged from the closet, only to return with a big cardboard box emblazoned with the words 'Incan Awakening', which he began to fill with the DVDs he had decided to get rid of. 'What's that box about?' I mumbled, to which Mr Someya replied, 'It's a type of potato.'

The proportion of his DVD collection Yamae Yamamoto had decided to part with was conservative in comparison with his initial decluttering experiments, but there were still enough cases to fill a box that once contained several kilos of potatoes. Yamae Yamamoto went to pick it up, but seemingly bowed by its weight, gave up on the idea, and instead pushed it out of the closet. When he got it as far as the entrance, he went back for his phone and placed a call.

'He must be phoning a courier,' Mr Someya said.

'Yes, it looks that way.'

Mr Someya now informed someone, presumably our guy stationed near Yamae Yamamoto's building, of the anticipated course of events. If a courier came to pick up the box from Yamae Yamamoto's house, our guy was to intercept him or her and request to check the contents of the box. He was allowed to hand over an incentive of up to 100,000 yen. Things were starting to feel a whole lot more real.

Apparently revitalised after packing up his DVDs, Yamae Yamamoto whiled away the time until the courier was due to come by brewing coffee. I switched the image over to the camera in the closet and, to give my nerves a bit of a rest, tried to immerse myself in the task of figuring out whether he had really given away the DVD with the contraband in. My eye paused on *Over the Hedge* and *Danny the Dog* as potentially fishy candidates, but then I reconsidered – he liked animations, and he had given his *Once Upon a Time in China* box set, another Jet Li offering, priority treatment, storing it carefully away in the plastic drawers – so I couldn't rule either of those out as native members of the collection.

Yamae Yamamoto put down his coffee, calmly got to his feet and moved quickly to the door. The courier had arrived faster than I expected. He was wearing a different uniform to the woman who usually delivered stuff, so I zoomed in to discover that the logo on his chest was that of the local used bookshop. It seemed he wasn't going to evaluate Yamae Yamamoto's offerings here, but had just come to pick them up. Still, the application form looked alarmingly involved – and it was giving Yamae Yamamoto a bit of trouble. Even through the camera, I could sense how profoundly listless this gangly delivery kid was. His spine looked bent, and from time to time he twisted his body off to the side to cough behind him. It seemed he spoke really quietly too, because Yamae Yamamoto kept asking him to repeat the answers to his questions about how he was supposed to fill in the form.

Mr Someya informed our guy that the person who had shown up was from the bookshop itself and not a third-party courier. He said the name of the shop, then apparently getting a reply that didn't sit well with him, cocked his head and said down the phone, 'No, I mean that maybe it won't be a question of money.'

'What do you mean by that?' I enquired. 'That it won't be a question of money?'

'I mean that there's a possibility that a financial incentive won't be enough to bring this kid around.'

The bookshop in question, I learned, had pretty strict rules. Part-timers like this kid, who were sent out to collect second-hand goods for sale, were forbidden from even stopping off at a vending machine for a bottle of juice, explained Mr Someya. He remembered one time when he'd popped into the shop around midnight before getting the last train home, and found the same guy working there as when he'd been in at lunchtime earlier that same day. Yikes, I thought. Sure, being stuck on a chair ceaselessly watching a specific individual was hardly a picnic, but working ridiculous hours in a sales job must be many times worse.

Finally finishing with the form, Yamae Yamamoto bowed his head at the kid and sent him on his way. It looked as though the Incan Awakening box was of a considerable weight, and I worried that a kid that skinny might not be able to carry it, so when I noticed a fold-up trolley waiting outside, I felt a strange sense of relief.

'The article has left the target's house. Intercept it,' Mr Someya said down the phone. Yamae Yamamoto, with an expression of profound relief, stretched out his arms, then lay down on the sofa, leaving the coffee maker and his full coffee cup right where they were. All that decision-making must have tired him out.

I figured that with everything in place for the person at the site to hand over a wad of cash to the bookshop guy, and check the contents of his package, my job was pretty much over too – but that turned out not to be the case.

'What? He can only give you fifteen minutes?' Mr Someya was not one for making his feelings known, and even now his voice betrayed only the smallest amount of surprise as he spoke into his mobile. 'If he takes longer than the permitted span of time he has to do two hours overtime, you say?'

What an awful place to work, I thought. No wonder he looked so lifeless. Still, we didn't have the authority to tell this delivery boy that there was a risk that the box contained something seriously dodgy and forcibly seize it, so our guy was reduced to opening each of the DVD cases in a corner of the building's car park, and checking them one by one.

'If only we could go and help him,' Mr Someya said with a wistful look.

On screen, Yamae Yamamoto had draped a blanket over his entire body, so it covered even his head, and was fast asleep. Mr Someya was having the person on the other end of the line read out the DVD titles and repeating them back to me. There was a *Harry Potter* film that seemed out of place to me, and I figured that might be it, but apparently it was clean.

With nothing in particular to be doing, I kept a close watch on the time displayed in the right-hand corner of the screen, and waited for the contraband to show up. I wondered if, in a case like this one, the oft-rumoured bonus would be split equally between me, Mr Someya and the guy at the scene. But then, there was no guarantee that the contraband would actually be found. However half-arsed Yamae Yamamoto may seem in the way he went about his life, there was still a possibility that he had enough sense to keep a borrowed DVD apart from all of the rest.

Time ticked on cruelly, indifferent to the fact that our treasure still hadn't shown itself. It wasn't in the *Cheburashka* DVD case, and *Oasis: Live* was a dud too. Mr Someya was calmly intoning '*Bewitched, Blades of Glory, Dinosaur Kingdom in 3D*,' and I was thinking about how Yamae Yamamoto seemed to have fallen out of love with Will Ferrell recently. I made a note of this observation, just in case.

'Ten seconds left,' Mr Someya said, glancing at his watch with a resigned expression.

'*Barking Dogs Never Bite, Madagascar*,' he read, and then the moment he said, '*The Butterfly Effect*,' I reflexively turned to him.

'Try that one.'

I couldn't say with confidence that it was the culprit, but I did feel relatively sure that Yamae Yamamoto hated Ashton Kutcher. I'd heard from

Mrs Ōizumi about a scene in *The Baboon Dance* where the protagonist explained to the baboon how Ashton Kutcher was an awful actor who'd left Demi Moore for a younger woman, and how he had decided to hate him forever, regardless of what he might do in the future. 'That's the way I've decided to live my life,' the protagonist tells the baboon. Also, I knew that Yamae Yamamoto was an animal lover, so the chances of him having owned the previous two titles seemed pretty high.

'You've got it?' Mr Someya said, dropping his shoulders and looking relieved. 'Okay, then buy that one off him and let the guy get back to work.'

Then he turned to me. 'Good work. You're free to go home today.'

He was making to leave the room, so I took the opportunity to ask what it was they'd found. It wasn't entirely clear whether my inspired suggestion had actually preceded our guy opening up *The Butterfly Effect* case of his own volition, but I still felt like I had the right to know.

'Gems. It's smuggled gems. I'll explain more tomorrow,' Mr Someya said at speed, then hurried out of the room. On screen, a still fast-asleep Yamae Yamamoto was gradually slipping off the sofa.

The following day, we were given a detailed explanation about the seized contraband. The acquaintance in question turned out to be a young female editor who Yamae Yamamoto had worked with a few times, and who had been smuggling illegal gems from overseas under the guise of researching a special feature on ecotourism. Before coming under scrutiny from our agency, she had been selling off the gemstones as soon as she got back to Japan, but this time, knowing she was likely to be called in for questioning, had entrusted them with Yamae Yamamoto for a while. Until now, since she hadn't been discovered in possession of the contraband, there hadn't been sufficient evidence to prove her guilt, but with the fingerprints from yesterday's DVD case, Mr Someya informed me, she could be convicted. When she was arrested, she had apparently explained that she had chosen Mr Yamamoto because, with so many DVDs to watch, she could be confident he wouldn't ever open the case. The gems that Yamae Yamamoto had been keeping warm were Madagascan sapphires.

'Thank goodness we didn't choose *Madagascar*, eh?' Mr Someya said with a grin, although in actual fact the search had apparently exceeded the allocated fifteen minutes, earning the kid a good 'telling-off' from his boss. This information was relayed to me offhandedly, but I could only imagine how grim the scene of that 'telling-off' might have been.

My Yamae Yamamoto-related tasks thus came to an abrupt end. After the explanation from Mr Someya,

I was asked to check through the facts of the case noted in a summary he had produced, and then I was through. I asked when the cameras would be removed, and was told that Yamae Yamamoto's entire building was due for a cable TV inspection soon, so they'd do it then.

It turned out that I really would be getting a bonus: 100,000 yen. It was a totally reasonable amount, very different to what I'd fantasised about, but still the sort of sum anyone would be happy to receive. 'Tomorrow it'll be exactly a month that you've been working here, so you'll be getting a contract renewal form,' Mr Someya told me, then added, 'I told my boss you've got what it takes.'

'It's just sitting and watching a screen, though. Is it really possible to be suited to it or not?' I asked, thinking as I said the words that, actually, it probably was.

'Oh yes. Some people end up patients of the psychosomatic medicine department.'

Holy shit, I thought. Mr Someya also told me I didn't have to rush into a decision. I crossed the street to my house, remembering what it had said in the job posting: *Permanent position, take-home monthly pay of 170,000 yen (with potential for raises), full insurance payments.*

It certainly didn't feel bad to be told that I had what it takes, and the working conditions were, if anything, slightly better than the minimum I would accept. But could I really go on doing this job?

I got home early for the second day running, and the only thing I could think to do was sleep, which I guessed was a sign that I was thoroughly accustomed to a lifestyle of overwork. My parents had both retired from their full-time jobs, but were still working part-time, so there was nobody at home. I sat down on the sofa and picked up the newspaper lying next to me. It was a flimsy one, so it must be the evening edition, I thought.

I made to look at the TV listings, then remembered that wouldn't be much use if it was yesterday's paper. Now I was holding it, though, I leafed slowly through its pages. My eyes slipped all over the place. Reading the words felt like more than I could be bothered to do, and even the photographs wouldn't lodge in my head. I must be really tired, I thought. Maybe it was the result of staring at a screen for days on end, or maybe it was that the fatigue from my old job hadn't entirely disappeared yet.

Even the idea of folding the paper up and putting it down felt like a hassle, so I let my eyes pass over its surface, when suddenly, under the culture section, my eyes alighted on Yamae Yamamoto's name. What? My eyes widened. I thought I just finished with you? The article in question was a throwaway opinion piece – really insubstantial. I deliberated for a while between tossing the paper on the floor and skimming through it before deciding on the latter:

I recently found myself in an embarrassing predicament for someone midway into his thirties: I became fixated by a ghost story I heard about on TV. For days on end, I kept having the feeling that something was standing behind me. I thought about ghosts while I was dreaming and while I was waking, and found myself unable to continue with my work.

Yeah, I know, I thought. Man, what an innocent life you lead.

It was a kind of self-imposed bondage. And mentioning bondage, my mind of course leaps to jibakurei: those ghosts bound to one fixed spot. Was my ghost a bound one or freely floating? When I was a kid, I always envied the freely floating kind. If you're free to float as you please, then surely you can travel all you want! You can go to Brazil whenever the mood takes you.

You bloody idiot, I thought. If you were a 'freely floating' ghost, then boats and trains and all other modes of transport would pass straight through you. The only way you'd have of getting to Brazil would be to walk there. Even if that was physically possible as a freely floating ghost, could you really be bothered to do it?

Jibakurei, in comparison, must have so much spare time on their hands. They have to stand there, in the same spot, doing nothing. If that was my fate, I'd like to be stationed in the living room with a house-wife who watched a lot of TV, or else in the cinema. But they can't choose, and that must be tough. I guess getting stuck in a place without any people would get lonely, but it would also be tough to be surrounded by really boring people. If there was a jibakurei in my room, for example, I'm fairly sure he or she would be incredibly bored.

I could feel my stomach producing a surplus of acid. I didn't turn around and look behind me Yamae Yamamoto-style, but the hands holding my newspaper grew weak.

I'll share with you a personal confession. Every month or so, I'm taken by the irresistible urge to chew my toenails. Now it just so happened that this urge visited me during my ghosting period, but I resisted it. I felt like my ghost wouldn't want to see that sort of thing. There was an etiquette that has to be upheld by those being watched, as well as by those watching, after all.

I shook my head, put the paper down on the floor, leaned my head back against the sofa and shut my eyes. Damn, was I tired.

I never wanted to know everything there was to know about Yamae Yamamoto, and I hadn't been under the illusion that I did, either, but I guess that somewhere in my head, I had been feeling like I had him pretty well down. Now, I discovered, there were simple, very superficial habits of his I didn't have the faintest clue about.

I felt a headache coming on. I made the decision, right then and there, not to renew my contract.

The Bus Advertising Job

I had to look for another job again, so there I was in the employment centre, letting my eyes roam over the latest vacancies while my brain was consumed by the question of where I should eat dinner on my way home, when I heard someone behind me say my name. Recognising the voice as that of Mrs Masakado – the recruiter who'd introduced me to the surveillance job – I resolved to be as polite as possible, turning around, bowing and saying how nice it was to see her, all the while thinking how much I wished she hadn't discovered me.

'I heard you didn't renew your contract at the surveillance company?'

'Yeah, no ... '

'The person who called us seemed very disappointed. He said it was such a shame when they'd finally found someone so well suited to the role.'

'Did he ... '

I was aware that I was saying pretty much nothing, and the longer the situation went on – with Mrs Masakado saying things of actual substance, and me just drawing her out – the guiltier I felt. Standing there, I sensed myself split between the intuition that I would feel a lot better if she would just leave me alone, and a more circumspect element that told me she might help me find another job so I'd better pull myself together. As I scrabbled around for an excuse as to why, in fact, I hadn't renewed my contract, Mrs Masakado took the opportunity to steer me towards the consultation space in the corner, saying 'We'd be better off having a seat, don't you think?'

She made me a cup of tea, then put on the gradient-tinted glasses hanging round her neck and ran her eyes over what I assumed was a record of our discussions. Waiting meekly for whatever it was she was about to say to me, I pondered the question of how old she was. To judge by the wrinkles on her face and hands, I would have guessed over sixty. She had a remarkably gentle manner, and certainly didn't give the impression of having worked her fingers to the bone all her life, but when I'd spoken to her of the problems I'd experienced with the people at my old job, she'd sympathised and said, 'Yes, people are the most important thing, aren't they? One feels like one can put up with a slightly lower salary so long as the people are okay.' The way she'd said this intimated to me that she did have a fair amount of experience in the world of work.

'It says here that you cited personal reasons as grounds for leaving.'

'That's right.'

I'd read on the internet that it was okay to cite 'personal reasons' for a whole host of circumstances. Even when submitting a full-blown resignation, the article had informed, good old 'personal reasons' would see you through in the majority of cases. Whether you'd had a boss who'd made barbed comments about you at a half-hourly rate, or you'd been blamed for the disappearance of a document mentioned on the job sheet that had never existed in the first place, or your colleagues had spread horrible rumours about you, or you'd been held responsible for ruining a business deal that had fallen through after you'd refused to go drinking with some guy at the client company – whatever your particular situation might be, 'personal reasons' was your man.

And yet, my 'personal reasons' didn't seem to be landing too well with Mrs Masakado.

'Might I ask you to explain a little? It might help me in finding work for you in the future.'

The truth was that, for reasons that weren't entirely clear to me, I'd panicked. The surveillance job hadn't been that bad, but it had felt weighty and involved in a way that I didn't feel capable of dealing with. Perhaps it just wasn't a job suited to a chronic over-thinker like me. I doubted I could ever feel the affection that Mr Someya clearly felt towards it, and I wasn't by nature as rule-abiding as Mrs Ōizumi. I could see how people like that could do the job without losing their minds, but I also understood that it was bound to send some-one like me funny in the head sooner or later.

'I found it hard to stay sitting at a desk for all that time. With all the overwork, I ended up doing very long hours.' I looked down uncomfortably as I came out with the reason that seemed the easiest to vocalise. 'It was a really great job, but I felt that if I carried on, I'd only end up inconveniencing the company.'

'Is that so?' said Mrs Masakado. 'I don't think that's something you can really know without trying it out first.'

Touché. I could see I would have to force my way to victory with the 'I found it physically challenging' tack.

'It was like, nothing really happened, and then all of a sudden something really dramatic would happen. That pace just didn't suit me.'

'I see. You requested a job that was like watching over collagen extraction, didn't you, and this one involved far more drama than you wanted. I'm sorry about that.'

'No, no! I mean, in essence, it was exactly the type of thing I requested, and it was entirely my fault I couldn't keep it up, I'm sorry.' In response to Mrs Masakado's apology, I too began apologising.

'Is it a question of wanting a very uneventful job?'

'Yes, I think so. Ideally there would be events of some kind from time to time, but nothing too sudden.'

'Do you still feel like a desk job is best?'

'Yes,' I said emphatically. I marvelled to myself at my cheek in requesting a desk job, even as I moaned about the hardship of sitting down the whole time, but I figured the best strategy right now was to go big and negotiate down if necessary.

Mrs Masakado opened up a different file and flipped through it at speed. *You really don't need to do that*, I advised her internally. I didn't mean that she didn't need to find me a job – but rather, she didn't need to be quite so zealous about it. Yet this was the person who'd listened with staggering forbearance to me going on about how physically and psychologically burned out I was after my old job, so I supposed I couldn't expect any less.

'There's one here that I think might be of interest,' she said, turning the file around to face me and reading out the job description.

'It says they're temporarily short of staff, so they're looking for someone urgently. They've put the duration as "one month to indefinite, depending on in-house demand".'

I pulled the file towards me and studied the posting. The salary was about the same as the surveillance job, but there appeared to be no health insurance provisions until you were appointed as a permanent employee.

'There would be a certain amount of variation, but in essence it's a calm, steady desk job,' Mrs Masakado said, as if reading aloud from an advertisement. 'I think it's exactly the kind of thing you're looking for.'

'There's something else I'd like you to do in addition to all that,' said Mr Kazetani, the head of department who had also interviewed me, his face assuming a peculiar expression. 'I'd also like you to keep an eye on Ms Eriguchi.'

The 'all that' to which Mr Kazetani referred was the substance of my new job – namely, writing audio advertisements to be aired on a particular bus route. My very first day, I thought, and already I was being lumped with more surveillance tasks.

'Is there some kind of issue with Ms Eriguchi?' I asked. Ms Eriguchi was the only other employee in my section, and was thus responsible for training me. She had gone home at five on the dot. Although she was significantly younger than I was, she seemed of a peaceable demeanour and generally quite reliable.

'You could say that there was, or you could say there wasn't.'

Mr Kazetani interlocked his hands and placed them under his chin with calculated gravity, then looked up at me. His oddly voluminous hairstyle had to be an attempt to make himself look younger – with this being my first day, that was the only thing about him I could find to pick holes in.

'What kinds of, erm, areas should I keep an eye on, exactly?' I asked.

'Oh, everything, really. Whether or not the content of the adverts is accurate, and that sort of thing.'

'Oh, so, checking the content of her work?'

'Not just that.' Mr Kazetani shook his head slowly in a slightly theatrical fashion. 'I'd like you to report to me if you notice anything at all about her behaviour.'

Well, thanks a lot! *If you notice anything at all about her behaviour* – I'd only met her for the first time today, so it stood to reason that I would notice practically everything she did. She breaks the Oreos she has for her three o'clock snack into pieces before eating them! She prefers thick-nibbed ballpoint pens to thin-nibbed! Was I supposed to be reporting these kinds of behavioural observations?

Surely not? And so I translated Mr Kazetani's words, which seemed to me somewhat oblique in their formulation, into something altogether plainer, and repeated them back to him.

'Okay. If I see her doing something I find strange, I'll tell you.'

'Right,' he said, and nodded. 'So, I'll see you tomorrow.'

With this, he took the daily report I held out to him. I bowed, noticing that he seemed rejuvenated after offloading this uncomfortable task on me, and then I left the office floor, passing by the other employees still hard at work. The offices of the company, which took up the second and third floors of a six-storey building in front of the station, were neither large nor small.

They were, in fact, of a resolutely ordinary scale. For a minimum of one month, I would be working, together with Ms Eriguchi, in a small space separated off by a partitioning screen.

What was the deal with this 'keeping an eye on Ms Eriguchi' stuff? The thing about her that had impressed itself most strongly on me so far was how much younger she was than me: she could easily have been ten years my junior. She was petite and softly spoken. The suit she had on reminded me of the iden-tikit 'recruit suits' that university students wore when job-hunting, which, together with her unmade-up face, gave a rather colourless impression. Yet, in teaching me how to do my job, she'd displayed a level of competence that seemed to me nigh on remarkable. It couldn't have been easy to show someone how to get across in a limited amount of words the key elements of the businesses wanting to advertise, but she'd managed it, and she kept on patiently offering me advice even after I'd written several drafts of copy that fell wide of the mark. In a sense then, I registered for the first time now, there was an inconsistency between the unsea-soned and slightly stiff impression she gave off, and her actual capabilities – but that was about the only noteworthy thing I could come up with. It would be no exaggeration to say that of all the people I'd met since coming into this office, she seemed the most innocu-ous of the bunch. With his attempts to look younger than he was, Mr Kazetani aroused a greater sense of wariness in me – although, of course, it was still only my first day, and I only had my initial impressions to go on.

I set off home, unable, for all my ruminating, to light on any valid reason why I'd been asked to keep an eye on Ms Eriguchi. The office was a little way from the previous one, far enough that I needed to cycle in. The surrounding area was relatively built up, with a couple of fast-food restaurants, a big supermarket and a DVD rental shop, which meant I could expect to feel less of a sense of suffocation than I had with the previous workplace that was slap-bang in front of my house.

Pedalling my bike along the main road, it struck me that since watching over Ms Eriguchi hadn't been part of the advertised job description, I might get paid extra for it. But then I shook my head and told myself to get a grip. Seriously, though, what was I supposed to be looking out for? Despite her unassuming appearance, was Ms Eriguchi secretly up to some kind of mischief? And if so, what kind?

The job itself – writing copy for businesses that wanted to advertise on the circulating bus – sounded promising, but the fact that I'd been asked to do something weird on my very first day weighed on my spirits. My best guess was that there was something bugging Mr Kazetani that he couldn't be bothered investigating properly, so he'd decided to enlist my services in tracking down evidence. I decided, for the moment, as my feet pumped the pedals, that I'd put his request to one side and concentrate on mastering my job.

The company-wide discussion over whether to abolish the Albatross town bus service had been dragging on for over half a year. Two years ago, when the Albatross had been doing badly – it had never exactly been in the red, but its profits were negligible – the company had announced that they would be getting rid of it, but were met with such a vehement backlash from local residents that in the end, they decided to keep it going. At the start of this fiscal year, however, the debate had been reignited. The time was approaching for the Albatrosses to be refurbished – and there simply wasn't the budget for it.

Deeming that they could hardly go around threatening to abolish the service in case they ended up rescinding their decision again, the bus company decided instead to increase the number of audio advertisements featured on bus journeys and see how far the revenue would go towards supplementing maintenance fees. Aware that asking freelancers to write the adverts would mean incurring additional costs, they took the decision to handle the work in-house.

'So I haven't always been doing this job,' Ms Eriguchi explained to me, 'and I won't be doing it forever, either.'

The same went for me, apparently. Yet, unlike Ms Eriguchi, I'd been employed with the explicit purpose of creating these adverts, which in turn were intended to pay for the buses' refitting, so it wasn't at all clear if I'd be able to stay on after the adverts had all been written. Ms Eriguchi had been in the admin department until the month before last, yet it seemed to me like she had a knack for the business of writing copy.

The workflow for advert creation, as Ms Eriguchi outlined it to me – prefacing her words with the disclaimer that she didn't know how it worked in other companies – went as follows. First of all, we placed 'Adverts Wanted!' notices in various town circulars and in the buses themselves so as to recruit restaurants, shops, companies and other facilities wishing to advertise their services. Once an interested party appeared, we'd get in touch with them and find out what they wanted in the advert, asking which aspects of their business they wished to highlight and conducting some light fieldwork if necessary, before presenting a draft of the proposed script to the client. If they were happy with it, we would ask one of our staff members with a 'good radio voice' to record the advert and send this to the client. After making any necessary final adjustments, we were done. Reading large, and even not so large volumes of text at a time still tired me out, so I had concerns upon hearing the workflow about whether I'd be able to cope with the reading material involved – but thus far I seemed to be managing.

The company's guidelines stipulated that we should aim for least two adverts in the time it took to get from one bus stop to the next. We had thus accepted requests for over thirty new adverts, and the numbers were rising. It appeared obvious to me that airing so many adverts would mean subjecting passengers to a non-stop commercial barrage, but the people at the bus company seemed confident enough that when the locals remembered past talk of the route being abolished, they'd understand that you couldn't make an omelette without breaking a few eggs.

The advert I was tasked with creating in my first two days at work was for a long-established Japanese confectionery shop. Every time I spoke with them, they would change their minds about the particular item they wanted to promote, which was a pain.

'What!? But I've never seen such a huge manjū! You bought it locally, you say?' And the surprises don't end there! Cut open the jumbo manjū to find more manjū inside, in red, yellow and green – how perfectly auspicious! For special occasions, look no further than jumbo manjū from traditional Japanese confectioner Baifūan.

This was the first I'd ever heard of jumbo manjū, but they were reputedly the go-to gift for people getting married and so on. As the advert suggested, a jumbo manjū was quite literally a very enormous manjū, its doughy outer layer stuffed with several entire regular-sized manjū, as well as the usual sweet bean paste. They also went by the name 'pregnant manjū'. The owner of Baifūan had initially said he wanted to advertise ume jellies, then he changed to mooncake and then rakugan confectionery. It was after I'd remade the advert three times that he finally settled on the jumbo manjū. Ms Eriguchi looked down the list of Baifūan's products and pointed out that each change marked an increase in price.

'I mean, the jellies are 180 yen each, the mooncakes are 210, the smallest box of rakugan is 500 and the jumbo manjū 4,800.'

'Wow, that's a big hike.'

'I suppose he realised he was better off selling a single jumbo manjū than ten ume jellies.'

Were there really that many occasions where people would buy jumbo manjū? I guessed if you managed to cement it in people's minds that felicitous events called for jumbo manjū, then there was a possibility that people would remember the shop when they heard news of an impending wedding. What was more, said Ms Eriguchi, there were lots of seniors living in the Albatross's circulation area, so the advert may have come as good tidings for elderly men who thought there was something distasteful about giving western sweets and cakes at a wedding ceremony. This seemed to me like very positive reasoning on Ms Eriguchi's part, exactly the kind of thinking I imagined the bus company hoped to instil in their advertisers.

While training me over the past two days, Ms Eriguchi had produced two advertisements of her own: one for an estate agency, the other for an ear and nose clinic.

'I might attract more customers if only my shop was a bit bigger!'
'Now the children have grown up, we should be thinking about moving home!'
If this is you, there's no need to fret alone! Come and talk to us at Maruyama Homes! The gorilla on our billboard would be so APE-Y if you stopped by!

'Argh, I've got a hot date tomorrow but my nose won't stop running!'
'It's my daughter's piano recital next week but my ears are blocked!'
Whatever your issue, drop into Takeyama Ear and Nose Clinic. You'll know us by the big tree in the garden – our name means bamboo, but our tree is a pine!

It seemed like quite a circumscribed category of individuals to whom these adverts would be relevant – self-employed people considering upscaling, empty nesters, men or women with runny noses and dates scheduled for the following day, and parents whose children's piano recitals were fast approaching. According to Ms Eriguchi, adverts landed better with listeners if you gave concrete examples of people who might use the service, even if these people were purely hypothetical – although of course, there was no knowing what effect the adverts would really have until they actually aired.

The sound recordings for the completed adverts would then be edited – a task we had to commence at least an hour before the end of the day – and sent out for airing on the buses the following morning. The immediacy of this implementation procedure was sold as one of the merits of advertising on the Albatross.

The job of recording the adverts also fell to Ms Eriguchi and me. At three o'clock, we would ask Ms Katori from the accounts department, who'd been with the company a good while, to read the adverts for us to record. When Ms Eriguchi and I approached the section of the office floor with the ACCOUNTS banner dangling from the ceiling, Ms Katori turned to look at us with her face screwed into a sour expression, fingers still glued to her keyboard, feigning extreme lethargy. 'Not *again*?'

'I'm really sorry,' replied Ms Eriguchi. 'We'll be finished in a month.'

'A month!? Despite what you may think, I don't come in to record the weird stuff you dream up, you know. I'm here to think about numbers!'

There was no doubting that Ms Katori had a good voice. She reminded me of a presenter on daytime radio. Her voice had both character and gravitas to it, the kind that would have suited a seasoned actor.

'I know, but please try to bear it as best you can, for our sake.'

'But I'm exhausted! I can barely talk any more,' Ms Katori said, swaying her body from side to side in a charade of reluctance. She clearly had something of a dramatic streak to her personality. 'Oh, is this the new recruit?'

'That's right,' I said, and introduced myself. Ms Katori got to her feet, pulled herself up straight and gave me a deep bow. 'Nice to meet you.'

Okay, I thought, despite the drama, she didn't seem like a bad sort.

'It's definitely snack time, isn't it, Ms Katori? Can I tempt you with this before we record?' Ms Eriguchi slipped a mooncake from her pocket and handed it to Ms Katori. Ms Katori frowned, opened her eyes very wide, and then with evident delight exclaimed, 'Oooh!' and took the mooncake from Ms Eriguchi. I was pretty sure it had to be from Baifūan.

'Swing by our section when you've finished, okay?'

'Will do.'

Ms Katori was already stripping the plastic film from the mooncake and biting into it.

'We're counting on you, Ms Katori!'

'Yeah, yeah, I know.'

And so, before long, Ms Katori came to the section in the corner where Ms Eriguchi and I worked – distinguished by a sheet of paper pinned to the partitioning screen which read ADVERT CREATION

DEPARTMENT – and gave us a very nice recording of several scripts. When we were done, Ms Eriguchi presented her with another mooncake, as if in reward for her services. 'Ooh, thank you!' said Ms Katori. 'Count me in for tomorrow!'

We wrapped up our recording session just before four, and Ms Eriguchi edited the advert until 4:55 p.m., at which time she sent it off to the operations manager. In her final five minutes she filled in her daily report, then left precisely at five. I was still writing up the notes I'd taken on editing the sound recordings, so I ended up submitting my daily report a little later.

I'd just placed my report notebook in the document tray on Mr Kazetani's desk and was saying goodbye when he beckoned me over. 'Do you have a second?'

Dutifully I went to stand by the side of his desk.

'Have you noticed anything … off about Ms Eriguchi yet?'

'No, not especially,' I replied. Not only had I not noticed anything 'off' – I was noticing on a moment-by-moment basis that Ms Eriguchi was exceedingly good at her job. Admittedly it was still only my second day, but it seemed hard to imagine a more ideal employee. I supposed that as I learned more about what the job entailed, I would grow to be more like her, but I was sure it would take me a long while before I could approximate the standards she set.

'Sooner or later, something will come up to make you stop in your tracks,' said Mr Kazetani, putting a hand up to his bouffant head of hair. I was mightily conscious that insofar as Ms Eriguchi was responsible for training me, any sense of distrust I developed towards her would make things harder for me, and so I commented internally, out of something like self-protection: this guy thinks he's in a play or something.

'What kind of thing are you talking about specifically?' I asked in the most laid-back, harmless-sounding tone I could muster. I knew it was pushy to be forcing the issue, but I figured I'd reached an age where I could afford to be a little bold when the situation called for it. Such was my excuse, anyway.

Mr Kazetani tilted his head, and after a little pause, opened his mouth and said gravely, 'Things appearing that shouldn't be there, or things that seem to have disappeared actually disappearing.'

'Ah-hhh.' It took me all I had not to cry out: *Whaaaat?*

'But look, don't worry about it,' Mr Kazetani said, waving his hand dismissively. 'Just let me know if you notice anything off, that's all I'm asking.' With that, he took the pile of daily reports from his tray and started flicking through them absent-mindedly.

Things appearing that shouldn't be there, or things that seem to have disappeared actually disappearing. What in the world was he talking about? Was this about office stationery? Had he got wind of Ms Eriguchi commandeering office supplies for her own personal use? But even if she was, surely that didn't merit a fuss on this scale? Not as long as she was doing her job properly.

Reaching the door to leave the office, I turned around to check what Mr Kazetani was up to, and saw him pushing the pile of reports disinterestedly back into the tray before opening up a large map of the area. This he began to study avidly, one hand to his head.

I don't want a part in this mess, I thought reflexively as I retired to the locker room. I knew I might have to leave the company in a month's time, but I still wanted to spend my days there peacefully. I didn't want to have any more feelings about my work than were strictly necessary. I was done with all that.

And so, I took the decision to ignore Mr Kazetani's concerns, or whatever they were. I couldn't deny that however much his ostentatious appearance marked him out as slightly untrustworthy, his perturbance seemed to be genuine. But if Ms Eriguchi was bothering him that much, why didn't he just ask her about it directly instead of trying to rope me into keeping watch over her?

However much I thought about it, I didn't arrive at any answers.

I reached the end of my first week at the bus company without noticing a single thing that was 'off' about Ms

Eriguchi, and when Friday drew to a close, I decided to take a spin on the Albatross. The nearest Albatross stop was a reasonable distance from my house, and if I needed to get somewhere, I mostly just took the train, so it was only once every couple of months that I had occasion to use the route. Getting on board now, though, it struck me for the first time that having a service like this for the cost of a mere hundred yen was not half convenient.

As well as taking in the large supermarket, the town hall and various clinics and hospitals, the Albatross also circulated around all the local spots one might need in an attempt to assuage one's boredom: the DVD shop, the bookshop, the pachinko parlour, the family restaurant, the shopping arcade and so on and so forth. But these places weren't close to one another, meaning the Albatross's circulation area was of necessity quite large – a single loop took a while to execute. That could potentially have been viewed as a drawback, but it seemed as though the majority of the Albatross's passengers were housewives, children and the elderly, who were more forgiving of its leisurely pace.

Hearing Ms Katori's voice coming through the bus speakers made me feel faintly excited. She had confided in me one lunchtime, in a somewhat bashful tone, that she herself took the Albatross to work and that the sound of her own voice made her feel a bit icky, but to my ears the adverts sounded as good in situ as if they'd been recorded by a professional voice actor.

'To think that just sitting still could be this painful … !'

Are haemorrhoids getting you down? Feel like you can't talk to anybody? Well, come in to Taguchi Colorectal Clinic and tell us all about it. Together we'll solve your problems! You'll never fear sitting down again.

There was real emotion vested in Ms Katori's voice, and her tone as she spoke the words 'To think that just sitting still could be this painful … ' sounded genuinely mournful. She had mentioned to me that through recording the adverts, she'd learned of shops and clinics whose existence she'd never previously been aware of – 'you realise there's so much about your own neighbourhood you don't know,' she'd said ponderously.

It wasn't large chain stores or well-known landmarks that were advertised on the Albatross; rather, the kinds of businesses you might have called niche. Thus far, there'd been several I'd never heard of before: a soba noodle works, a coffee bean supplier, an official dealership for a foreign road-bike brand. All lay just off the main road, and the adverts provided an easy explanation of how to reach them from the relevant Albatross stop. As yet, I'd only written adverts for places right by the bus stops, which made me think that perhaps Ms Eriguchi had been giving me the easier adverts to handle.

Ms Katori's pronouncement about how little we knew of our own neighbourhood transpired to be spot on. Riding the Albatross that day, putting the scenery outside the window together with the contents of the advertisements, I made a lot of new discoveries. In the past, I'd travelled to work on a bus whose route had overlapped part of the way with the Albatross's, but now I still saw lots of things I'd not seen before.

As I was basking in this revelation, thinking that maybe I'd actually landed myself a decent job this time, that perhaps leaving in a month would feel like a shame, the bus pulled into a neighbourhood through which I often passed on my bike. In three more stops, I would have done a complete loop. Gazing out the window at the road I knew very well, feeling encumbered by the realisation that I still hadn't decided what to have for dinner, I suddenly jumped at the sight of a five-storey building in a vivid cherry red.

Do you like the sun? Dancing? Javier Bardem? Then pop in and see us at the Far East Flamenco Centre, for lessons in Spanish, cooking and – of course – flamenco!

All of the windows in the building had yellow curtains. It was Spain after all, I reasoned to myself. But the 'Far East'? Who had been responsible for such a grandiose naming choice?

Gaping up at the red building, which I assumed had to be the Far East Flamenco Centre as it moved past the window, I half doubted my eyes. Had it really always been there? Sure, this wasn't an area through which I passed on a daily basis, but the largish bookshop and a good udon restaurant brought me here a fair amount – I'd say, maybe twice a month.

So how was it possible that a building like that had escaped my notice? Was it just that riding the bus disposed me to be more observant of those parts of the buildings above ground-floor level? Or rather, with my bookshop visits taking place mostly in the evenings, had it simply been too dark for me to see? Of the two, this second hypothesis seemed the more likely.

In any case, this really was a new discovery. The Albatross went by, gobbling up its stops one by one, and I got off at the same place I'd boarded. Even with my feet on solid ground, I was still swaying under the force of this revelation. Perhaps this was simply a case of having it proved to me how little I knew my neighbourhood, just as Ms Katori had said, but I couldn't shake my sense of amazement at having overlooked something so sizeable.

Overwhelmed by an unquenchable desire to go back and check, I walked in the opposite direction to my house, towards the Far East Flamenco Centre. My question was, just how well would the ground-level shopfront have to blend into its surroundings so that I could have missed the cherry red facade extending up from its first floor?

Behind the glass door to the building, printed with the words 'La Institución Española del Extremo Oriente' in gold, I didn't find mannequins dressed in flamenco costumes or FC Barcelona kit, but rather, a couple of bookshelves home to a selection of serious-looking books. In comparison to its red exterior, it was certainly a tame window display. Beside the door was a small noticeboard, close inspection of which revealed a sign in rather limp handwriting: 'Basque cakes to buy, 340 yen each. Please come in.' It didn't look like the writing of anybody who was involved in flamenco dancing, so perhaps it was that of a Javier Bardem fan.

I opened the door and made my way unsteadily inside the Far East Flamenco Centre. The Basque cake was nice and everything, but it didn't help assuage my feeling of astonishment, which lingered until I went to sleep that evening.

From that point on, I began periodically riding the Albatross without any particular reason for doing so. I would invariably ride in the evening, after work, so possibly the darkness aided in bringing out different aspects of the scenery, but even so it seemed to me like my rate of new discoveries was on the high side.

The number of advertisements aired on the bus increased steadily until there were at least three per stop, and the Albatross had become much like an audio version of a town bulletin. I still felt the same worry I'd had from the beginning, that the passengers would find it too intrusive, but Ms Katori's voice was really quite pleasant to listen to and I never heard of any complaints. Since I'd joined the company, Ms Eriguchi had edited the recordings single-handedly. It seemed to me, by rights, that an underling like myself should be handling the mechanical compilation of the adverts rather than their creative composition, and so I would occasionally apologise to her for the fact that all my time seemed to be taken up with writing – but she would always respond good-naturedly, 'No, no, not at all. You take all the time you need.'

At the beginning of my third week in the company, I finally got around to editing the audio data by myself, a task that entailed using special voice-editing software to add in new advertisements to the existing reel, and checking that the total length of the adverts didn't exceed the time it took the bus to travel from one stop to the next. Currently, all the adverts fitted into the gaps between stops, although the stop after Station Crossroads: North Side – where the Far East Flamenco Centre was located – only had space for about one more. I wasn't sure if it was a particularly well-off area, or it just happened to be home to a lot of businesses wanting to advertise.

For the time being, we updated the advert reel about once every three days. There would have been nothing to stop us from doing so daily, if our output had merited it, but when you factored in time for calling the business wanting to advertise, recording their advert and getting them to check the copy we came up with, we found that between us we could complete at the most two per day – or if things went exceptionally well, then three. If things weren't progressing particularly smoothly with our clients we'd often go out and visit them, even if they didn't explicitly invite us to do so, and if on such occasions we happened to fall into the clutches of a company director with far too much time on their hands, three or so hours of the morning could easily be eaten up.

The company didn't complain about the pace at which Ms Eriguchi and I were creating adverts. They didn't tell us to hurry, nor did they advise us to slow down. Our sole instruction was to squeeze as many adverts as we could into the slots provided.

So there I was, doing the editing, playing back the reel for the stop for which I'd just added a new advert, when it came: my 'stopping in my tracks' moment.

'It's my son's baseball match this weekend, but the Parents and Teachers Association don't have any plastic bento boxes to give out to the kids!'

'I've worked out how to make great take-away food – now I need some take-home containers for my customers!'

Mums, shop owners, look no further than Itō Packaging! Providing containers to fit all your diverse needs.

The advert was one of Ms Eriguchi's. I waited until Ms Katori's voice had moved through the usual roster of specific consumer profile, shop name and business outline and then, as the recording shifted to announce, 'The next stop is Umenoki Primary School,' I hit pause.

Was there really a packaging shop near Umenoki Primary School? I felt relatively confident that I'd know about it if there were. I was a big fan of wrapping paper, disposable lunch boxes and that sort of thing, so it was the kind of place I was highly likely to have stopped by at least once.

Besides, I'd gone past the Umenoki Primary School stop on the bus the day before yesterday, and there'd been no trace of any such shop – although I suppose there was no way of seeing from the bus what was happening in the backstreets, so if it was an old shop tucked away, out of sight, then there were no such arguments to be broached there.

Above any specific desire to go and check the place out, my initial reaction was one of pure suspicion. Something seemed awry: that was my feeling. I finished the editing task, sent off the file, wrote my daily report, let Ms Eriguchi go home and then stepped out of my section in search of an area map. The maps were kept on the shelf behind Mr Kazetani's desk. Affecting an air of casualness, I made a beeline for it and picked out this year's map for the area around Umenoki Primary School.

Flipping through the pages until I found the school itself, I began to carefully scour the vicinity, but I could see no sign of any Itō Packaging. Squinting, I ran my finger across every building on the Umenoki Primary School page. No Itō Packaging. I did the same for the pages before and after it. My vision started to swim. Still no Itō Packaging. I couldn't even find any houses registered in the name of Itō.

Standing there by the bookcase, staring down at the map, I suddenly became aware of Mr Kazetani hovering beside me.

'What do you think?' There was something about the formulation of this question, from which he left out not just the subject but almost everything else, that felt overly familiar to me – and so I replied, 'About what?'

Mr Kazetani took a step back and began muttering, 'Oh, erm, I … no, I just … ' which made me feel immediately guilty. I was starting to think that maybe he was actually just a slightly weak person.

'Sorry, I mean … I was just checking that the actual location of a shop matches up with what it says in our advert.'

'Oh, I see.' Mr Kazetani nodded and returned to his chair. Should I have been a bit more empathetic to his concerns? Maybe. But the truth was, I didn't yet feel clear enough about what was going on to fully empathise. It wouldn't do to admit that I suspected there was something up with the adverts Ms Eriguchi was making – not at this stage.

After handing in my daily report, I left the office and got on the Albatross, half wild with impatience by now. Neither the scenes passing by outside the window, nor Ms Katori's words entered my head. I sat there simply waiting for the voice to announce Umenoki Primary School, then got off the bus.

By now it was totally dark outside. There was something eerie about the way the school playing field looked in this light like a stagnant lake, but there was a glow emanating from one of the windows on the ground floor – I assumed it must have been the staffroom – which reassured me a little. The Baifūan confectionery shop diagonally across from the school entrance had its shutters half down, preparing to close. When I realised that all the other shops were already done for the day, it occurred to me that this was perhaps an area where shops shut particularly early.

Maybe I should have held on until the weekend so I could have visited when it was still light, I thought, as I set off down the pavement on the Baifūan side of the road, inspecting the shop names written on the shutters – but there was no sign of any Itō Packaging. Just as it struck me that maybe I should phone the office and get Mr Kazetani to come out here, I saw a light a little way down a wide alley leading off from the road. A shop down there, it seemed, was still open.

It was the two large flowering plants that I first saw as I made my approach, the lavish kind that businesses gifted to other businesses when they first opened, and then I took in what lay behind: towering columns of circular canapé platters, crimson bento boxes with transparent lids and black sushi trays adorned in gold, enormous cardboard boxes filled with bundles of disposable chopsticks and thousand-packs of bento-dividers fashioned into the shape of bears' faces in pink, baby blue and yellow. Up close, I could see that the plant pots had notecards stuck in them, with messages from two local businesses congratulating Itō Packaging on their opening.

With a thousand-pack of bear-face-shaped bento-dividers in hand, I stood there looking around the brand-new shop in a state of bewilderment. Before long, a man in his fifties came to greet me, an apron tied around his waist.

'Irasshaimase!'

'Oh, hi … '

'Are you looking for something in particular?'

'No, no. Did you, erm, open recently?'

'Yes! Just yesterday.' The man nodded cheerfully, shooting a look in the direction of the potted plants. 'Until not long ago, I was working at the company that manufactures those very bento box dividers you've got there, but I decided to follow in the footsteps of my late father and go into the wholesale packaging trade.'

'Your late father … ?'

'Ideally I'd have liked to have opened this place while he was still alive, so he could have seen it.'

The man turned his head to cast a look around, a sentimental expression shifting across his face. There were a handful of customers in the shop: a young woman examining the selection of paper wrappers for crêpes, a middle-aged man holding a large cardboard box printed with the words DISPOSABLE ALUMINIUM SAUCEPANS: 400 PCS, and two women in their mid-thirties who were pointing at brightly coloured aluminium cups as they spoke.

'Do you make your own lunches?' he asked me now.

'Ah, no.'

There was both a convenience store and a bento shop near the bus company, and besides, one of the things I looked forward to after spending the morning visiting clients was finding a restaurant in the vicinity to eat lunch in. In fact, in all my working life, I hadn't once made myself a packed lunch. If there were any spare seconds in the morning before work, I wanted to spend them sleeping.

'Well, if you do start, then come back and pay us a visit. Our disposable bento containers are excellent value. Using a fresh container every day is the most hygienic solution, after all.'

'Right, yes ... '

I knew what he was saying was true, but I also knew that realistically, there was very little chance I was ever going to follow his advice. Perhaps guessing at the contents of my mind, the man clasped his hands in front of his waist and beamed at me.

'By the way,' I said, 'on the residential map of this area, there isn't anyone listed as Itō as far as I can recall. Did your father live a little way away?'

I judged that so long as I didn't give away that I was from the bus company, it was alright to be a bit nosey. Still grinning at me, the man shook his head. 'No, no. I changed my name when I married, as it happens, so I have a different surname to my father.'

'Oh, I see.'

'Itō is my wife's family name. My birth name was Nashiyama.'

Nashiyama, Nashiyama … Yes, I was relatively confident I'd seen that name on the map. 'I could have called it Nashiyama Packaging, of course, but I'd have felt bad for my in-laws.'

Mr Itō went on to tell me that his wife was an only child, and he'd decided to take her name to prevent Itō from dying out completely – but then, as it transpired, he and his wife had only had one daughter, so there was no telling what would happen to the name now. Around about then, he was called over by another customer and went to help them out.

There was nothing more I wanted to know, so I left the shop and returned to the bus stop outside Umenoki School. So that's all there was to it, said one part of me, while another remained not entirely satisfied. The bus came and I got on, thinking that I couldn't be sure whether this sensation I was having was the feeling of something not being quite right of which Mr Kazetani had spoken, but regardless, I now knew that his unease wasn't totally unprompted.

Whatever way you looked at it, it was too early for Ms Eriguchi's advert to be aired on the bus. Naturally I was aware that brand-new businesses handed out flyers and other promotional material in the interest of spreading word of their existence to those in the vicinity, but it wasn't flyers and other promotional material that Ms Eriguchi was dealing with – it was bus adverts.

Of course, part of my and Ms Eriguchi's job was to recruit potential advertisers, placing notices in the buses and town circulars and spreading news by word of mouth – but now it appeared that she had some particular means of accessing information about shops that were about to open and their desire to advertise – although she had never once spoken about it to me, and, in theory, our job didn't involve any sales activities.

Rocking gently from side to side in my seat on the bus, I passed the Far East Flamenco Centre again. Looking up at the windows framed in their yellow curtains of an almost eerie radiance, it occurred to me that maybe the problem wasn't how little I knew my neighbourhood. Maybe it was that my neighbourhood was morphing into a place I didn't know.

The next morning, I set out to visit a piano academy wishing to advertise on the Albatross. The teacher was a perceptive sort, and our conversation was wrapped up quickly, so by 2 p.m. I found I'd finished my tasks for the day. All that remained was to get Ms Katori to record the advert I'd written and to call the client whose advert I'd be making the following day to check a couple of things. To give myself a little break, I headed to the kitchen to make a cup of tea. It was just as I was opening the lid of the green tea canister that Mr Kazetani came walking down the corridor.

I saw him stroll past the door, and then the next moment he was back. I didn't like being in the kitchen with other people, so I made to excuse myself and leave, but Mr Kazetani moved straight towards me, proffering a can of coffee.

'Here,' he said. 'Have this.'

'Oh, no,' I said, waving a hand. 'I couldn't.'

'Is this brand no good?' he said, checking the can.

The coffee in question was unsweetened and it definitely wasn't a make that I liked enough to buy, but I began to feel sorry for poor old Mr Kazetani, and in the end I took the can. I got the sense that he wasn't a bad sort, all told. Although I was also aware that in a workplace context, people could become bad sorts as and when the situation required, so maybe it was more accurate to say he wasn't always a bad sort.

Relieved of his load, Mr Kazetani stretched out a hand, leaned against the door frame and began: 'About what I was saying to you a while back … ' Here we go, I thought. Still, recalling the peculiar feeling that had come over me yesterday with the Itō Packaging debacle, I felt I could understand why he was so fixated on this topic. 'Have you noticed anything off?'

I had absolutely no complaints with Ms Eriguchi, but I couldn't deny I was experiencing a vague discomfort around the connection between the adverts and the world outside them, so I nodded and said, 'Well, yes, just a little. There's been a couple of times when I've sensed that, erm, how should I put this? Changes are very quick to be reflected.'

I decided not to mention Ms Eriguchi's name. I had simply noticed something off – I had no intention of implicating her specifically.

'Is it a case of things appearing that shouldn't be there?'

It hit me in that moment that this phrase, which Mr Kazetani had repeated to me several times by now, was a more or less perfect description of what was happening – but I didn't want to wholeheartedly agree with him only to find myself roped into watching out for yet something else, so I kept my agreement as tepid as I could and said, 'Yes, well, something like that.'

But perhaps even such tepidness was enough because now Mr Kazetani, who had never previously been forthcoming with any concrete details about his concerns, began to talk.

'You know, one time, when I came across a shop that I thought had materialised out of the blue, I tried waiting a little and then deleting the advert from the audio data before sending it off to air, just to see what would happen. Of course, I didn't tell Ms Eriguchi that that was what I was doing.' Mr Kazetani's face wore a pained expression, as if the deed to which he was confessing was a truly heinous one. 'And when I went back to the spot where the shop had been, it had closed. Its sign taken down and everything. If I hadn't been searching for it, I'd never have noticed it had even been there. It was like it had just vanished.'

With a heavy feeling in the pit of my stomach, I asked, 'And has it stayed closed?'

'Seems so,' Mr Kazetani answered.

'Are you sure that it wasn't due to close anyway?'

'Of course, I can't rule that out as a possibility,' he said. He went on to tell me that the place in question was a nail salon, run single-handedly by a woman in the converted garage of her husband's family home, where she now lived. It didn't seem like a business she'd staked her livelihood on or anything but, by all accounts, it had not been doing too badly. Mr Kazetani's wife had once had her nails done there.

'Maybe there were family circumstances which meant she couldn't keep it open. It's hard to say for sure.'

Then someone came down the corridor to tell Mr Kazetani he had a phone call, and he went hurrying off. Standing there alone in the kitchen, clutching a can of coffee of a make I didn't even particularly like,

I fell deep into thought – except I didn't have enough material to facilitate particularly deep thinking, so my thoughts circulated the same territory over and over. Eventually, I left the kitchen having arrived at a single decision: I'd give the can of coffee to Ms Katori.

All that week, my kitchen encounter with Mr Kazetani played around my head. In essence, he'd been suggesting that when an advert disappeared, the business it was advertising also disappeared, which made no sense whatsoever. But by now, I'd encountered a couple of instances of what could be termed the reverse of this phenomenon, and I felt that I couldn't simply dispense of the idea as total rubbish. After all, Mr Kazetani had run up against the disappearing phenomenon through his attempts to confirm it was the adverts that were making the businesses appear in the first place.

But no, this was insanity. Mr Kazetani must be having some kind of midlife crisis. Maybe he was suffering from depression? When things had been really unbearable for me at my old job, I'd fallen prey to paranoid thoughts several times, suspecting that my boss was stealing my stationery and that someone was deliberately hiding my documents so as to ensure I'd miss my deadlines. In fact, it transpired that both the stationery and the documents had been disappearing thanks to my own organisational mismanagement.

Meanwhile, Ms Eriguchi was performing her job as efficiently as ever. Just this morning, she'd received a thank you postcard from a client: 'Thanks to the advert on the Albatross, our revenue is now three times what it was when we opened!' The postcard was from a burger joint serving Sasebo burgers – the original American-style burgers to be served in Japan – which had opened up near the Station Crossroads: Higashi-dōri stop not long ago. I had felt doubtful about whether there'd be any demand for a new Sasebo burger joint in this day and age, but it seemed the offer of a three-quarter-sized burger with fries and a drink for a very reasonable 650 yen was going down a treat.

'Aah, I'm craving a filling, juicy burger. But it's so hard to find one just the right size … ' Look no further than Doctor Sasebo! Our burgers come in every size, from full and three-quarter down to half-size and mini, so we're bound to have just what the doctor ordered! We've got a range of different fries too!

From what I could see, Doctor Sasebo was another example of a business materialising out of nowhere. One day, on one of my after-work bus journeys, I spotted a brightly coloured canopy of the kind often seen festooning restaurants, which had appeared outside a previously unoccupied shop on the corner beside the Station Crossroads: Higashi-dōri stop. By the following day, the burger joint had opened, and the bus was playing its advert. It was all a little too neat. There were several other cases that fell into this pattern of shops whose adverts were played from the very day they opened, but the strange thing was that it was only ever Ms Eriguchi who dealt with these. All the adverts I was entrusted with making were for shops or clinics or companies or academies that had been around for a while, and who were taking out adverts to boost their sales. When I was told about the business I'd be covering for my next assignment, its name would always be vaguely familiar to me. The places Ms Eriguchi was charged with making adverts for, though, would often just have appeared out of the blue.

As far as I could see, it wasn't like Ms Eriguchi was receiving secret perks for penning adverts for spanking new shops, and nor did it seem that she'd been driven by some desperate love of all that was new to request first dibs on any virgin businesses that came in. Besides, it wasn't as if the clients contacted us with requests directly – our instructions about which adverts to create always came via the advertising department. In other words, even if Ms Eriguchi was making adverts for all these new places, it wasn't as though doing so held any particular merit for her, just as there were no disadvantages for me in producing adverts for businesses that had been around for a while.

All of which had to mean that Mr Kazetani's inter-pretation of the situation was nuts. I reached the conclusion that the closure of the nail salon must have been sheer coincidence. And yet, despite arriving at that verdict, I was taken by an impulse that ran something like this: if it really is sheer coincidence, there's no harm in checking to make sure.

The devil had got into me, that was the truth of it. No, maybe that wasn't the truth of it – maybe it was silly to use that sort of phraseology about work-related stuff, when it was clearly all my own doing. But either way, it was a very devilish state of mind I found myself in that afternoon when I was entrusted with editing the sound recordings on my own. What harm can a single day do? I thought. Besides, as it happened, the following day when the recording reel would be aired was a Wednesday: the day off for the Far East Flamenco Centre. Which just so happened to be the place whose advert I was considering deleting.

Given that the nail salon Mr Kazetani had spoken about was in a converted garage and had been run as a kind of passion project, it was, in a sense, the type of place you could imagine folding pretty unceremoni-ously. But there was no way that a five-storey bright red building like the Flamenco Centre could vanish just like that. Having its advert deleted for a single day wasn't going to do anything, especially if said day was its day off.

After inserting the data for the advert I'd created and recorded that day, I pressed delete on the Far East Flamenco Centre advert in the Station Crossroads: North Side reel, and sent the data off to the operations manager, all with great composure. I could only assume that Ms Eriguchi trusted me; in any case, she didn't check my work. I felt more than somewhat guilty to think that I was turning the company's laid-back working structure to my advantage, but I consoled myself with the belief that resolving doubts for oneself was a crucial part of ensuring one could keep on doing one's job properly.

The shock came the next day, when we were recording the adverts – a shock so great I genuinely thought I might faint. Ms Katori came right out and said it. 'Is it true that the Flamenco Centre's going to close?'

I whipped around to look at her.

'Sometimes on days when I feel like treating myself, I borrow a company bike and cycle down there at lunchtime. You know, they do really good tapas, at a reasonable price. Anyway, when I went today, the shutters were down. That's weird, I thought, and then I remembered that today is their day off, but when I looked closer it seemed like it wasn't just that.'

'What do you mean?'

'There was a sign up saying that the owner had suddenly been taken ill, and they're closing indefinitely.'

This can't be, I thought, as I felt the blood rushing from my head. Next to me, Ms Eriguchi said in a tone that suggested genuine regret, 'Oh no, is it really closing?' Then she added, 'I guess I'd better update the audio data sooner rather than later.'

Even in my current state of mental disarray, I retained enough circumspection to realise it wouldn't do for it to get out that I'd deleted the advert, so I raised a hand and said, 'Oh, I'll do it!'

'Are you sure?' she said. 'In that case, I'll just call them to confirm,' and with that, she left her seat.

'It's a very fancy-looking building, isn't it?' said Ms Katori to me. 'It didn't half give me a start when it suddenly appeared there last year.'

'Yes, absolutely.'

'It's such a shame that it's closing. The tapas really were good quality, and I used to like going to that cafe bit on the ground floor to relax.' Ms Katori looked wistful. A little while ago when we'd had lunch together, she'd told me that she'd got married in her early thirties, but had divorced and been single ever since. After work, she said, she rode the Albatross to the gym, but it was too much to exercise every day, so on her days off she liked to go to cafes and just take it easy.

Now, this influx of additional information about Ms Katori's relationship with the Far East Flamenco Centre left me at a loss for words. Without meaning to, I'd stolen her favourite relaxation spot from her. Ms Eriguchi returned very shortly, shaking her head. 'I can't get through,' she said. 'I'll call them again tomorrow and see. But it won't do to advertise if they're saying they're closed, so for the moment let's delete the advert from today's data.'

I nodded. As I nodded, I wondered what would happen if I were to do the opposite: if I were to rein-state the advert. Maybe, then, the Flamenco Centre would renege on its decision to close. Of course, it was sheer conjecture on my part, but putting together what Mr Kazetani had told me with what had just happened, it seemed as though if deleting its advert could cause a place to disappear, then reinstating that advert may well bring the place back again.

Later on that day, I added the Far East Flamenco Centre advert I'd deleted the previous day back into the audio track, sent it off to the operations manager, then boarded the Albatross for an end-of-day loop. When the bus approached Station Crossroads: North Side, I sat up from my seat so as to get a good look at what was going on in the cherry red Flamenco Centre. Despite reports of it having shut, the lights on all the floors were on. Were they doing some post-closure clearing?

The strangest thing was that the yellow curtains in the windows had all been replaced by black ones, as if the building itself were in mourning. I shook my head and sank as far back in my seat as I could go. What on earth had I gone and done?

The call from the operations manager came about an hour after I got into work. I felt intensely relieved that it was me who picked up the phone. As it happened, Ms Eriguchi was out doing some research work for the advert she was assigned with creating that day.

The operations manager had heard from the bus driver that the advert for the Flamenco Centre had been disappearing and then appearing again. Which was the newest version, the manager wanted to know, and could I send them the most recent data? Omitting to mention that I'd deliberately deleted the ad, I said, 'Oh, the latest version of the reel includes the advert.'

'But isn't it closing?' said the manager. This, it transpired, they also knew from the bus driver. Sensing something awry when he'd seen black curtains in the building's windows, the driver had stopped in to check on his way home, and found the notice announcing its indefinite closure.

'The driver said he was wondering if the advert had vanished because it was the centre's day off, but when he saw it was closing down, it all made sense. When the advert appeared again today, though, he started wondering what was going on.'

So the bus driver was actually listening and looking at what went on around him. I felt like the greatest idiot the world had ever known. There was no trace of blame in the operation manager's tone, yet still I felt full of self-loathing.

'Okay, I'll sort it out when I'm editing the audio today,' I said, not specifying whether 'sorting it out' would mean deleting it or leaving it as it was.

'Okay, thanks!' said the operations manager cheerily, and put down the phone.

The rest of that day at work, my mood was very bleak. I felt an unusually piercing sense of shame about both the effects that my bad deeds – or rather, my selfish experimenting – had wrought upon the world, and the fact that such effects were utterly out in the open, known to all those around me. What was I playing at, honestly? Here I was with fourteen years' work experience behind me, and I was still acting like a brazen, conceited teenager.

Ms Eriguchi came back just before I went on my lunch break, and handed me a bento box with rolled omelette, grilled salmon and rice boiled with wild shoots, which she'd been given by the delicatessen she'd just visited. I ate it for my lunch but I was so busy mulling over what I'd done, and the question of how to tell Ms Eriguchi about it, that I barely tasted the food. Ms Eriguchi and Ms Katori were in high spirits as they ate their bento boxes, remarking over and over again how delicious they were.

Even once we resumed work in the afternoon, I found myself unable to divulge my bad deed to Ms Eriguchi. I plodded on glumly with my work, deciding at some point that at three o'clock, I'd have a cup of tea and a breather, and then at four o'clock, I'd confess.

Ms Eriguchi was busy polishing her draft for the delicatessen advert, putting in a call every hour or so to the Flamenco Centre. I guessed she kept getting the answerphone, because each time I'd hear her politely repeat the words, 'I'm sorry to keep calling,' and 'If you wouldn't mind giving me a ring when you have a moment, that would be great,' before setting down the receiver.

My stomach hurt. My confidence in my ability to work, which I had been accruing little by little since leaving university, was now in tatters. *No, you've got me wrong,* I imagined saying, *I really do take my work seriously, this thing that's happened, it's just, well, it's all because of this conversation I had with Mr Kazetani, and then, I don't know, there was a lot going on and the devil got into me, and …* No, it was no good. Invoking Mr Kazetani's name like that would make me the lowest of the low, and as I'd already established, saying that the devil had got into me was just silliness. That wasn't something that working adults went around saying.

Three o'clock came, the time when we recorded Ms Katori reading the adverts, and I still hadn't managed to get my thoughts together. There was only one hour left until the time I'd decided to spill the beans. Just as Ms Eriguchi opened up the box where she put all the sweets and other edibles she'd been given by our advertisers, examining the selection to decide what to present to Ms Katori, a call came through on the internal line. I picked up, and the woman from the admin department said, 'I've got someone from the Far East Flamenco Centre on the line. Can you put Ms Eriguchi on?'

I felt cold sweat form instantly on my brow, and my stomach wrenched as though it were about to split open. I passed the receiver to Ms Eriguchi.

'Yes, this is Eriguchi,' I heard her say. 'Thank you very much for calling back. I'm sorry for leaving so many messages.'

I passed my eyes several times over the script that Ms Katori would be reading for us that afternoon, but I couldn't take in a single word. As she told the person on the other end of the line how surprised she'd been to hear from a colleague of their closure, Ms Eriguchi's tone was perfectly flat, and it was impossible to predict whether my position was about to take a turn for the better or for the worse. Oh, come off it, I admonished myself, there's no way it's going to take a turn for the better, don't kid yourself, and with that I began to imagine the contempt with which Ms Eriguchi was about to shower me.

If I was only going to be in this job until all the advert slots had been filled, a part of me thought, it didn't particularly matter what was said to me. And yet, for some reason, I had come to feel quite strongly that I didn't want to be looked down on by this colleague of mine, who was plausibly ten years my junior. Of course, I didn't really want to be looked down on by anybody, but I was especially averse to ruining my relationship with Ms Eriguchi. I didn't really know why. It was possible I was coming to feel towards her something best described as a species of awe.

'Oh, really, he's improving?' Gripping the receiver in one hand, Ms Eriguchi gave a series of small nods. There was a trace of animation in her voice now. 'And you've found someone to take over from him? Right, right, I see. But you don't yet have a fixed date for when you'll reopen? Oh, no, not at all. It's down to all your hard work! What would you like to do about the advertisement?' There was another pause, and then she said, 'Yes, please let me know! Okay then, speak soon, goodbye.' She put down the phone, and turned around to where I was sitting, rod-straight and barely breathing.

'They haven't got an exact date for when they'll be reopening, but they want to keep the advert playing for the moment. So we'll add it back into the audio data we send off today.'

'Right,' I said, 'I see.' I found myself nodding over and over again, totally meaninglessly.

'Can I get you to edit the data when we're done recording?'

'Er, actually,' I replied immediately. I had the urgent sense that it was better that I didn't involve myself in this affair any further – that I left the entire thing to Ms Eriguchi. 'My vision is a bit funny today, all kind of blurry, and also my ears feel like there's air trapped inside, so everything sounds a bit muffled. Would it be alright if I left the computer stuff to you?'

'Gosh, are you okay? Do you need to go home early?'

'Ahh, no, no, it's not that bad.'

'Okay, sure. Come to think of it, I have been leaving all the editing to you of late.'

Even-tempered Ms Eriguchi didn't even challenge the absurd excuse I'd come out with. Holding an ume jelly in hand as an offering, she stood up, saying, 'I'll go and get Ms Katori.'

'Thanks.' I waved at her as she stepped out of our section, then immediately after she had gone, slumped down onto the desk, exhausted. The next moment, I remembered that if I was going to let Ms Eriguchi do the editing, I needed to swap the most recent data over for a version with no Flamenco Centre advert, so I dived towards the computer and overwrote the current data with the version from two days ago.

Ms Katori's recording session went off without a hitch, and when it was done, Ms Eriguchi began editing the data.

'Hmm, that's weird!' I heard her remark at one point. 'This is saying that the file was last revised today.' There are no flies on her, I thought, but managed to give a reply smooth enough to evade suspicion: 'Oh, I opened it up this morning to remove a bit of background noise.'

On my way home, in a state of total exhaustion, I did a circuit on the Albatross. Hunched over, clutching my cramping stomach, I sat up when the Flamenco Centre came into view in the distance, but the curtains were still black and there were no lights on inside. I returned home feeling utterly miserable, and went to bed without eating dinner.

The following day, the Flamenco Centre was so much on my mind that I left the office at lunchtime and walked down there. The shutters were still down, but the closure notice had disappeared. Moving a little distance away, I saw that the curtains on the first and second floors had been replaced by the original yellow ones again. As I stood there watching, I spotted someone moving about by the third-floor windows and looked up, only to find myself witnessing the very moment of the curtains being switched over. When I thought I saw the curtain-changer glancing in my direction, I quickly hurried away from the building.

On Thursday that week, as he took the daily report I handed him, Mr Kazetani said to me, 'We're having a meeting first thing tomorrow.'

I felt the blood drain from my face. What was this about? Had Ms Eriguchi discovered the truth about the whole affair and taken it to her superiors without confronting me about it? *But I haven't even been in this company for very long,* I protested internally. *You really don't need to be organising a meeting on my behalf. All I deserve is to be called out to the end of the corridor, shouted at for fifteen minutes, then told not to bother coming in the following day.*

Such were the thoughts on which I stewed constantly from the time I left work that evening till the time I returned the following morning. As it turned out, all my fears were needless. The meeting had not been assembled to call me out on my peculiar behaviour, but rather, to discuss a new announcement to be added into the Albatross audio reel.

The meeting was attended by Ms Eriguchi and me, Mr Kazetani, the head of advertising, the head of sales and six young employees from the sales division. The head of sales upped and left after the first ten minutes. Since I'd started at the company, my headspace had been taken up so entirely by the Albatross ads that I'd never given much thought to the company's other functions, but of course, it also ran regular bus routes. It turned out that my and Ms Eriguchi's official job title was Albatross Advertisements Creation Supervisor. A young man called Mr Shōda from the sales division referred to us as the 'Alba-dross team', then immediately pulled an 'Oops, I've gone and put my foot in it now!' face, but Ms Eriguchi and I, who collectively formed said Alba-dross department, both kept our cool. It seemed like a good opportunity to make it clear to this upstart how revealing disdain for other people's work could be just as humiliating as being the target of that disdain.

According to the head of advertising, the sales department had learned of several incidents of a stranger harassing children at points along the Albatross route and it had been suggested that a warning announcement be played on the bus. Looking down at the documents she'd brought along to the meeting, Ms Eriguchi provided for the assembled company a concise explanation of which stops still had space for such an announcement. Trust her, I thought. There was no way that I could have said with any degree of precision which stops were full and which still had space without the actual recording data in front of me. I knew that generally speaking, free slots were more plentiful in residential areas like Umenoki Primary, and less so in more commercial zones, like the shopping arcade and around the station – but that was as far as my knowledge on the matter went.

'We're not expecting any new advertisements in those areas, either,' Ms Eriguchi said in conclusion, her voice loaded with a strange conviction. This lodged with me instantly, and I noticed Mr Kazetani shoot her the sort of look with which one might regard an unearthly being, but neither the head of advertising, nor those from the sales department, seemed to pay her comment any mind. Instead, they went on to request that Ms Eriguchi create an advert that 'would lead to a remarkable improvement in the image of the

Albatross, not to mention the entire bus company'. That's easy enough for you to say, I thought. As if a remarkable improvement in reputation could be affected by a single advert! But Ms Eriguchi nodded and said with a serious expression, 'Understood.'

Those at the meeting had all seemed genuine in their motivation to do something about the issue, yet even after returning to our seats, Ms Eriguchi and I couldn't shake our feelings of disquiet about the developments just relayed to us. 'I always thought this was a peaceful, crime-free area,' I said.

Ms Eriguchi nodded. 'I moved here four years ago, straight out of university,' she said, 'and all the time I've been living here, I've not once had cause to feel scared.' It was unusual for her to divulge things in this way, and I stopped what I was doing to listen. As a rule, Ms Eriguchi didn't speak about herself or her life outside of work. Her contributions to conversations with Ms Katori and me at lunchtime were mostly limited to replying to whatever we said, and I'd not once eaten out with her or anything, so this seemed like a precious opportunity to get to know her better.

Until graduating university, Ms Eriguchi told me, she'd lived with her parents in a house they'd built in a residential district in the suburbs. The area had been newer and less rundown than the one that the Albatross circulated, and yet there had been several incidents that had left her feeling uneasy. There were few people around on the streets, and night seemed to come early. Once every couple of years, on her way home from school, a stranger would speak to her in way she found unnerving.

'I really like this neighbourhood, and I can't stand the thought that this is happening here.'

I realised that, to my astonishment, Ms Eriguchi was openly showing anger. By way of response, I told her I'd been born and raised here, and I'd never heard of anything like this happening before. I'd encountered the sort of crimes that befell people regardless of their age – my mother's bag had been snatched by someone on a motorbike as she was walking by the crossroads, my father's wallet had been stolen at the station, I'd almost been run down by a high school boy on a bike, and so on – but this was the first I'd heard of children being targeted specifically.

The warning announcements were to be aimed at parents and other concerned passengers. Mr Shōda had told us that the predator was using the promise of sweets and video games to lure children on their way home from school, so after talking it through, Ms Eriguchi and I decided to go for content that didn't mess around:

There have been reports of strangers offering children sweets in an attempt to lead them away. Do not, under any circumstances, accept gifts from someone you don't know, or go anywhere with them.

We went over to show our script to the head of advertising, who, probably because his hands were full with other routes and matters, approved it immediately, adding only, 'Oh, and so that it stands out from the other adverts, you should probably get someone different to record it. A man, maybe?'

'A man?' Ms Eriguchi repeated.

'A man's voice might stand out better, given that the other adverts are read by a woman.'

'Would you like to do it, in that case?' asked Ms Eriguchi.

The head of advertising waved a hand in front of his face, forcing a cough as he said, 'Oh no, you don't want someone with a voice like mine.'

'How about Mr Shōda?'

'Ah, yes, now we're talking. Although he won't be back in the office until the evening.'

The head's tone implied that, really, it was all one to him who read the advert. He began stuffing assorted papers inside his briefcase, then, saying he had a meeting with a big client for the regular buses, hurried out of the office, leaving the issue of who would read the advert unresolved.

Not the most helpful of advice, eh? I was about to say in Ms Eriguchi's direction, when Mr Kazetani, whose desk was not far from the head of advertising, approached, a strained expression on his face.

'Erm, Ms Eriguchi!'

Surely, as her boss, there was no call for him to be nervous around her, I thought, although I imagined that in some sense, he genuinely revered her.

'Would I do? For, er, recording the advert, I mean.'

'Yes, of course,' Ms Eriguchi said, nodding matter-of-factly. In age terms, she may have been considerably Mr Kazetani's junior, but she seemed to command more authority in the workplace – which, for a third party such as myself observing their interactions, made for a rather confusing spectacle.

'If you've time now, we can do it right away.'

'Oh, right,' said Mr Kazetani. He glanced towards his desk, then said, 'I'll try and have this thing I'm working on finished by three.'

I snuck a look at his computer screen. His desktop background was a photo of a woman about the same age as him – I imagined she must be his wife – with her arm around a girl of maybe ten. Taken against a background of a field of cosmos flowers, the two of them looked very happy. His wife had a gentle, kind-looking face, and the daughter beaming out at the camera was adorable. I knew that Mr Kazetani lived within the area circumscribed by the Albatross, and that he took the bus to work.

While eating lunch with Ms Eriguchi that day, I came close on several occasions to suggesting that perhaps Mr Kazetani's concern for his own daughter was part of the reason he'd suggested broadcasting the announcement on the Albatross – but in the end, I couldn't get the words out.

At three o'clock on the dot, Mr Kazetani appeared at the door to my and Ms Eriguchi's section. He wasn't an old hand like Ms Katori was, and hesitations and trip-ups rendered his first three attempts unusable, but after that he got the hang of things and the final recording sounded heartfelt, as if he was genuinely worried about the welfare of the neighbourhood.

Afterwards, as I was editing the audio data and Ms Eriguchi was reading over the information about a pickle shop dating back to the Edo period for which she'd be writing an advert the following day, we somehow wound up sharing our opinion that in the end, we'd managed to record a reasonably high-quality advert. Ms Katori's output was of a consistently high calibre, but there was a humble aspect to Mr Kazetani's effort that was very effective.

I turned around, intending to tell Ms Eriguchi that I thought this job was a good one, only to find that she was putting in a call to the pickle place, and once again I found myself unable to come out with the thing I'd been meaning to say.

A week after Mr Kazetani's announcement began to air, one of the teachers at Umenoki Primary School got in touch to thank us. It was someone from the sales department who took the call, and on asking if the school had been seeing any effect, they'd been told that incidents of kids being approached by strangers had gone down from nine a week to just two since the announcement had been implemented. Coming over to inform us of this development, Mr Shōda seemed positively jubilant, and enquired whether we couldn't broadcast Mr Kazetani's advert between all the stops where there was space to do so, but Ms Eriguchi replied in a businesslike tone that he would need to consult the head of advertising about that.

Ms Eriguchi's shocking confession came at lunch-time the following day. As she dug into the quinoa salad accompanying her three-quarter-sized Doctor Sasebo burger, she informed me that when she was done making all the adverts, she was planning to leave the company. So great was my astonishment that I bit the inside of my mouth while chewing the batter of my deep-fried chicken, causing myself extreme pain – but I felt like it was hardly the time to be complaining about woes of that ilk. Ms Katori, on the other hand, showed no surprise at all, saying, 'Oh yes, you've been saying that since last year, haven't you?' The matter appeared to have been settled some while back.

'Um, I, I hope you don't mind me saying, but that actually comes as a real surprise to me,' I said with trepidation.

'Oh, I'm sorry!' said Ms Eriguchi. 'For the company, though, it's just a drop in the ocean, and it's not like the end date for this job has been fixed yet.' She did seem slightly guilty, though, and apologised several times.

She also said that if I did decide to stay on at the company, she was sure they'd find someone to take care of me and show me the ropes for whatever new role I took on. I'd be fine. Ms Katori patted my arm and said cheerily, 'If you come over to accounts, I'll make sure you're looked after!'

'Everyone's really great here, whatever department you're in,' Ms Eriguchi went on. Yet despite these attempts to comfort me, the news had left me dazed. My body felt cold and shivery, and my vision slightly blurred.

Ms Eriguchi seemed certain that what with requests for adverts still dribbling in, she wouldn't be leaving right away, but to me, it was clear that our work was gradually winding down. The 'Adverts Wanted!' posters were being taken down from the buses and the notices withdrawn from the website.

'I'll be lost without you,' I told her. What with fourteen years' work experience under my belt, I knew that wasn't strictly true. But it wasn't pure flattery, either. If my co-worker left, it was inevitable that I'd fall into a temporary state of confusion, even if it was equally inevitable that I would eventually acclimatise. I'd come to feel a great deal of respect for Ms Eriguchi during my time working alongside her. There I'd been, thinking I wanted to work with her for as long as possible. Now those hopes had been crushed in a decidedly offhand manner.

I understood that Ms Eriguchi had her own life to live. When I thought back to my own reasons for quitting jobs in the past, I surmised that hers might not be all that easy to explain to another person either – but still, as we were working later on that afternoon, I found myself enquiring if she was planning to take a break after leaving the job. Ms Eriguchi informed me placidly that some of the elder members of a club she'd been in at university had set up their own small business, and she was planning to go and work with them.

'What type of club was it?' I asked out of sheer curiosity.

'A mountaineering club,' she said. 'I was at a women's university, so it was an all-women's mountaineering club.'

There was really no point getting upset about all this when I didn't even know what my own fate would be once this project was over, when today there was barely any work to be done and when everything was up in the air anyway – trying, and failing, to make myself feel better in this way, I headed to the kitchen at four o'clock to make a late cup of tea when I ran into Mr Kazetani coming down the corridor the other way. For reasons unbeknown to me, he was holding a square bag of pink cloth, with a pink felt appliqué crocodile on its front. The bag was such an unexpected item for him to be holding that I found myself ogling it in spite of myself.

'Yeah, I guess you're wondering about this.' Mr Kazetani said as he entered the kitchen. 'Look, do you mind keeping quiet about it to other people in the office?'

'I guess not.'

'It's my daughter's,' he said, setting the bag down on the table. I now recognised it as the kind of home-made bag that primary schoolkids often carried around. It was bulging with heavy-looking objects.

'She had library class today. At Umenoki, they have these lessons where the whole class goes to the school library, and my daughter always takes out the maximum number of books, which is five. They looked very heavy, so I let her keep one and brought the rest home with me.'

'Right,' I nodded, although I was still no clearer as to why it was that Mr Kazetani had his daughter's bag with him at the office.

'I had to pop out earlier, you see, and take her to after-school care club. It's a little way away from the school, and yesterday a man followed her on her way there.'

'Oh! But I thought the adverts were working?'

'Well, I think they are working to a certain extent, but it looks like the problem hasn't been totally eradicated.'

'You mean maybe there's more than one culprit? The one giving sweets has stopped, but there's another one still lurking?'

For a moment I violently regretted saying this, thinking I'd gone and blurted out something highly insensitive, but Mr Kazetani just nodded and said, 'Yes, maybe.' He went on, 'Both me and my wife work, you see, and my wife commutes into town on the express train, so she can hardly come back to pick up and drop off our daughter. Even if I take it in turns with my mother-in-law, that still means ducking out of work every other day, which isn't really tenable. I'm not sure what to do.'

I felt like I understood his predicament well enough, but I didn't know what to say. I could hardly offer to join the pick-up rota so he'd only have to go once every three days. All I could do was agree, limply, that his situation was a tough one.

'I'm sending her to after-school care specifically to make sure nothing bad happens to her, and now this is happening on the way there,' he said, moving a hand to his head.

'What about getting back?' I asked, to which Mr Kazetani replied that his wife collected his daughter on her way home from work, so that wasn't a problem.

It occurred to me that, for the moment, it might be a good idea to create a warning announcement slightly more specific in nature, so after having a cup of tea with Ms Eriguchi, I pulled the appropriate area map from the shelf, took it over to Mr Kazetani who was now back at his desk and asked him to indicate the spot where his daughter had been followed.

'Just here,' he said. 'The road that runs between this narrow triangular corner plot and the park.'

The park was deserted, he told me, and even if there were people around, the large trees by the road-side served to block off the view of the street. The three-storey building in the corner lot had once been used by a designer as a live-in office, but they'd moved away a while ago and the building had stood empty since. Thinking about it, I could see how this narrow triangular patch of land would appeal both to those looking for a place to live, and those seeking a location for their business. Next to the corner plot was a launderette. I could imagine too, how this sort of area could suddenly feel quite deserted.

I tried suggesting that Mr Kazetani's daughter change routes, but he said that the after-school care club was held in a private house at the end of the same street as the park, which just so happened to be a dead end. I crossed my arms and groaned in frustration at this news – although, ultimately, I recognised that it was very much not my problem. Back when the club had started up, said Mr Kazetani, the designer's office had still been there, and the launderette had been a cafe.

It crossed my mind to suggest that his daughter went straight home instead of going to after-school care, but I couldn't bring myself to say it. 'Can't Ms Eriguchi do something to help me?' Mr Kazetani mumbled vacantly to nobody in particular. 'Ms

Eriguchi is just a regular bus company employee,'
I replied, the voice of perfect reason. Yes, I may
have observed with my own eyes phenomena which
implied that Ms Eriguchi had the power to pre-empt
what happened to the Far East Flamenco Centre and
similar places, phenomena which seemed to suggest
that she was in fact deeply connected with the very
existence of such places, but the possibility that
this was sheer coincidence couldn't be discounted.
Rather: the phenomena I'd observed could still be
categorised as the result of coincidence, according to
a common-sense view of the matter.

I returned to my workspace and told Ms Eriguchi
about the situation at hand, eliding Mr Kazetani's
name and instead reporting the event as something
that had happened to an acquaintance.

'Hmm, it sounds like it was bad timing for that
designer to leave,' she said, a note of regret in her voice.
Then she added, 'If it really is not just one stranger
but several, all using different methods, then we're in
trouble.'

'And even if we warn people about that particular
location, the culprit may well just find another spot.'

'Yes, we'll just end up playing cat and mouse,' she
said. To my disappointment, she didn't seem particularly stirred.

'I suppose so … ' I said, not agreeing entirely.

'For the moment, shall we have the sales team report
it to an Umenoki teacher?'

Ms Eriguchi went online to look up the address of the location I showed her, then put in a call to Mr Shōda on the internal line. She didn't use the speakerphone, but Mr Shōda's voice was powerful enough that I could hear it leaking from the receiver, as he said, 'Aaahhh' over and over again in a way that suggested he didn't really get the point. Three times he asked for the address to be repeated. Each time, Ms Eriguchi read it out in exactly the same tone as before. It seemed to me highly dubious that the necessary information would ever be conveyed to any Umenoki Primary School teacher.

Eventually Ms Eriguchi put down the phone. Had it been me, I would have been shaking my head and sighing, but Ms Eriguchi simply returned to her work, her expression unaltered. Having heard that the historic pickle shop had decided to run an advert on the Albatross, a green tea shop with a similarly extensive heritage located by the next stop along had also requested an advert, so she was reading through their material and working on a draft. With us not having made a single advert either today or the day before, there was no editing work to do, so I had begun organising the documentation of the adverts we'd made up until this point.

'If there was a police box there, that would put an end to it,' I said.

I'd put Mr Kazetani firmly in his place for alluding to Ms Eriguchi's power for 'making things appear that shouldn't be there', but now here I was, attempting to avail myself of them.

'You don't hear of new police boxes being created very often though, do you?'

Ms Eriguchi's tone was thoughtful enough, but I didn't feel satisfied. I knew I was being selfish, but I couldn't help but think that of all people, Ms Eriguchi was the one who could solve this problem.

As the number of adverts placed far exceeded initial expectations, and with the host of glowing reports about their beneficial effects from advertisers, not to mention the positive contribution that the bus was making to the local community through its work in issuing warnings about dangerous individuals, word began to spread around the company that the Albatross's continuation was more or less assured for the next few years.

But with ever fewer adverts to write, and the fate of the Albatross now ostensibly secure, the vocation of those in what Mr Shōda had so charmingly referred to as the Alba-dross department was rapidly vanishing.

Straight after lunch on the day of Ms Eriguchi's farewell party, I was called in by the head of advertising, who informed me that although Ms Eriguchi had been scheduled to return to the administration department, he thought it might be better for me to take this success under my belt and seek work elsewhere.

'If you want to stay on here,' he told me, 'then of course you could go to admin in Ms Eriguchi's place. But when I told one of our clients that the Albatross advert department was taking a break, they seemed very keen for either Ms Eriguchi or you to go and work for them.'

The hourly rate, he said, would be 150 yen higher, and the company was located just one station away from here. Unlike this company, they offered health insurance even to limited-contract employees.

'You wouldn't exactly be making adverts, no,' he replied when I asked about the nature of the job, 'but there is some crossover. And I mean, we've no intention of updating our adverts for a while, either, so it's not like you'd be doing that type of work if you stayed. Your work there would probably be more the kind of thing you're used to than if you started from scratch in admin.'

I couldn't tell from his tone and expression whether he was trying to get rid of me, or whether he genuinely wasn't bothered if I went or stayed. I guessed probably the latter: this wasn't a particularly toxic working environment, and from his point of view, if I wasn't going to be his subordinate any more, it probably didn't matter either way. Nor did this seem to be a political-marriage type situation, where sending me to the other company would mean some sort of gain for him. It really was all up to me.

The head said he'd asked the admin department to explain the situation to Mrs Masakado, so it was fine to discuss it with her. I said I'd mull it over and let him know, and got up from my seat.

There hadn't been any fixed date set for Ms Eriguchi's leaving the company, but the fact they were throwing her a farewell party suggested her departure was incontrovertible. The party was held in a chain izakaya advertised on the Albatross at the Shopping Arcade Entrance stop, and upon arrival we were given a very warm welcome and told that business was flourishing. Before placing the advert, a staff member now told us, they'd been concerned about their profits, but since the airing of our advert plugging the buffet lunch they'd started offering, the izakaya had seen a surge in custom from office workers and elderly people in the area:

'It's easy enough to eat meat and rice, but why do I find it so hard to get the vegetables and seaweed that I need?'

If you're worried about your vitamin intake, then come along to Sanumaru Izakaya, just inside the arcade. Our all-you-can-eat buffet is full of exciting vegetable and seaweed dishes. And of course, there's plenty of meat and rice too!

The advert was one of Ms Eriguchi's. Ms Katori had gone along to scope out the place, and delivered her verdict thus: the meat selection was limited to fried chicken and meatballs, but the rice was mixed grain, and at 720 yen a head, it wasn't at all bad value for a buffet.

The evening menu wasn't all-you-can-eat, and they served fancier dishes like roast beef. Ms Eriguchi repeatedly praised the food as she ate. She seemed positively carefree in her demeanour, although she did say over and over again both to me and other people that it was a real shame to have to say goodbye, and she wished she could have worked with us for longer. Despite paying for the entire thing, Mr Kazetani left after thirty minutes, saying he had to go and collect his daughter.

When someone from the sales department had checked in with Umenoki Primary School that day, they'd been told that there had been two cases of kids being followed or approached by strangers this week. The teacher had been kind enough to say how grateful they were that the number of incidents had fallen thanks to the bus announcements, but it irked me that it was still happening at all. The head of advertising had found me a better-paid job, but I didn't feel capable of cutting myself free from this one until the matter had been resolved.

And yet there was Ms Eriguchi at her farewell party, acting as though she'd as good as left the company already, saying thank you so much, it's been great. I knew that there was nothing anybody could do, but I couldn't help feeling as though I'd lost a valuable ally.

As far as the Far East Flamenco Centre was concerned, that was all in the past. Despite the various cold sweats and bizarre states of mind which the affair had brought on at the time, thinking about it now brought on a feeling akin to faint nostalgia. It marked the peak of my immersion in my advert-writing job. The head of advertising hadn't given me a date by which I needed to decide about my next steps, and I hadn't volunteered one either, but now I wondered if I was going to be capable of making that decision. Just having to choose felt stressful. I wanted to return to that period when all I needed to do was work, and the time would pass of its own accord.

'I need to advertise, but I don't know the first thing about marketing!'

'I want to create some nice postcards to promote my business!'

Sound familiar? Then get in touch with Hanabatake Ads! Our services include photocopying, scanning, USB printing and laminating. We also make business cards and pamphlets!

So ran the advert Ms Eriguchi created on her final day at work. Unusually for her, Ms Katori muffed her lines twice while recording, apologising profusely. The ad was to fill the last remaining slot for the Umenoki stop. I imagined that Hanabatake Ads must be a combination of an advertising company and commercial convenience store, serving the assorted needs of small businesses. How would they fare in a location like that, I wondered initially, but then it occurred to me that maybe some of the schoolteachers might find use for them. Come to think of it, there weren't many places offering design and copy services in the Albatross circulation area, so maybe it wasn't a bad business concept.

Mr Kazetani was still ducking out of work once every other day to collect his daughter from school and drop her at after-school club. It didn't seem to be causing any impediment to his job performance or necessitating any overtime, but the situation appeared to be weighing on him a lot. I knew this because each time I ran into him in the kitchen or the elevator, he'd tell me how worried he was. I never knew whether to feel sympathy for him or to find it all a bit much. I guessed the fact that he could hardly get anyone higher up to officially okay his excursions was making the whole situation feel precarious, even though in practical terms, he wasn't inconveniencing a soul.

'Surely there's no need to fret about it that much,' I tried saying, but he would just shake his head and say, 'Oh no, but it can't go on like this.'

Apparently the suggestion had been raised among the after-school club parents that they pool their funds and employ someone to escort the kids from school to the club. I asked naively if the teacher couldn't go and pick them up, but was told that they had set up the school after retiring and now suffered from leg problems, so that wouldn't be possible.

Meanwhile, I had more or less decided to move company. I say more or less because I felt that I should consult Mrs Masakado before making my final decision, and I supposed that if she came up with multiple reasons why it was better to stay on at the bus company, there was a chance I'd change my mind. It was the Friday before a long weekend, so I planned to go and speak to her after work, and then announce my decision to the head of advertising when I came back on Tuesday.

Leaving aside the influx of people from a variety of different departments who stopped by our section to say goodbye, Ms Eriguchi's last day passed mostly without incident. Every time we saw her, Ms Katori would say, 'We should go out for dinner one day, the three of us!'

The farewell party had been the first time that I'd eaten out with Ms Eriguchi, and the same appeared to be true of Ms Katori, which reinforced my belief that Ms Eriguchi divided her personal and her private time quite rigidly. But then, I remembered, she'd told me about the club she'd been in at university when I'd asked her, so it didn't seem like she was desperately secretive as a matter of principle.

What with all the people stopping by our section, it was later than usual when I went to the kitchen to make tea. There I found Mr Kazetani returning from his trip to his daughter's school, his step rather lighter than usual.

'Welcome back,' I greeted him.

'A new office has opened up in the corner plot!' he said, his voice more animated than I'd ever heard it before.

'The corner plot?'

'You know, the one I told you about before. The blind corner.'

'Oh.'

Thus reminded of the issue of the Umenoki Primary School predator, I felt instantly glum to realise that in the end, both Ms Eriguchi and I would be leaving the company without solving the problem – yet Mr Kazetani went on cheerfully.

'I saw some activity in that building recently – people carrying things out or taking them in, I wasn't sure, but I decided not to get my hopes up. When I went past today, though, they'd built a glass shopfront. I spoke to a woman inside and she told me there's an advertising and printing services company opening up there.'

'Well, that's great news.'

'It really is great news! There'll be three employees permanently stationed there, and they've got a meeting space that looks out towards the park.'

Mr Kazetani said that, on the spur of the moment, he'd decided to tell the woman about the after-school care facility that was close by, and about what had happened to his daughter, and she'd said that she'd keep a lookout in that direction. Their days off were Sundays and public holidays, which meant they'd be open every day the school was.

With a look on his face that suggested a great weight had been lifted, Mr Kazetani went striding off down the corridor. Well, that's one problem solved, I thought, as I watched his receding figure, feeling all the while something niggling at me.

That day, Ms Eriguchi edited the data with characteristic efficiency and sent it off, then she and I took it easy until home time came around. All that remained for our section to do was pass on the information about our audio and text files to the advertising department, which I would be doing when I came back after the long weekend. I was set to finish work at the end of the following week.

Sitting there behind our section of the partitioning screen, Ms Eriguchi and I talked about the various advertisers we'd dealt with and our most memorable encounters with them. Ms Eriguchi said that the president of Maruyama Homes was a very tall, thin man who'd reminded her of a giraffe, so his determination to include the gorilla on the shop sign in the advertising copy had made her laugh. I said I found it hard to forget the astonishment I'd felt upon first laying eyes on the jumbo manjū from Baifūan.

As we wallowed in our unremarkable reminiscences, five o'clock soon came around. 'Thank you so much for everything,' Ms Eriguchi said, and left the office as she always did. And just like that, she was gone.

In my last week at the bus company, I swung by Baifūan. One of my friends was about to have a baby, and a group of us had decided to give her a jumbo manjū to celebrate, which I was sent out to buy. The plan had almost been abandoned out of concern about whether it was advisable for a pregnant woman to eat a manjū that enormous, but one of our group recalled that the friend's husband had a sweet tooth, so we planned to give it to her under strict instructions that she share it with him.

Once all the adverts had been written and I'd passed on all the handover files and data to the ad department, I was left with a lot of spare time on my hands. In the few days remaining, I set myself the task of creating a comprehensive list of said files and data, but it was only with multiple trips to make tea, bursts of tidying the office and endless breaks that I could fill up the hours.

Mr Kazetani had stopped skipping out of work, but now, as if in his place, I found myself filled with a burning desire to leave the office – to pop out shopping or something. Ms Katori would sometimes drop by to see me where I sat behind the partition all by myself, and talk at length about nothing in particular. She told me that the Far East Flamenco Centre, apparently not content with flamenco lessons, had now started offering Spanish guitar classes, and that after much deliberation she had decided to sign up.

After my penultimate day at work had ended, I set out to Baifūan to buy the giant manjū. As it turned out, giant manjū weren't something that you could just turn up and buy, it had to be ordered specially. Baifūan would deliver the manjū on the buyer's specified date, the shop clerk said. Standing there in the shop, consulting via text with my friends, I composed an awkwardly intrusive sort of gift note to the tune of: if you eat the whole thing in one go, it might harm your baby, so you should share it with your husband and eat one bit at a time. This I handed over to the shop clerk. If the gift necessitated going to such ridiculous lengths, one might well think, surely it would have been better just to buy her something else instead – but I felt I simply couldn't pass up on this perfect opportunity to give someone a jumbo manjū.

I came out of the shop just as it was closing, and remembered that this area was home to the corner plot of which Mr Kazetani had so often spoken. Of course, if there were perverts on the prowl targeting primary schoolkids, then there was a risk that something bad could have befallen me too, but given the reputed appearance of this well-lit glass-fronted office, I imagined I'd be okay. From the beginning, I'd sensed a faintly naive aspect to Mr Kazetani's personality, and I was taken by the urge to go and check if what he said was really true.

The area around Umenoki Primary School stop wasn't particularly dark, but the shops shut early, and there were barely any people around. I stood beneath the bus shelter and opened up the map on my smartphone, attempting to locate the park that Mr Kazetani had mentioned. Three blocks from the school I found a large green patch labelled Umenoki Sports Park, and the triangular corner plot across the road marked Yamamoto Architects. Mr Kazetani had said there had once been a design office there, so I figured that must be the place, and that the smartphone map simply hadn't been updated.

From the stop directly outside the school, I set out walking towards the park. There were a number of houses and shops around, but I could see at a glance that many of the houses were unlit, and could well have been vacant, and with their shutters down, it was hard to know whether the rice shop and the kimono shop were still in business or had closed for good. Without doubt, it wasn't the sort of place you wanted to be walking through alone at night. My guess was that, even in the day, it was not what you'd call a lively area, aside from when the kids came out of school.

The road I walked down wasn't narrow, but it still managed to feel quiet and tucked away. It was when I hit the corner by Umenoki Sports Park that I was suddenly greeted by a large patch of brilliant light. It was coming from a sizeable ground-floor space that looked a lot like a convenience store, but it wasn't – it was a glass-fronted office. I could see at least two photocopiers, and next to them, a large plotter. Several four-seater tables had been positioned looking out over the trees planted along the side of Umenoki Sports Park. A boy and a girl wearing the uniform of a nearby high school stood beside a laminating machine, puzzled expressions on their faces. It seemed that they hadn't quite grasped how to use it. After consulting each other with tangible awkwardness, they turned around to the counter and waved, calling out to the woman working there.

I moved a little closer to the office and squinted, taking in the stainless steel sign above the door that read Hanabatake Ads. One of the women behind the counter moved over to where the two schoolkids were standing, and skilfully produced three card-shaped objects. The kids nodded, then began operating the laminating machine as she'd shown them, churning out one card after another. The woman who'd come out from behind the counter bowed, then returned to her former station.

It was Ms Eriguchi. Standing there, I recalled Mr Kazetani's words: 'Can't Ms Eriguchi do something to help me?' Hanabatake Ads' business hours were 10 a.m. to 9 p.m., meaning it would definitely be open any time that kids were being taken to after-school care club.

It appeared that Ms Eriguchi had, indeed, done something.

The Cracker Packet Job

I knew that the next job awaiting me was still a limited-contract one, but that it would pay 150 yen more per hour, as well as provide health insurance, which made a big change from the bus company.

'That doesn't mean I'll be expected to work excessive amounts or be given unfair responsibilities, right?' I asked Mrs Masakado at our meeting, where she told me that she, too, believed it was wise for me to move on.

'I did look into that possibility, but there haven't been any complaints about the employer.' Mrs Masakado went on to tell me that the company in question posted a call for part-timers every six months or so, but they didn't have an especially high turnover rate, and current company employees whom the agency had interviewed hadn't voiced any pronounced dissatisfactions.

The job that the head of advertising had found me was with a rice cracker manufacturer that had been going for forty years. The story went that the second-generation owner of a small rice cracker shop had one day been seized by a determination to produce better-quality crackers, and so, snapped up a manufacturing company on the verge of bankruptcy. The brand wasn't exactly a household name, but was shelved in supermarkets alongside the more famous types, and had plenty of stockists, as well as its fair share of diehard fans. It seemed a reliable enough prospect. When it came to savoury snacks, I was more of a crisp person, and rice crackers were not something I regularly bought, but Mrs Masakado informed me that she often indulged. 'Are they nice?' I asked.

'They are,' she said. 'The Supersize Squid and Mirin ones are especially good.' Hearing the name, I had a feeling these were the same crackers I often saw my mother tucking into at home.

Back when I'd met with the head of advertising, he'd explained to me that there was 'some crossover' between this new job and my role at the bus company, a statement which I thought I'd understood, but realised upon thinking about it now that I hadn't. When Mrs Masakado enquired about the nature of the position, she was told it was 'composing content for cracker wrappers'.

'Don't they ask people from outside the company to do that kind of thing?' I asked her.

'The director told me that it was considered a really crucial role, and they didn't want someone to be doing it alongside other work.'

'They want someone who's there exclusively to think about cracker wrappers?'

'It seems so.'

The words 'really crucial role' made me feel an instant sense of pressure. Mrs Masakado must have sensed this because she went on to say, 'Why don't you at least meet the director? If it doesn't seem like something you can manage, you don't have to take it.'

'But I suppose if I do go and meet the director, there'll be no going back to the bus company?'

'No, I imagine not.'

'Ah, what a bind,' I said, although I knew that however much of a bind I might have felt my current situation to be, it didn't alter the fact that I had to keep on working, which meant I had to keep on moving forward. Yet I was also very clear that I didn't want a job that carried too much responsibility. My current assessment was that the bus adverts job had also carried a reasonable amount of responsibility, but I had no memory of any such pressure put on me at the recruitment stage, and besides, I'd had a reliable role model in the shape of Ms Eriguchi.

'I hope I have someone helpful showing me the ropes.'

Mrs Masakado stared down at the document in front of her and angled her head slightly.

'It says that, essentially, you'll be working alone. Your predecessor was a man of forty-three, who is now off work with depression.'

You had to be kidding me! I shook my head incredulously and Mrs Masakado stretched out a hand and waved it at me, as if to remonstrate with my interpretation. 'It says here that the cause was fatigue brought on by his search for a wife. The fact that he reported it was depression shows honesty, and his reason seems valid enough. But nobody's forcing you to go if you don't want to.'

I wasn't so convinced that fatigue from looking for a wife was a valid reason for depression, but at least it seemed unrelated to the job.

The company director, who looked to be in his late sixties or so, explained the product range to me with impressive enthusiasm. So impassioned was he, in fact, that I had to wonder if he hadn't mistaken me for a buyer from a major supermarket chain, as opposed to someone seeking a temporary post at the company. But he also divulged that the company motto was 'Doing our utmost for the happiness of our customers and our employees!' so maybe as a potential employee, I'd been deemed a suitable target for his utmost.

'I love all our products, but if I had to choose just one then it would be these Supersize Squid and Mirin!' The director took a sizeable individually wrapped cracker from a basket on the desk containing a selection of the company's products and handed it to me. The same cracker that Mrs Masakado had mentioned, I noted.

'Oh yes?' I said as I took off the wrapper. The cracker was indeed super sized: about the size of my hand. According to the director, deep-fried rice crackers of this sort were usually four to five centimetres in diameter, and although the taste was moreish, certain customers found them troublesome to eat because one needed to keep returning one's hand to the bag, and they were slightly too small to be individually wrapped. These big ones worked because they lasted a while, and if you didn't want sticky fingers, you could hold the wrapper around them as you ate. Moreover, he told me, squid and mirin flavouring was usually reserved for starch products, but the company had identified an untapped desire among customers for squid and mirin flavouring in fried rice products too. To date, they were the only rice cracker brand making them in this flavour. The cracker I chomped through as I listened to the director's explanation was genuinely tasty.

'It's big enough that people feel inspired to adapt it in various ways, adding okonomiyaki sauce or mayonnaise or what have you,' he said, going on to tell me that the company's website featured recipes with shredded seaweed and dried bonito flakes. You could also smash the crackers up, sprinkle them over rice and pour in tea to make a unique version of ochazuke. The individual wrapping meant you could crush them in the bag, he told me, as if relating something truly wondrous.

'My other top recommendation would be Nattō and Cheese Thins.' He plucked another specimen from the basket, this time a slimline fried cracker whose surface was sprinkled with cheese and soybeans, and set it down in front of me.

'We're very particular about what nattō we use – we've made sure to use the least odorous brand on the market. There are a lot of diehard fans of this product, and once a year we release a limited-edition version with wasabi, which is also very well received.'

He went on proudly, 'But really, all our crackers are excellent. We create and sell the kinds of crackers we ourselves want to eat.'

The Nattō and Cheese Thins were also good – sufficiently good, in fact, that I felt I could see why he was carrying on like this.

'We think it's important that people enjoy themselves when they're eating crackers.'

'Well, yes, of course.'

'We aim to make products where the customers can enjoy the taste, enjoy the experience and in addition, feel like they've gained something. Turn over to the reverse side of the wrapper, the side without the logo.' Slightly startled by this sudden shift into instruction mode, I turned over the Supersize cracker in my hands. The unexpected words 'The Voynich Manuscript' jumped out at me, and I peered down at the packet.

Mysteries of the World #17: The Voynich Manuscript

This handwritten manuscript using an unknown writing system was discovered in Italy in 1912. It features beautiful illustrations of plants and women, but to date nobody has figured out what the text says. Its script has been variously interpreted as a code, a musical notation, and having no meaning at all.

Though I felt sure I'd heard about the Voynich Manuscript somewhere before, it was very much not the kind of topic one expected to encounter on the back of a cracker packet. The mystery was marked #17, so I plucked another Supersize cracker out of the basket to find Mysteries of the World #6: The Jersey Devil. The last one in the basket was Mysteries of the World #13: The Roanoke Colony.

'What do you think? They're good fun, and isn't it better if people come away feeling they've learned something?' In his excitement, the company director leaned in slightly across the desk, his eyes sparkling.

'Yes, I can see that,' I nodded, taken in by his enthusiasm.

'Have a look at that one,' he instructed, and I turned the packet of the Nattō and Cheese Thins over to find Poisonous Plants of Japan #7: Narcissus. The text warned readers not to confuse the narcissus with Chinese chives, as they looked very similar. Was there really anyone out there who'd confuse them? A different packet featured Poisonous Plants of Japan #9:

Japanese Star Anise, and informed me that the while the poisonous Japanese version was similar-looking to non-toxic star anise, the two could be told apart by their smell: the Japanese version had a bitter scent while Chinese star anise was sweet.

'We want our customers to savour our packaging as well as what's inside them. We'd like to give mothers something to teach their children, or provide a minute's conversation to a couple on a date struggling for things to say, or fill a few moments of solitary relaxation.'

'I understand,' I said. And truly, it didn't seem to me like a mistaken policy. There was something slightly startling about topic choices like the Jersey Devil and poisonous plants, but I could see how that hint of darkness would mean they were more likely to spark conversation. I wasn't entirely sure that this made suitable material for mothers to teach to their children, but as a child myself I'd much preferred learning about the Seven Wonders of the World or poisonous plants than famous tourist destinations or seasonal flowers. It seemed as though playing it safe wasn't a concept that existed in the dictionary of my 43-year-old predecessor – or, for that matter, of the company director.

The director went on pulling cracker after cracker out of the basket, commenting, 'This is our Dictators series which became a real hit online,' and 'This is our Six-Second Recipes series, featuring simple recipes you can read in six seconds.'

'We had someone doing this job before, but while on refreshment leave from the company, he began looking for a wife, you see, and ended up being terribly betrayed. That brought on a bit of a breakdown, so he's currently off work.'

What with my on-the-job experience writing the Albatross advertisements, the director went on to say, he was keen for me fill the gap.

'It was mostly my colleague who was writing the adverts,' I informed him. 'I was just helping out behind the scenes.' I knew that writing adverts was in a sense already 'behind the scenes', but when it came to on-the-job-experience, Ms Eriguchi was leagues ahead of me and I felt I couldn't just sit back and assent to his version of events.

'But you wrote the advert for Baifūan and the Morimura Piano School. And for Étoiles Astrologists and Zozo Salad Lab! And Ishikawa Haematologists, and others besides, no?'

'I did.'

It was flattering to hear the director reeling off a list of the jobs I'd been involved with, and I found myself feeling suddenly a lot more optimistic.

'In that case, you're exactly the kind of person we're looking for.' The director nodded deeply, and then excusing himself, took out a cracker labelled Seaside Ume from the basket in the centre of the table and opened it up. This was a cracker whose dough was sewn through with nori strands, and flavoured with sour plum. He passed me the bag across the table and, thanking him, I looked down at the back:

Rhino Trivia: A rhino's horns are made of keratin, which is also found in hair. Rhinos have one baby at a time, and they raise it with love and care.

'What do you think? Would you like to come and work for us?'

I turned the Seaside Ume packet face up on the desk and said, 'Yes, I would.'

International News Trivia #89: Pussy Riot

A Moscow-based punk rock group composed of up to eleven women of ages ranging from twenty to thirty-three. In March 2012, three of its vocal-ists were arrested for performing anti-government songs in a Russian Orthodox Cathedral. One was released in October that year, and the other two were released in December 2013.

International News Trivia #90: 'Tax Haven'

This English phrase refers to countries or terri-tories which, having no reliable industry of their own, do away with taxes or create extremely low tax rates to lure companies and wealthy people from other nations. Prominent examples include Monaco,

San Marino and the Cayman Islands. Don't confuse 'haven' with 'heaven'!

When I went to show these drafts to the director, who personally vetted all the text on the back of the cracker packets, he made little suggestions: 'the word "prominent" is too high-level, so let's go with "famous"' and, '"singers" is easier for the elder generation to understand than "vocalists"', so I adjusted the text as he advised.

The first task assigned to me at the cracker company was to continue working on the job my predecessor, Mr Kiyota, had left unfinished when he'd gone on his refreshment break. This turned out to be the International News Trivia series, which had been printed for some while now on the back of the Black Bean Koban crackers, salted and studded with black soybeans, and which derived their name and shape from an oval gold coin used back in feudal times. There was a sister product called Black Bean Curry Koban. The women from the factory told me at lunch that Mr Kiyota had started the International News Trivia series back when he first joined the company, and it had been going on so long that it could be considered his life's work.

'He should have talked to us if he was that concerned about finding a wife!' said Mrs Terai wistfully, pouring me a cup of green tea from the pot. Mrs Terai was a part-timer who, having found me dithering at the back of the queue on my first visit to the staff canteen, had explained the lunch-room system to me: you picked up a tray and chopsticks first, took as many side dishes as you wanted and were then served the main dish by the canteen staff. As my sides, I'd taken a vinegared salad of cucumber and small fish, and kombu parcels. The main dish was oyako-don – a rice bowl topped with chicken and egg.

'Did you have someone particular in mind?'

'Well, no … '

The five women around the table, who seemed to be something of a set lunch crew, looked at one another and laughed. They hadn't had any leads, they said, but still, they thought it was a bit unfriendly of him to have feigned disinterest. The group, which was made up of two full-time employees and three part-timers, said that they'd always had lunch with Mr Kiyota and had given him lots of advice about wrapper topics. You didn't find many men of forty-three who would eat lunch every day with a bunch of middle-aged women, I thought. The fact that something like that had happened here made me feel that the vibe at this company couldn't be too bad.

'They take our opinions into account,' said Mrs Urakawa, another part-timer who looked like the youngest of the five as she closed the lid on her size-able navy bento box that I suspected must be one of her sons' cast-offs.

'In what way?' I asked.

'We vote on the topics,' someone else answered immediately.

'They hold a lot of votes here,' added Mrs Terai. 'There are votes to decide on the flavours of the new products, too.'

Ms Kawasaki, a full-timer who, in direct contrast to the rather ample Mrs Terai, was petite and rather thin, now started to speak quickly: 'I can't deal with spicy stuff, though, and I can't stand the wasabi they put in the Nattō and Cheese Thins, so I thought we could get the people on the line to vote as a bloc, but no one was having it! They were just like, "Get over it, Kawasaki, they're delicious!"'

'Well, they are delicious, but who spoke to you like that? Was it Yamamura?'

'Oh, I don't want to say … '

Their conversation progressed, moving further and further away from the original subject. In a bid to pull it back, I asked, 'So you vote on topics for the backs of the packets then?'

All five women, wearing the same knowing facial expression, turned to me and started saying, 'Oh yes!' I'd been aware that the company consulted the tastes of the director and employees when determining the flavours of the crackers, but it hadn't occurred to me that they'd ask for opinions about the backs of the packets as well.

'Is the International News Trivia going to end soon?'

'I learned so much from that series, I was able to answer one of my son's homework questions for social studies.'

'I bet he looked up to you after that!'

'I think it made him see me in a different light, yes.'

'Sheesh, I wish my son would see me in a different light. But he's already twenty-five, so the chances of that seem slim.'

'I was thinking, you know you were saying his pay was low? You should have him take the civil servants' exam. Stuff from International News Trivia crops up in the general knowledge section on there, too.'

'Aaah, now there's an idea!'

There's no way that's going to work, I thought to myself as I brought my bowl up to my face and shovelled the remaining rice into my mouth. The oyako-don had been really good. Thinking about it, I supposed it figured that companies manufacturing food products would have high-quality staff meals. I was looking forward to seeing what they dished up tomorrow, and at the same time, feeling slightly anxious about this new job of mine whose contours I still hadn't fully grasped.

I was assigned a smallish, well-lit office at one corner of the ground floor. Most of the floor was given over to the so-called Rice Cracker Museum – which show-cased products the company had made over the years, information about its history and various bits of rice cracker trivia – so I was the only employee working on that level. There was no reception desk at the company; visitors would be let inside by the security guard, Mr Fukumoto, then take the elevator directly to the floor of whomever they were visiting. The Rice Cracker Museum sat between the elevator hall and my office, which meant that none of the visitors came by where I sat, and without my trips to the factory block at lunch-time, it would have been possible to go the whole day without encountering a soul. For the moment, I was saved from complete solitude by occasional visits from the director – which I guessed were testament to the fact that I was still something of a novelty – and the appearance at a fixed time each day from the person in charge of placing the company's stationery order, asking if I needed anything.

Customer feedback about the packets was sorted by the customer service representative Miss Ōtomo, and would be printed out and handed to me along with my daily report sheet. Most of the responses were favourable, but not without their troubling elements. A letter written in beautiful handwriting complete with illustrations – 'I would very much like to see a series featuring flowers from the forty-seven prefectures of Japan' – came from a sender who had allegedly written in every week for a year. And there were occasionally some more ominous missives: 'I'm impressed by your selection of weighty topics. Please can I have a job at your company? I don't mind how much the pay is. If I was given a job, I would create a Serial Killer Series. The first in the series would be Ed Gein. The second would be John Wayne Gacy. The third would be Peter Kürten. The fourth ... '

That wasn't what we were after, said the director. Ōtomo said the same thing, as did the employees with whom I ate lunch. Of course, text that made people prick up their ears and even gave them a little start was good, but we didn't want anything gory or scandalous on the company's packets.

I would nod along as these opinions were voiced, but as I did, it occurred to me that I might one day find these very words used against me. Sitting in that room on my own, I began to feel quite overwhelmed by the thought of what lay ahead. For a little while to come, my working days would be taken up by getting through the list of International News Trivia topics I'd inherited from Mr Kiyota, but he hadn't left behind any ideas for future series, so once they were done, I imagined I'd have to come up with something myself.

That day, I wrote the text for #91: Joseph 'Sepp' Blatter, #92: Edward Snowden, #93: The Tunguska Event, #94: Vermont Yankee Nuclear Power Plant and #95: Malala. Each piece of trivia had to be between 45–50 words. That wasn't long by any reckoning, and you'd be forgiven for thinking that a text of that size could be dashed off in no time, but the director's stipulation that each piece of trivia needed to be easily comprehensible to everyone 'between the ages of ten and ninety' ensured they were no piece of cake to write. For example, I really wanted to say that Blatter, President of FIFA, was also the former president of the World Society of Friends of Suspenders. The director of this company roared with laughter at this suggestion, but he soon resumed his composure and flatly rejected my suggestion, saying 'I think it would make the old ladies blanch.' It seemed that the director had fixed in his mind an image of a young child and his grandmother enjoying a packet of rice crackers together. In his understanding, the kid was ten, and the grandmother was ninety. Afterwards, it occurred to me that there were very few ten-year-olds with ninety-year-old grandmothers. I fretted about whether or not to tell him.

Over lunch, I spoke with Mrs Terai and my other newly acquired lunchmates about the ninety-year-old woman with the ten-year-old grandchild, and the World Society of Friends of Suspenders. The feedback I received on the former issue was: 'If the grandmother had given birth to the mother at forty and the mother at forty-one, then it's totally possible.' The feedback about the latter was: 'People like us might find it amusing, but it could easily be awkward if young children or elderly people were reading.' There was just one lunchmate who was fervent that the World Society of Friends of Suspenders should make it into the trivia: a full-time employee called Ms Tamada, who was divorced. 'She always goes for the saucy stuff,' teased the other women.

Ms Tamada, perhaps two or three years older than I was, did have a something of a come-hither air to her. Until three months previously, she'd been going out with the security guard, Mr Fukumoto, who was also divorced, but they'd split up after it was decided that his children would be coming to live with him. Prior to that they'd been considering getting married, but apparently Ms Tamada felt that bringing up someone else's children was another proposition entirely, and she needed to think over the matter more carefully. It was alarming to me that I was privy to such personal information less than a week after joining the company, but the truth was that my lunchmates kept on revealing all this stuff about themselves. It was a very different situation to that with Ms Eriguchi, about whom the sum total of my knowledge – having worked with her for all that time – was that she'd attended a women's university where she'd been part of the mountaineering club.

Likely as a result of having been long-time lunch-mates with my predecessor, the factory women seemed very eager to discuss the cracker packets. When I said I was pleased they were taking such an interest and enquired if everyone in the company felt similarly, I was told that, broadly speaking, the employees could be split into two: the flavour camp and the trivia camp.

'Just between us, the people who are obsessed with flavours are always going out for drinks with the product development team, and lobbying when there are new product votes. It gets really tiring.'

'But weren't you saying the other day you were trying to organise a bloc vote when there was the suggestion to add wasabi to the Nattō and Cheese Thins?' I asked.

'Ah, but you see, Ms Kawasaki has a foot in both camps.'

'That's not true!' protested Ms Kawasaki. 'It's just that I really can't stand wasabi. That was a one-off thing. I'm a hundred per cent moderate trivia person.'

So there were moderates and extremists now? I thought, astounded. Or maybe there weren't – maybe these women were making it all up for my benefit. Regardless, though, I could sense that even in this company set-up where everything was decided democratically, a degree of conflict still remained.

I went back to my office rubbing my stomach, a nebulous sense of anxiety swilling around inside me. Lunch had been stir-fried ginger pork, and once again, it had been excellent. Passing in front of the Rice Cracker Museum, I saw a man sitting on the sofa in the middle of the room, reading a book. Hmm, I thought. The people I'd eaten lunch with were uninhibited and fun, but it might get tiring doing that every day.

My mother was pretty happy about the new job I'd found for myself, because it meant I would now frequently bring imperfect cracker specimens home with me. The day I brought home two packs of Nattō and Cheese Thins (With Wasabi!) she was delighted, exclaiming, 'They only sell these at special times!' This put me in mind of an occasion shortly after I left my old job, when I'd basically become a kind of recluse. One day, I'd had a craving for salty snacks but hadn't wanted to leave the house, so I'd gone rummaging through the big jar where my mother stockpiled her crackers and eaten all of the Nattō and Cheese Thins (With Wasabi!), of which there'd been about five. I remembered now how my mother had yelled at me, 'But they're rare, those ones!' On the back of this memory, I also recalled an occasion when she'd been eating crackers and surprised me by saying out of the blue, 'If you, me or your father were freemasons, we might be able to find you an easy job.'

This surprising outburst, I realised now, had almost certainly been prompted by one of Mr Kiyota's bits of trivia. When I informed her that my job now involved writing those bits of trivia, her only comment was, 'Another complicated role!'

Eventually I finished the next batch of the International News Trivia series that Mr Kiyota had left behind, and then, finally, it was time for me to create some new topics from scratch. The Seaside Ume packaging was being redesigned, and so the decision had been taken to rewrite the trivia as well. The previous series had been Animal Trivia, a relatively innocuous offering by Mr Kiyota's standards, but when I suggested to the director that I'd go away and research some animals that fit the previously established pattern, he'd said quite forcefully that no, I may as well create a new series.

Remembering the cards featuring reproductions of famous ukiyo-e prints that I'd collected as a child from packets of shredded seaweed for ochazuke, I first made the utterly amateurish suggestion that we do a series introducing famous paintings. The director smiled and said simply, 'Unfortunately, we have to think about printing costs,' and that was the end of that. It made sense. The packets for Seaside Ume were a solid dark green, a colour chosen so that the pink of the sour plum flesh would show up better. Introducing various famous paintings would necessitate using a good number of different colours on top of that, and I could imagine production costs quickly getting expensive.

The director had dismissed the famous paintings suggestion more or less out of hand, but with my subsequent suggestion of a 'What Happened Today?' series of strange anniversaries, his verdict was slightly more considered: 'It's not bad, but isn't it overly reliant on when you read them?' He went on to explain that if you were reading in June about a day in May, it wouldn't be until the following year that that day would come around again, so unless the anniversaries were really fascinating in and of themselves, there wouldn't be that much of a hook. Even if you staggered the days according to when the packets were printed, there would doubtless still be a certain amount of slippage. Again, I could see he had a point. It seemed to me that the director was in a far better position to be coming up with ideas for the backs of the packets than I was, so I asked perfectly seriously if he could provide a broad framework for a topic and just leave the finer details for me to hone – but he replied with modesty, 'Oh no, no, I'm far too old for that.'

I didn't really understand what age had to do with anything, but I got the impression that the director was very concerned that the packets remain edgy. I was seized by the desire to explain to him that it was just Mr Kiyota who was edgy, and that I was in fact a very run-of-the-mill sort of person, but I could also see how that was quite a pathetic thing to come out with – especially for someone who'd been taken on in virtue of her work at the bus company – so I resisted.

'Okay,' I said. 'If we need to make it accessible to everyone from ten to ninety, and also avoid anything too safe, I wonder if maybe it's best to go really niche? Like, this is just an example, but how about well-known psychology experiments or something?'

'Yes, I think that could work!' said the director. Even as he spoke, he was already raising his body slightly from his seat, so I quickly shook my head and added, 'I mean, that's just one extreme example.'

As if coming back to himself, the director nodded as he lowered himself again into his chair, and said, 'Yes, I suppose it is a little extreme, isn't it.' He looked slightly disappointed.

Eventually, the three options put to the employee vote were: World's Smallest Countries, Nobel Prize Winners and a Source That Word! series about etymology. The voting system was simple: employees would write the name of their chosen series on a slip of paper and cast it into the ballot box placed outside the staff canteen. There was no obligation to vote, but from my furtive observations at lunch, it seemed that a healthy proportion of people were scribbling things on the company memo pad placed beside the box and posting them. The voting period was five working days.

At the end of each day, the voting box was retrieved by Ms Ōtomo, who would send me the daily results in a word file. On the first day, there was a total of twelve votes, with World's Smallest Countries receiving six and the etymology and Nobel Prize Winners series each receiving two. One voting slip read, 'Lacking punch,' and another, 'What about 100 Famous Japanese Mountains?' 100 Famous Japanese Mountains was a good shout, I realised, but I felt considerably disheartened by the 'lacking punch' comment. The director's slightly underwhelmed reaction to my suggestions had left me with the sense they didn't quite cut the mustard, but having this stated to me in no uncertain terms still affected me a lot. The next day brought six more votes: two for World's Smallest Countries, two for Source That Word!, none for Nobel Prize Winners, one saying, 'Can you not think of anything a bit more entertaining?' and one more for 100 Famous Japanese Mountains. With two votes apiece, the Japanese Mountains and the Nobel Prize Winners were now tied. Possibly the Mountains would sneak into the lead tomorrow.

At lunchtime I confessed to my dining companions that while I worked on the International Trivia Series, I would think constantly about the 'lacking punch' comment and the 100 Mountains suggestion, and as a result, my work wasn't proceeding very quickly. They all banded together to cheer me up, telling me that it was okay, that Mr Kiyota had sometimes felt down too and that there was no way it was going to go swimmingly from the very beginning – but it niggled with me that none of them actually said that the topics I'd landed on were okay. Of the five of them, only one had voted so far: Mrs Urakawa, the youngest of the group, mother to two boys of sixteen and thirteen, who said she'd voted for the Source That Word! series because she thought it might help her sons with their studies. The others said things like, 'It's an important choice, so I'm going to give it a bit more thought before voting,' or 'I always leave my vote to the last day.' This was hard for me to hear, when an early result felt like it would be so much easier for me to take psychologically. It was better that they were straight with me than shower me with meaningless flattery, I tried to think, yet still it played on my mind.

'When I suggested well-known psychology experiments as a joke, the director seemed to take to the idea.'

'Aah, that's a good one!' said Ms Tamada, setting down her chopsticks and narrowing her eyes in thought. She was the one who'd said several times that there was no way that it would go swimmingly from the very beginning.

I hurriedly made the excuse, 'The problem is, I think I could only come up with a maximum of five or six.'

'Oh, really?' Ms Tamada bit into a sprig of broccoli with a disappointed expression.

'Look, as long as they're a bit distinctive and different from what the other brands are doing, that's all that matters,' Mrs Terai said, obviously trying to cheer me up in a way that immediately made me feel guilty for being so needy.

It may indeed have been true that there was no way it would go swimmingly from the very beginning, and that as long as the topics were a bit distinctive that was all that mattered, but it was clear to me that it wouldn't do to take that type of so-what attitude from the outset. Even if I managed to scrape through this Seaside Ume job with a passing grade, I'd have to up my game before next time.

After completing my quota of International News Trivia for the day, I set about researching Mr Kiyota's past work. The texts he'd created were all saved on the office computer, but thinking I'd rather see the real things, I set out for the Rice Cracker Museum. When I left my office to go to the toilet, I'd sometimes catch sight of people in the museum who were clearly skipping off work, which made me a bit wary of setting foot inside now – but luckily there were no skivers in evidence today.

The Rice Cracker Museum was about as big as a medium-sized meeting room. A timeline of the company snaked around its four walls, together with showcases of products arranged chronologically through the ages. As might be expected, the older products were just replicas in glass cases, but as the display moved into the last decade, it featured actual product specimens. For cracker lines from the past three years, the display comprised the packaged product at the back with its contents in front, laid out on a round wicker tray. In the centre of the museum floor stood a plinth, low enough that a primary school child would be able to see it, reproducing the manufacturing process of a basic soy-sauce-flavoured rice cracker using what looked like the plastic replicas one saw outside restaurants. A pretty fancy exhibit, I thought, impressed. One Saturday a month, the company held a tour of its factory, and I guessed they showed visitors around the museum then.

I picked up a packet of Nattō and Cheese Thins from last year, and turned it over to see the tagline 'Bizarre Japanese Bylaws'. The example in question was the 'Everyone Enjoy the Snow Bylaw' from the town of Kutchan in Hokkaido, which stipulated that townspeople should join forces in overcoming the hindrance that snow presented to their lives, making an effort to utilise it as a resource. Another packet featured the 'Bylaw Promoting the Consumption of Kyoto-Produced Sake'. Next to these was a packet of the Nattō and Cheese Thins (With Wasabi!), boasting an Illustrated Wild Birds of Japan series, complete with illustrations of cormorants, herons and the like. So, Mr Kiyota had an artistic sense as well, had he? The Supersize Squid and Mirin packets from three years ago taught consumers the words for 'Help!' and 'Call the Police!' in various languages of the world: in Russian, 'Help!' was 'Pomogitye!' and in Finnish it was 'Auttakaa!' On the back of the Sea Urchin Bitesize (Big Bag!) was an entry from a series called 100 Pasta Sauces, explaining the difference between vongole rosso and vongole bianco. The Black Bean Curry Koban from earlier this year had a series on the World's Baddest Women, with the packets I examined featuring Agrippina and Bloody Mary. There were plenty of other series for which I assumed Mr Kiyota was responsible, including World Dictators, Original Ideas for Onigiri Fillings, Deities from Around the World and An ABC of Ethnic Cultures.

Making ponderous noises, I sat down on the sofa in the centre of the museum, the skivers' spot of choice. I was Mr Kiyota's successor, which meant that even if I wasn't capable of it now, at some point in the future at least, I would have to do as good a job as he had done. The thought made me feel a bit woozy. In theory, the job seemed enticing enough, but when I'd been instructed to come up with a new series I hadn't been able to think of anything decent, and having the choices put to the vote set the bar even higher.

And yet, my museum outing had at least helped me form an image of the kind of work I would be doing from now on. I decided that for the time being, I'd leave the rest of my tasks until tomorrow and look through the files Mr Kiyota had left on the computer. With that in mind, I stood up from the sofa just as someone entered the museum from the other door. Slipping quickly into the corridor, I moved in the direction of the toilet so as to get a better look at the person who'd come to skive off. A young man in factory uniform carried over a wicker tray containing a cracker packet onto the sofa, and now sat examining it, his gaze casual yet intent. He must have come in here for a change of scenery, I thought. Feeling like I'd been set straight in some way, I went to the toilet, then returned to my office.

In the end, it was a dead heat between the World's Smallest Countries and the Source That Word! series, and it was decided that the backs of the new Seaside Ume packets would be home to a series on Japanese etymology. According to Mrs Terai, who'd reputedly had numerous conversations about the matter with colleagues over their breaks, it had seemed at first as though the smallest countries were set to win, but then the view began to emerge that, of all the company's crackers, the Seaside Ume had the most classically Japanese image and were therefore better suited to a feature on the Japanese language, so the tide of opinion began to turn.

'Thinking about it, we've never really done anything about our own language before,' said Mrs Urakawa, who was adamant that the cracker packets produced at her place of work should contribute to her sons' education in some way. She went on to say that, with the exception of maths, which was hard to tackle in this format, most school subjects had been covered: the International News Trivia and Historical Figures series had helped with history and social studies, the Calling for Help Around the World series dealt with foreign languages, while the various plants and birds trivia had focused on science. Japanese, however, was virgin ground. Aha! I thought when she pointed this out. So even Mr Kiyota, with his interests ranging from world history to the culinary arts, had left certain stones unturned.

'What do you think, though?' I asked. 'Is it a good idea to venture into new terrain?'

'Well,' said Mrs Terai, who had been working in the company the longest of the five, 'so long as you're following the general precedent that's been set, I think it's fine.' The self-declared 'trivia moderate' Ms Kawasaki agreed, saying, 'If it's interesting, there's no problem,' while Mrs Nihei, the eldest of the group with a son aged twenty-five, shrugged, 'As long as there's nothing offensive in there.' Ms Tamada, who had recently gone on another date with the security guard, nodded, 'I think that's better, honestly.' Mrs Urakawa, with the two teenage sons, said, 'Ideally they'd be the kinds of things people can learn from.' Each time she took some crackers home with her, she would take a photo of the backs of the packaging on her phone to show her sons. Apparently they never came out and asked to see the photos, but the younger son would sometimes take packets lying around the house up to his room.

'Would more stuff in the Japanese vein be a good idea? Introductions to famous writers and so on?'

'Yes, that could work. Or what about something to do with names?'

'Names?'

'Yeah, like weird names.' Ms Tamada smiled, screwed up the corners of her mouth into a slightly embittered expression, then grinned again. It transpired that the daughters of the security guard – her ex or perhaps current boyfriend – had rather glitzy names: Mianna and Mioria.

'Couldn't they just have gone for something a bit more normal like Anna and Mio?' I asked, only to be informed that his ex-wife had been vehement that Anna was too run-of-the-mill, and the particular characters chosen to write Mioria made it 'look like a gemstone', which had struck her as a good thing. Apparently Mr Fukumoto hadn't had it in him to go against her wishes.

'I'll be mother to those two, if I end up with him,' Ms Tamada said with a sigh. She added that she'd been told off for commenting that his daughters' names were 'cool' because they 'sounded like princesses from a computer game'. I felt quite enthused about the prospect of doing a series on weird names, but I could see that that the theme would likely invite all kinds of controversy, so I simply said, 'That's a tough situation.'

'All the kids in my sons' class have spangly names like that though,' said Mrs Urakawa flatly.

As I riffled through the dictionary in search of inspiration for words to include in my etymology series – my first original series at the company – my mind would wander over the kinds of topics Mr Kiyota had and hadn't covered in his past efforts. Maybe, as Mrs Urakawa had suggested, it was a good idea to categorise them in terms of school subjects. On a nearby memo pad, I scrawled the word 'Japanese'.

Source That Word! #10: ご馳走 *(go-chisō)*

As in 'go-chisō-sama-deshita', a set phrase said at the end of a meal to thank one's hosts. 'Go' is an honorific particle, while 'chisō' means feast. Comprised of characters meaning 'rush' and 'run', the original meaning of chisō was the running around to prepare the feast; the meaning of 'the effort put into hosting people' came later.

Source That Word! #11: 横好き *(yokozuki)*

As in the phrase 'heta no yokozuki', meaning a person who is passionate about something they show no particular talent for. Here 'yoko' ('side') indicates something peripheral to one's main career, while 'suki' means like.

The etymology series may have been my own innovation, but coming up with the individual entries was no mean feat. I'd think, and then it'd occur to me – ooh, mean feat! I could talk about the etymology of that phrase! – and so I'd make a note of it and then move on to the next one. Before long, I started wanting to look into the etymology of 'etymology' and 'phrase', and so on, ad infinitum. My research would have me passing between the Japanese dictionary, the kanji dictionary and the internet, and then moving on to my next idea before my thoughts for the first had really been consolidated. This went on for hours as I flitted from one word to the next. The World's Smallest Countries would have been a breeze in comparison – all I'd have had to do was assemble information on San Marino and Andorra, for heaven's sake! It struck me how Mr Kiyota had always been wise enough to choose topics that could be researched and explained with relative simplicity. And yet, I knew full well that it was way too late to be having such thoughts. I was stuck with etymology. After a while, I came to the conclusion that I'd find the entries easier to write if I stipulated an imaginary reader, and so I envisioned myself writing them for Mrs Urakawa's thirteen-year-old son, although in truth I had no faith that my text would be sufficiently interesting to entice him to carry packets of Seaside Ume to his room.

The staff vote had thrown me off balance by making me feel so much at the mercy of others, but now I found myself landed with the opposite problem: having to write the text all by myself in a solitary room hidden away at the back of the museum. I supposed it wasn't so different in nature to what I'd done at the bus company, but at least there we could go out to meet our advertisers, and there'd been Ms Eriguchi and Ms Katori to talk to. Mr Kazetani's need to be perpetually worrying about something – be it Ms Eriguchi's movements or his daughter's route to her after-school club – may have rubbed me up the wrong way, but I had to admit that even speaking to him had offered a kind of respite.

Now I was utterly alone. Sure, from time to time I would discuss the texts I'd written with the director, or Ms Ōtomo would bring around the customer feedback, and at lunch I chatted with Mrs Terai and the others, but basically I was working in solitude. It wasn't that such a way of working was at odds with my nature, but at times when I couldn't light upon any suitable topics to write on, or found myself incapable of composing coherent sentences despite knowing what I wanted to write, I would be seized by the certain knowledge that I was a total and utter idiot and descend into bouts of self-loathing, cursing myself for stealing the company's money in the guise of undeserved wages. The fact that my office was so sunny also made things hard. The director had told me it was fine to go and work in the local library, but when I actually tried to do so I found myself drawn exclusively to books with no relation to the subject I was supposed to be researching, in what was clearly a subconscious bid to escape the reality of my present situation – meaning I made no progress whatsoever.

Still, when the packets for which I'd written content went to print and found their way onto the market, I began at last to understand what was good about this job. My lunchmates responsible for product inspection, Mrs Nihei and Mrs Urakawa, told me that they'd been so engrossed in reading the backs that they'd barely got any work done, and that they'd been the envy of all the others on the line for getting the first look at the new packaging. I was also grateful for the customer feedback which Ms Ōtomo collected from various social media sites and passed on. Admittedly the majority of the responses just said things along the lines of 'I noticed there's a new series on the back!', but there were also a few comments like, 'That was eye-opening!' or 'I enjoyed reading the trivia, and it made me want to buy another packet,' which made me very happy.

Next, it was decided that the Sea Urchin Bitesize (Big Bag!) was to have a package revamp, and that the trivia on the back would also be redone. There was talk of using the World's Smallest Countries series, which had scored highly in the previous round of voting, but capitalising on Ms Tamada's suggestion, I proposed a series called 'Know Your Name!' which focused on kanji often used in names, but whose meanings weren't widely known. The proposal was met with a favourable response from the director, and it was decided to put that to the vote along with the World's Smallest Countries, whereupon the names came out on top.

It was at this point that, as arrogant as it sounds, I began to feel like I'd somehow got the knack of the job. In any case, I began to actively enjoy the task of writing the rice cracker trivia, and also came to feel some sense of motivation for my work. The first name of Mrs Nihei, with whom I ate lunch, was Yoshino. She said that her parents had died relatively young and she'd never had the chance to ask them properly about why they'd chosen the name for her. When I decided to feature her particular character for 'yoshi' (佳) in the first instalment of the series, divulging that it carried the meanings 'beautiful', 'excellent' and 'good', she was delighted, and told me that she'd presented a sample packet as an offering at her home altar. That was really nice for me to hear. Nowadays, when I was sitting eating lunch, people would come up and say they'd heard from Mrs Terai that I was the person doing the text for the packets, and would I look into their names, and so on.

With all that going on, I started to understand better the director's huge emotional investment in the packets, and why Mr Kiyota had felt encouraged to continually diversify his knowledge and tackle new fields. As I went about writing texts for the various series on which I was working, I found myself coming across more and more suitable topics for rice cracker packets. I knew by now that to hit the mark, they had to have a decent number of possible entries which there was clear merit in introducing, and so I thought of: characters from the four great classics of Chinese literature, the locations of Japan's prefectural capitals together with their famous landmarks and products, types of embroidery stitches, Agatha Christie novels ... Seeing a football player sporting an afro on TV, the idea came to me of World Hairstyles, Past and Present. When the staff lunch one day was mixed tempura, it occurred to me to make a series of all the different foods that could be eaten as tempura. I'd previously been worried that I wouldn't ever be able to come up with any good ideas, but gradually I was coming around to a different mindset: if you fired off enough ideas, you were bound to eventually hit upon a winner. The key was to keep churning them out.

Almost every day at lunch now, someone would come up to me to request that I feature a character from their name, or to check back in about a kanji they'd asked about, and to ask, just by the by, if it'd be possible for me to highlight one from their friend's name as well? And so, slowly, I began thinking about potential topics from the perspective of what would most benefit readers. I had to produce work of a quality that was more than just passable – that much was apparent to me.

After having to leave my old job because of burnout syndrome, I was rationally aware that it wasn't a good idea to get too emotionally involved in what I was doing, but it was also difficult to prevent myself from taking satisfaction in it. Truthfully, I was happy when people took pleasure in my work, and it made me want to try harder.

'For the present, I don't recommend falling into a love–hate relationship with your work,' my recruiter Mrs Masakado had advised me at our very first meeting. Rather than doing the kind of job where I'd be involved with lots of people and become a central pillar of the establishment, I was better off in a role that I could fulfil calmly and peaceably. The surveillance job, the bus adverts job and this current job had all passed Mrs Masakado's audit in this regard, and yet I couldn't help but feel that this position was turning out to be rather different than I expected.

After I got home in the evening, I'd spend hours trawling the net in search of possible series ideas, weighing up their respective merits. How about this one? Nope, not enough potential entries. Ah, this one's better, but could present problems in terms of age – might it make a ninety-year-old grimace? The research didn't make me unhappy or present any detriment to my health, but I was gradually forgetting Mrs Masakado's warnings and falling head first into thoughts of rice cracker packets.

Know Your Name! S-Kanji #1
  佐 *(sa): To help; to assist.*
  惣 *(shō): All, in general. Often used to mean 'eldest son'.*

Know Your Name! R-Kanji #
  亮 *(ryō): Bright; true; to help.*
  玲 *(rei): The melodious chinking of gemstones.*

All of my kanji choices were drawn from real people: Mrs Terai's name was Misa, while Mrs Urakawa's husband's was Shōichi, Ms Ōtomo's brother was called Ryōta and the director's wife was Reiko. The Know Your Name! series proved something of a hit, though I say it myself. The responses online and on social media with which Ms Ōtomo presented me were overwhelmingly positive – and the staff members who'd had kanji from their names featured welcomed the series too. The director's wife Reiko was particularly overjoyed, and one day a bunch of preserved flowers she'd made turned up at my desk. When I relayed this news to my lunchmates, they showed evident surprise, saying, 'Wow, she must have been really over the moon!' It appeared that Reiko had among the employees if not exactly a bad reputation, then at least something of a gloomy one. At the New Year party, she'd burst into tears while talking about how she felt unable to ask her friend from a class to a newly opened tea shop. 'I mean, what could you say other than, "Why don't you just invite her?"' said Ms Kawasaki. But apparently in response to that very question, Reiko had said, 'But what if she refuses me? Then I'll never be able to go back to class,' and had grown visibly more miserable. It seemed that for a person like that to have sent flowers was quite something.

Reiko may have had something of a mixed reputation among the employees, but she clearly commanded a sizeable influence over the director, because now each time I put forward a suggestion for a new series for the packets, the director would say that he wanted to consult his wife, and then inform me the following day that she had deemed it a wonderful idea. I had the feeling that those ideas of mine that had been vetoed at the beginning, like the famous paintings series, might well make the cut now. The director was by all accounts a devoted husband.

My lunch companions suggested jokingly that I accompany Reiko to the tea shop. 'You've got to be kidding, I could never,' I said, secretly starting to fear that such an event might in fact come to pass. And it was around this time that the announcement came that a new product, which had been in development for some while, was finally ready to go on sale.

The product in question was named Ms Fujiko's Soy Sauce, and it combined two different types of crackers: bite-sized triangular crackers with rounded corners that were dusted with cheese, and larger circular ones flavoured delicately with nori and soy sauce. The company had asked a freelance illustrator to design a character for the product, Ms Fujiko: a smiling mountain that looked a bit like Mount Fuji, a pink carnation adorning her peak.

The packet was produced entirely of white matt paper of a washi-like texture, with a centrally positioned illustration of Ms Fujiko smiling, her eyes closed – altogether a very tasteful, soothing design. Above the picture of Ms Fujiko appeared the slogan 'Cheese and Soy Sauce: Mild and Mellow as the Mountains', written in an elegant calligraphic hand. A photograph of the crackers appeared on the back. It was the first time the company had used white and entirely opaque packaging – also the first time they had created a cartoon character for such a purpose.

The concept was a cracker with a soft, gentle ambience – different to what the company had produced in the past – and which had been inspired by an event involving the sister of Ms Sakemoto from the product development department. The story went that Ms Sakemoto had a niece who'd been refusing to go into school, a situation that worried Ms Sakemoto's sister so much that it was affecting her work, with the result that she too had ended up taking time off. During this spell at home, as Ms Sakemoto's sister was sitting munching on some rice crackers Ms Sakemoto had given her, and watching a TV programme she'd recorded showcasing mountains from around the world, her daughter said, 'God, it depresses me just to look at you.'

'I feel the same about you!' the mother snapped back, immediately bursting into tears. This had sparked off a full and frank exchange of feelings. In the end, the two of them had sat there talking, and eating rice crackers, until it got dark. The upshot was: the daughter had ended up going back to school and Ms Sakemoto's sister had returned to work. The rice crackers the mother and daughter had been eating at the time were the Black Bean Koban, the most orthodox of the company's range.

The impetus to create Ms Fujiko grew out of the question of whether there mightn't have been a better, more suitable type of cracker for that particular situation. The mother and daughter had sat eating crackers for five hours straight, and although their overall feedback was positive, they admitted that by the end they'd grown tired of the flavour. Further, the International News Trivia series featured on the back of the Black Bean Koban had felt a little remote from their concerns at that moment, and hadn't contributed to advancing their conversation in any way. The company's reaction to this anecdote was, of course, one of delight that their crackers had played some role in facilitating a turning point in the lives of this mother and daughter – but it was still clear that the best possible outcome would have been if the pair hadn't got bored with the crackers in the slightest, even after eating them continuously for five hours. And so, they had set about developing a product with a mild taste and some textural variation.

As far as the back of the packet was concerned, my instructions were to do whatever I liked, just as I'd been doing up to now. Yet, hearing the story behind the inception of Ms Fujiko, it seemed clear to me that a similar approach wouldn't fit the bill. I couldn't go writing about dictators from around the world – not on the packet of a product working so hard to generate a sense of serenity. And yet, with a cartoon of a smiling Ms Fujiko on the front, I could hardly run with summaries of literary classics or anything else overly highbrow.

However much I mulled it over, I couldn't come up with any promising ideas, so I decided to put the decision off for the moment and concentrate instead on writing the next instalments in the existing series. This was what I was doing when I was sent the final packet design. I had no particular issues with the front of the packet, its large calligraphy letters reading 'Ms Fujiko's Soy Sauce' – but when I laid eyes on the reverse, I immediately cradled my head in my hands. Emerging from the small Ms Fujiko on the bottom left-hand side of the packet was a speech bubble.

Surely this meant that whatever I wrote had to function as the direct speech of Ms Fujiko? If that was the case, there was even less scope for writing about dictators; poisonous Japanese plants and mysteries of the world were out of the window too. And it wasn't just Mr Kiyota's topics that were no good – my Smallest Countries wouldn't work either, and the Source That Word! and Know Your Name! series would have somehow seemed overly biased in one particular direction.

No, I thought, what was needed in this situation was to consider Ms Fujiko's personality. And so I got in touch with the illustrator responsible for designing her, who wrote to me: 'Ms Fujiko is kind-hearted and a bit of a busybody. She can be quite scatterbrained and is prone to worrying. Her favourite moment of the day is taking it easy with a nice cup of tea.' This only served to confirm my suspicions that the method I'd used to come up with ideas hitherto would be redundant. Until that point, I'd scraped through by focusing on the realm of linguistic issues, which lay outside my predecessor's preferred spheres of recipes and general knowledge in the fields of humanities and sciences.

Now I would have to try and find some kind of theme suitable for Ms Fujiko, the kind-hearted busybody.

The Ms Fujiko cartoon printed on the back of the packet came in three variations: there was the illustration which also featured on the front of the packet where her eyes were closed in a smile, one where she was frowning and looking slightly troubled, and one where her mouth was open as if midway through dispensing advice. I would have to think up text to go with each of the expressions.

With the date for the vote on the Ms Fujiko packet text looming ever closer, I was no longer in a position to put off thinking about it any more. If the company had gone to the lengths of having a character created especially, you'd think that the director could at least give me some advice, I fumed resentfully, while understanding at the same time that responding to this type of situation was exactly what I was being employed for. As I went on doing my other tasks and pretending that nothing untoward was happening, I thought endlessly about Ms Fujiko. She came to haunt me in my dreams, so I would wake up with a start in the middle of the night and find myself unable to get back to sleep before it was time to get up for work. Even the day before the submission deadline, I still hadn't thought of any decent topic ideas.

'Ms Fujiko is getting on a little in years, but she's still something of a girl at heart, and her appearance is the same as it ever was. As a result of living so long, though, she's accumulated a lot of wisdom. And I know I said she was scatterbrained, but that's just when it comes to the little things – her attitude towards life in general is quite deep.' Such was the illustrator's reply when pressed for more information on Ms Fujiko. 'When I met with the director and someone from the product development team, they mentioned the phrase "rice crackers for exhausted people". In the end they decided that that was a step too far, and it was omitted from the overall concept, but I think in a certain sense that was in the back of my mind when I was designing Ms Fujiko.'

Deadline day came, and with no other options on the table, I decided to submit 100 Famous Japanese Mountains and Summaries of All Fifty-Four Chapters of *The Tale of Genji* as contenders – but I hadn't come up with a topic that I really wanted to emerge victorious. As soon as I got into work at 9 a.m., I printed out the illustrator's emails and spent the entire morning poring over them, yet still nothing occurred to me. In desperation, I decided to put down the World's Smallest Countries series, which had showed relative popularity in past voting rounds but even so hadn't been used, simply to make up numbers. The vote would most likely go to 100 Famous Japanese Mountains, which hadn't even been my idea in the first place, but that was fine, I honestly didn't care any more, I thought, as I headed to the canteen.

Standing there slumped in line for food, the phrase ran through my head – 'rice crackers for exhausted people'. They would probably suit me very well in my current state. The main course today was meat loaf, which would have been welcome news if work had been going a bit better, but my mind was so taken up with Ms Fujiko that even the rich, aromatic smell seemed like something troublesome clinging to me.

Unable to summon up any desire for meat loaf, I put some pasta salad, chilled tofu and a couple of onigiri on my tray, then sat down. As my lunchmates chattered away like usual, I chewed my food silently.

Ms Kawasaki, who was sitting opposite, reached out a hand towards me and waved it in front of my face, saying, 'You're looking a bit off-colour. Are you okay?'

Feeling strangely guilty about being visibly out of sorts, I deliberated about whether to confess about the impasse I'd come up against, or to declare the matter over and reply with great self-possession about how the vote seemed set to go to 100 Famous Mountains of Japan, but even the fact of having to make that call started to seem unnecessarily stressful, so I just shook my head and said, 'No, no, I'm fine.'

'Come to think of it, isn't today the deadline for submitting the new topics?'

'Oh yeah! Did you manage to decide in the end?'

My lunchmates had plentiful intuition and a total absence of mercy.

'Well, yeah, I have until five today, so I'm going to keep thinking up until the last minute,' I lied.

'Well, that's good.'

'We were saying in the locker room you've been looking really worn out of late.'

'Yes! You should take a bunch of the new crackers home with you, that'll sort you out!'

I felt pretty pathetic that my worries had got out, despite my best intentions. And here I was, pretending that I was going to finish lunch, go back to my room and think very hard about the topics to put to the vote, when in fact what I intended to do was settle for a massive compromise. Perhaps even that much was obvious to them, because after wishing me luck, my lunchmates returned immediately to their previous conversations.

Mrs Urakawa was saying that her elder son always left cake and crisp crumbs scattered across his bedroom floor. After her twentieth time asking, he'd finally taken a plate up with him from which to eat from. 'But then he went and broke the blooming plate!' she said, clearly outraged. It wasn't an expensive plate, but it had been a favourite of hers, and was now broken cleanly into three. She'd been so saddened by this development, she confessed to us with a pained expression, that she'd cleared away the pieces into a paper bag to try and remove the evidence, but was unable to bring herself to throw away the bag.

Mrs Nihei, meanwhile, was conscious that she wasn't eating enough vegetables. In a bid to amend this state of affairs, she'd bought lettuce, tomatoes, daikon sprouts and red peppers, planning to eat a ton of salad, but had forgotten to buy dressing, so in the end she'd contented herself with just smearing mayonnaise on the vegetables. It tasted okay, she reported, but it was hard to make it stick. 'Seems I'm getting more forgetful of late,' she said.

'Speaking of forgetting to buy things,' broke in Ms Tamada, going on to relate how she'd run out of shampoo and conditioner and failed to pick any up in the shops, so had ended up washing her hair with soap. As a result, her hair today was all coarse, and she didn't want us looking at it.

Mrs Terai listened to these various accounts in silence, a grim expression on her face. When the others had said their piece, she leaned forward and said, 'Mine might get a bit long, do you mind?' She then embarked on the story of how her mother-in-law had suddenly started buying lots of expensive kimonos, and Mrs Terai was concerned she was going to spend all of her inheritance from her husband, who'd died the previous year. Mrs Terai was usually so cheerful, but she seemed genuinely perturbed, narrating this tale. Up until that point, the other women had all been adopting an attitude which seemed to suggest their own concerns should take priority, but now a subdued atmosphere fell across the group, and they all murmured, 'Oh gosh,' and 'Dear, oh dear.'

Last of all, Ms Kawasaki piped up with her contribution, lightening the by-now rather leaden air and making everyone smile with her tale of a very expensive pair of shoes she'd bought on impulse last year. Since she'd worn them out in the rain one day, she confided with a self-deprecating air, they'd begun to smell terrible, and now she couldn't get rid of the stench.

My current concerns were, needless to say, all about cracker packets. The three topics I'd decided to submit to the vote were starting to look utterly pitiful to me.

With lunch over, I returned to my office at the back of the Rice Cracker Museum and began attending to my other jobs, only to discover there was literally nothing else left for me to do. Resignedly I opened up the text editor and began to compose the outlines for the three topics to be put to the staff vote: 100 Famous Japanese Mountains, *The Tale of Genji* Chapter Summaries and the World's Smallest Countries. I had told the director the previous day that it would likely be those three, and he'd said that sounded good. The outlines were written in no time.

I killed some minutes by polishing the outlines more carefully than usual, but I still had a while left before the end of the day. I made some tea and opened up a bag of Ms Fujiko's Soy Sauce that I'd been given to help me form an image of the product. They really were delicious, quite possibly the best of this company's crackers that I'd tried. Our packet sizes tended to be on the large side in comparison to similar products produced by other brands, and Ms Fujiko was no different; it took a good while to get through a bag. The bite-sized mountain-shaped pieces dusted with cheese were hard and crunchy. As I munched away at them, I stared down at the image of Ms Fujiko that I'd printed out and apologised to her, saying that even if the overall topics weren't great, I'd do my best with the individual content.

Still, I had time on my hands, so I was looking over the customer feedback that Ms Ōtomo had passed on for a second time, when I suddenly remembered what Mrs Urakawa had been saying at lunch about her son breaking her favourite plate. That itself was proof that I was fed up with thinking about work. Plates were tricky things, I mused. However much you liked the colour, pattern, shape of a particular type, it was not unusual to find when you went to buy the same one again that they were no longer being made. The plate Mrs Urakawa's eldest son had broken had been pale turquoise in colour with a wave design on it, and Mrs Urakawa had bought it four years ago. It seemed doubtful that line would still be in production. I searched the online shop for the brand in question, but I couldn't see any sign of a plate like the one she'd described.

It wasn't like I'd seen the plate itself, but from the air of genuine disappointment with which Mrs Urakawa had spoken about it, I could easily imagine how lovely it had been. I went on an online auction site to have a look but couldn't find anything similar, which got me thinking once again about how irrevocable an act breaking a plate was, and it wasn't long before I arrived at the conclusion that surely the best thing in such a case would be to try gluing it back together.

I entered the words 'repair', 'broken' and 'ceramics' into the search box, and immediately arrived at the brand name of an adhesive specifically for repairing ceramics. The web page in question, which featured a discussion about the various ways to bring your broken ceramics back to life, also mentioned kintsugi – the technique where you stuck together the broken parts using lacquer and dusted it with powdered gold. The gold seams gave the repaired item a certain stylishness you didn't get from just sticking the pieces together using glue.

Unable to wait to tell Mrs Urakawa about this idea, I decided to message her. It was three o'clock, so I figured she might well be on a break. 'I was thinking about your plate … If you just want it to be serviceable you could use ceramic adhesive, but another option to consider is kintsugi!' It seemed she was indeed on her break, because her response came almost imme-diately: 'Ah, thank you so much! I'll google it on my way home!'

For no apparent reason, I was inordinately pleased by this enthusiastic response, and so I began carrying out searches related to what Mrs Nihei had been saying about forgetting to buy salad dressing. I discovered that you could make French dressing with just salad oil, vinegar, salt, pepper and sugar, while for a Thousand Island dressing you only needed to mix mayonnaise, ketchup, vinegar and sugar. Either could be rustled up with things that most people kept in their kitchen.

I jotted this down on a piece of paper. Then I recalled Ms Tamada's issue, and Ms Kawasaki's, and Mrs Terai's, and eventually I ended up searching for solutions to the problems presented by all five of my lunchmates. When I was done, it was almost five o'clock, and time to go home.

I opened up the file containing the outlines of the candidates for the employee vote, and deleted 'World's Smallest Countries'. In its place, I wrote the words 'Ms Fujiko's Helpful Hints':

Ms Fujiko provides simple solutions to familiar problems that crop up in daily life, such as: 'I broke my favourite plate!' or 'I'm in the mood for salad but I don't have any dressing!' or 'I've run out of shampoo and conditioner!' or 'I bought something I don't want any more!' or 'I can't get rid of the smell in my shoes!'

The following week, Ms Fujiko's Helpful Hints narrowly defeated 100 Famous Japanese Mountains at the polls. Having received comments from conscientious employees like, 'The broken plate example convinced me!' and 'We can do the mountains any time, but it's only this character which the Helpful Hints will work with,' it was decided that the back of the Ms Fujiko's Soy Sauce packet should feature hints and tips from gentle-spirited Ms Fujiko.

The first batch of hints I wrote comprised solutions to the problems provided by my lunchmates, as well as addressing a concern from Reiko about how long it took to scrub tea stains from cups, a query of my own about the best times to drink caffeine and a question inspired by the 100 Famous Japanese Mountains series about what to do if you got lost up a mountain. Ms Tamada had taken on the suggestion I'd made of rinsing her hair with citric acid after washing it with soap, and Ms Kawasaki's shoes, after she'd placed unwanted teabags inside them, had recovered to a degree where she could once again keep them in the doorway of her house.

When Ms Fujiko's Soy Sauce made it onto the shelves, its combination of exceptional flavour, pretty packaging and cute characterisation made it an instant hit, and reports flooded in from all our stockists saying that they were selling out fast. Ms Fujiko's Soy Sauce crackers had been longer than usual in development and were undoubtedly tasty, I told myself, so that surely accounted for a lot of the product's success, yet it did appear as though the backs of the packets were also going down well, and every day Ms Ōtomo would cheerfully pass on feedback received on blogs and through social media. As well as comments like 'At first I didn't think the tips would be relevant to me, but in fact they came in handy,' and 'A bit of harmless fun,' we also had comments from people who appeared to have been tracing the evolution of the company's trivia for a while saying things like 'Different to any of the past series,' and 'I'm glad you're finally featuring things that will actually help people rather than stuff nobody cares about,' which I was grateful for.

However, as I said to the director, there was a limit to the amount of problems faced by people like my lunchmates and the director's wife, with whom I had a direct connection, and so the decision was taken to install a Worry Box in the Rice Cracker Museum, to collect concerns from a wider spectrum of staff members. The box only received one or two submissions a day, but that was, in fact, a perfect amount. Unlike with previous research items, 'worry topics' were not restricted to any particular field, but were pulled from a range of different spheres, so researching each one and presenting the simplest solution was actually quite a time-consuming task. 'The nose pads have come off my glasses but I've no time to take them in for repair,' read one entry; 'I can never find a rubber when I need one,' said another; while a third complained: 'I don't know what to cook for dinner.' People's troubles were truly wide-ranging. As far as the nose pads went, it turned out that, as with broken plates, there was a specific adhesive available, so I suggested gluing them back on for the moment until the wearer had time to get to an optician. With the problem of never having a rubber to hand, I advised building up a stock by buying one every time the person saw one for a whole week. I couldn't think of a decent answer for the dinner issue, so I consulted my lunchmates, and several of them recommended winter hotpots on the grounds that they were both easy and nutritious, so I went with that.

In terms of its popularity among staff and favourable reviews online, Ms Fujiko wasn't all that different from the company's other products. The real game changer was the product being featured in the paper – not just a trade paper, either, but a national newspaper. What was more, the article in question was specifically about Helpful Hints.

My husband got lost in the mountains one night and, by sheer coincidence, on the back of the rice cracker packet I'd given him was the advice: 'Don't try to hurry down or descend via mountain streams.' And so my husband, who had been searching for a stream, stayed where he was eating his crackers, where he was found by a local rescue worker and returned to safety.

What was more, the name of the woman who had written in was Fujiko, which was deemed a very strange coincidence. Ms Ōtomo had brought me a letter that related a similar story, so I guessed it must be the same person.

The newspaper clipping was stuck up in the entrance hall outside the Rice Cracker Museum, and the sales team started adding it into their sales pitches to clients. It turned out that they had never explicitly mentioned the trivia before.

A week after the article was published, we were contacted by a journalist from the lifestyle section of a newspaper company, who came to interview the director together with Ms Ōtomo, and Ms Sakemoto from product development. I was asked if I wanted to come along too, but I refused, saying that I didn't really have anything to contribute. I was up against it with my work as it was. Unlike with the other kinds of trivia, writing Ms Fujiko advice necessitated researching various arguments both supporting and countering all the suggestions I was considering making, which made it all the more time-consuming. Added to that, I was struggling to find topics about which Ms Fujiko would plausibly be knowledgeable. Broken plates were okay, but I could hardly have her talking about repairing electrical appliances; and while she might know a thing or two about how to make crispy tempura, a Japanese woman of her ilk was not likely to know how many minutes to cook spaghetti for.

Since starting the Ms Fujiko job, I'd come to the realisation that I was really bad at giving advice, and that I knew absolutely nothing about anything. More and more, I'd find myself stopping mid-task. Now, even when writing copy for the other series which I'd previously got through at a handsome pace, my research became increasingly detailed and I'd stall because I couldn't find any conclusive evidence, eventually abandoning the topic entirely.

As if inversely to my job performance, sales of Ms Fujiko soared. People throughout the company were celebrating, and there were even rumours circulating of special bonuses. As all this was going on, I sat there in my office behind the Rice Cracker Museum, worrying about my ever-diminishing work rate.

It transpired that the woman who'd written into the newspaper had also been contacting TV stations, explaining the highly coincidental fate that had befallen her and her husband, and attaching a clipping of the newspaper article written about them. I was starting to suspect that this woman simply had more time on her hands than she knew what to do with, but either the TV stations were desperate for content or there was something else at play, because one station actually ended up coming into the company to film.

Needless to say, the director welcomed this development and told me that this time I should definitely be interviewed, but unable to put all the work I had to get done out of my head, I refused, instructing him and Ms Ōtomo to tell the TV people that I was just extremely shy. I found out afterwards that they had indeed said this, and everybody had laughed, and it had helped break the ice.

At some point, by the sounds of things, the cameras moved inside the Rice Cracker Museum. From my office where I was sitting, I listened to the laughing voices of the presenters and crew, of the company director and other employees, as I pondered the question of whether advice that read 'If you find your kitchen sponges wear out too quickly, try using acrylic scourers!' was appropriate for Ms Fujiko to be dispensing.

Thanks to TV appearances, Ms Fujiko's Soy Sauce's sales shot up further still. The presenters who'd come to film the TV programme had sampled the product on-air and waxed lyrical about its taste. A different station had featured an interview with the mountain climber's wife speaking again about how grateful she was, and this had apparently blown up online, with lots of people commenting on how hilariously dopey she was. At lunchtime, Ms Tamada voiced the opinion that this woman was using our company as a stepping stone in order to satisfy some desires of her own, but I sensed that if I got involved in the conversation, I'd find myself unable to carry on doing my work, so I just let her words wash over me.

Now, thanks to all the media exposure, members of the general public had begun to write in with their worries. As she handed me the list of problems, Ms Ōtomo said she understood it wasn't an easy situation for me to be in, but it'd be nice if I could feature at least one of these among the concerns submitted by employees. Scanning the list, I could see soon enough that it was all pretty heavy stuff: 'Since quitting his job, my husband just sits around at home all day. I don't know how much longer I can take living with him,' and 'I'm in debt and I haven't told my son,' and 'My daughter can't find a husband. Is it because she's too ugly?' The discovery only whetted my despair.

As I was trudging wearily back from one of my toilet trips, which had grown rather frequent of late, I heard the director call my name. When I explained my current predicament in a relatively pared-back way, he responded with a very unexpected suggestion: 'Why don't we invite the mountaineer's wife in as a guest respondent?' I felt like I might faint on the spot. 'She's cheerful and kind,' the director went on, 'and she's said that she'll do it for free, as a gesture of gratitude. And what's more, her name just so happens to be Fujiko.' Surely the issue wasn't a financial one? I desperately swallowed back the words that had risen to the back of my throat – *Just how far is she going to try and worm her way in?* – an effort which only left me feeling more exhausted.

'Why don't you at least try talking to her?' the director suggested. 'She's really a wonderful person.'

Excusing myself by saying that I was somewhat too busy for that at the moment, I scurried back to my room and picked up the list of problems Ms Ōtomo had given me. I managed to read one before I put the list down. After a while, I picked the list back up, read another question, and then gave up and put it down again. A good few times I repeated this pitiful process. The truth was that none of the problems submitted were the kinds for which I had any hope of providing solutions, I thought in desperation – and then my eye caught one that read, 'I quit my job because I wasn't getting on with my colleagues. Hearing my friends talk about all the nasty people at their workplaces, I don't feel like ever working again. Does working make you meaner?' Including my first workplace, which I'd quit because of burnout syndrome, I'd worked in four different places so far, and sure, there had been people with whom I hadn't especially got along, but I'd never experienced anyone being out-and-out mean to me. It seemed that if people had any scrap of energy to spare, they preferred to put it to use either in doing their job, or in their private life, rather than in being cruel to others. But then, when I thought back to the part-time jobs I'd had as a student, I realised I had endured my fair share of unpleasant run-ins, so it wasn't like

I couldn't understand this person's point entirely. I didn't have a diverse body of work experience, but as time went on, I'd come to understand the simple fact that every single workplace had an entirely different set of people working there.

Working makes you irritable, but it doesn't make you meaner. Mean people are mean even when they aren't working. Try thinking of colleagues you get along with as a bonus, rather than a requisite, and look for a workplace of a size where you feel comfortable.

The answer was totally out of character for Ms Fujiko, I thought, and immediately felt my stomach clench. I had done what Ms Ōtomo had asked, but it felt like, very possibly, the real-life Mrs Fujiko who was writing into a million different media outlets, would have been able to come up with a better answer. She seemed to have plenty of confidence, and wouldn't feel overly pressured. She was exactly the sort of person who would be able to waltz in and dispense life advice. I was clearly lacking in the self-belief this role necessitated.

On my way home from work, I found myself reflecting more and more on how I was not well suited to this job. Up until now, through a combination of following the precedent Mr Kiyota had set, and something like momentum, I had managed to write the texts required of me – but it had never occurred to me that I would struggle this much when trying to write things from scratch. I tried asking various people – the director, Ms Ōtomo, and my lunchmates – if they had any suggestions, but they all told me that they didn't, that they thought I was doing just fine. Maybe I should give the Ms Fujiko job to real-life Mrs Fujiko, I thought, and just step into the role of assistant, helping her and working on the other packets – but then it struck me that this would mean working closely alongside her, a prospect that left me feeling utterly despondent.

Though I knew it was wrong, I began to foster the hope that Ms Fujiko sales would start to ebb – but in vain. Ms Fujiko was mentioned in lists of 'the cutest mascots', and her reputation only continued to grow. She was clearly getting too much for me to handle.

It was the day after I began dipping out of work to buy stomach medicine that I heard the news that Mr Kiyota would be returning to the company. Ms Tamada had heard it from Mr Fukumoto, the security guard whom she was no longer dating but remained on good terms with. According to Mr Fukumoto, who was drinking buddies with Mr Kiyota, it seemed he'd been through an intense period of distress, and then quite abruptly worked it out of his system. He still hadn't found anybody to marry, but he'd decided to build a new life for himself based around his interests, which included rail holidays and visiting historical ruins.

If Mr Kiyota – the cracker packet trivia ace – was returning to work, that doubtless meant I was out of a job. I found the thought of doing a different job anxiety-inducing, but so long as it meant being liberated from my current one, I felt certain I could bear it. Whatever job I ended up doing next would be tough until I got used to it, but it was bound to be something to which I was better suited.

At home time that day, the director called me into the meeting room and told me officially about Mr Kiyota's return.

'I think it's great he's coming back,' I said, my tone unprecedentedly light. 'I really respect the work he does. He's the one who should be writing this company's packets.'

'He's a good person,' said the director. 'I think you two will get along very well.'

'Huh?'

'If it feels awkward to work together, just the two of you in that office, we can make a space for you on the admin floor.'

This conversation was panning out rather differently to how I'd expected. The director was talking as if I was now going to be working alongside Mr Kiyota, even though I'd been employed as his cover.

'You mean I'm not going to be made redundant?' I asked. It seemed to me best to start from the basics.

'Of course not!' the director replied with vehemence.

'Surely it'd be better if I moved to a different department, then?' I said, adding, 'I really like this company, and I'm happy to take on any kind of role.'

'Oh no,' said the director, looking a little taken aback. 'We're not even considering that. In fact, in our meeting just the other day, we took the decision to up the priority level for the backs of the packets. We're thinking about maybe increasing the number of texts featured.'

He went on to explain that Ms Fujiko had shown the world how serious the company was about its packets, and it seemed like the time to consolidate that impression with an extra push.

'And we've decided to create a sister product, a plain salted version, with the same series on the back.'

'Helpful Hints, you mean?'

'What else?!' said the director, looking almost vexed at having to cover such obvious ground with me. 'After all, people keep writing in with requests for advice.'

It seemed as though the response about working, which I'd written in a state close to resignation, had been judged pragmatically sound advice. 'Did nobody comment that the text didn't really fit with Ms Fujiko's personality?' I asked, to which the director replied casually, 'Oh, anything goes, I think.'

'Really,' I nodded. I felt as though air was seeping out from a hole in my back. So that was how it was – *anything goes*. I could see how, if that was your way of thinking, it would seem perfectly okay to have the real-life Mrs Fujiko come in and respond to people's requests for advice.

It wasn't like I felt that the director had his head in the clouds, but it did seem that his thinking was more simplistic than I'd believed. If this was how things were, then I'd rather he moved me to a different department, but I could see that wasn't the way things were going to go.

'We talked at the meeting about having the real-life Mrs Fujiko writing a few answers, and the suggestion was met with positively, so I'd like you to seriously consider it as a possibility.'

All I could do was nod and say, 'Right, sure.' The celebrity rating of the real-life Mrs Fujiko had shot up along with that of the cartoon character. I surmised that sooner or later, I would have to go along with his plan.

On the way back from the meeting room to my office, I thought over these impending changes to my working situation, and felt my shoulders slump heavily. It wasn't that I now disliked my job. I didn't, and I knew full well that it was a mightily common occurrence in the world of work for forces from above to intervene and stir things up, and yet I couldn't deny that this had hit me hard.

Back in my room, I recalled that the illustrator who had designed the Ms Fujiko character had shown a very good understanding of her personality, and so with trepidation I put in a call to the director, suggesting that we ask the illustrator to help out instead, but he didn't seem keen, saying he preferred not to delegate work to someone from outside the company. Faced with a choice between real-life Mrs Fujiko whose face was now well known and who would work for no money, and Ms Fujiko's true parent whose services would cost money and whose name wasn't even on the packet, I could see why you would go with real-life Mrs Fujiko.

After that, I composed five new additions for the Know Your Name! and the International News Trivia series, writing about the characters 亘 (kō, wataru), 佑 (yū, suke) and 拓 (taku, hiro), and about black box flight recorders and the Scythians. It wasn't that long ago that writing these kinds of texts had formed the main bulk of my job – the thought made me realise just how much had happened in such a short time.

I ate dinner out. Back at home I opened the fridge to get a drink, and my mother, who was sitting watching TV, called out to me, 'Your company was on the telly again.'

'Yeah. There's so little going on in the world of late they need stuff like that to fill up the holes in their schedule,' I replied thornily.

'It was that couple,' she informed me. Great, I thought. 'They were doing a reconstruction of the night that he got stranded on the mountain.'

'Were they now.'

'I thought those crackers looked good, so I've been keeping an eye out for them at the supermarket, but it seems like they're sold out almost everywhere. If there are any lying around in the office, do you think you bring some home?'

'They're hardly going to be just *lying around* in the office, are they, if they're sold out everywhere!' I snapped back at her unthinkingly.

'Oh, okay. Well, just if you happen to see some.'

'The other types are nice too, you know? The Supersize Squid and Mirin are good, and so are the Seaside Ume, and the Nattō and Cheese Thins (With Wasabi!). You used to love them, remember?'

'What are you getting so worked up for?' my mother said, shrugging as if to say 'you're a weirdo,' then turning back to the screen. From the jar in the corner of the kitchen where my mother stockpiled her snacks, I retrieved the three varieties of crackers I'd just mentioned and took them to my room. I made some green tea and ate them one after another. Just as I'd said, they were all perfectly nice.

Though I knew it wasn't reasonable, I felt angry with lots of different people. I was angry with the real-life Mrs Fujiko, and with the director, and with all the people who had featured Ms Fujiko in the media, and even with consumers of rice crackers around the world. None of them had any discernment.

For a moment, Mrs Masakado's words passed through my mind – 'for the present, I don't recommend falling into a love–hate relationship with your work' – but another part of me snapped back at her: *Just shut up!*

At lunch on Friday, Mrs Terai asked me out of the blue if I was free that evening. When I said I was, she told me that she and the lunch crowd were having dinner together, and asked if I'd like to come. I had no reason to say no, so I said yes. We ate lunch together most days, but this would be our first evening outing.

After lunch, I put paid to ten new items in the Source That Word! series, and then passed an eye over the list of Ms Fujiko advice requests that had been sent in. As usual, the topics tended towards the weighty side: 'I'm married, but I've fallen in love with someone at work who says she feels the same. Should I split up with my wife?' and 'My mother-in-law blatantly prefers one of my twins,' and 'My son spends 100,000 yen a month on anime figurines.' We also received an entry that seemed to form a perfect pair with the 'I'm married' one, revealing, 'I've fallen in love with my married boss,' so it seemed entirely possible that the writers were co-conspirators. I had no conception of why such people had decided to seek advice about such things from a rice cracker company. Was there no limit to how inappropriately a person could behave?

As I went on reading through the list of problems, I started to feel the urge to write a response to one of these questions that served as a secret dig at someone – maybe the director, or maybe the character Ms Fujiko. Honestly, my strongest impulse was to provide no constructive answer at all – to say: *I don't care what you do! I have no idea! It's got nothing to do with me! I don't give a toss! Do whatever the hell you want!* But then I started wondering whether, rather than approaching the problems from an ethically enlightened perspective, I might not be able to shed light on them from another direction, and began looking into the going rate for the kinds of damages the man could be hit with if he did go ahead and have an affair. This kept me occupied until home time came around and I cut my research short. I could easily have stayed on, but I knew Mrs Terai's restaurant reservation was for fifteen minutes' time, so I hurriedly got ready and left.

The restaurant in question was a small Italian place not far from the company. It made a real change to see my lunchmates in their own clothes as opposed to their factory uniforms, and the sight even made me a little nervous. They'd ordered wine, but being allergic to alcohol, I asked for a Perrier and we clinked glasses. Mrs Terai thanked us repeatedly in a weirdly formal way, before announcing, 'We got 1.5 million yen back!'

Apparently, she'd managed to return several of the kimonos that her mother-in-law had bought. Ms Fujiko's Helpful Hints had noted that items bought from visiting salespeople could sometimes be returned by content-certified delivery. After writing the text, I'd printed out my research and handed it to Mrs Terai. She said that with her lunchmates' help, she'd managed to fill out the form in between working, household cleaning and chores, and convincing her mother-in-law.

'I had no idea that Ms Kawasaki used to work in the legal department at her previous company,' she said.

'I developed a panic disorder and had to leave, though,' said Ms Kawasaki. She went on to say she'd spent two years at home as a recluse before returning to work, and had eventually found a permanent-contract job at the cracker factory. Ms Kawasaki, who was single and lived alone, said how glad she was that she'd renovated her house before getting ill. Mrs Terai bowed her head at me so often that I said, 'Honestly, I did nothing!'

'This wouldn't have happened if you hadn't featured it on the cracker packets,' Mrs Terai said to me, patting me on the shoulder. 'It would have ended as a story of my mother-in-law being conned and losing all her money.'

Mrs Terai hadn't herself benefitted financially, but she said she felt as though she'd put the problem behind her, and had wanted to celebrate. Everyone at the dinner said over and over how glad they were too. It struck me, not for the first time, what a genuinely good bunch of people they were. I began to feel myself in a very good mood, and told Ms Tamada that I'd looked into Mr Fukumoto's daughters' names on several name-horoscope sites and it turned out that, although Mianna Fukumoto was pretty inauspicious, Mioria Fukumoto got very high ratings all round. I'd also found out that there were a number of complex conditions you needed to meet in order to officially change your name, but one way seemed to be to use a new name for a number of years and then amass a lot of post addressed to that new name. 'Hmm,' said Ms Tamada, 'that's interesting. It does seem as though the elder one, Mianna, isn't really keen on hers.'

After that, the conversation turned to Mr Kiyota's return. All the women were clearly fond of him, and were looking forward to seeing him again. It seemed as though they, too, were convinced that his return meant I'd be removed from my current role, and were kind enough to say that they'd look out for me if I came over to the factory. This made me rather emotional and I felt in danger of welling up, so in the end I didn't manage to tell them that I would be continuing to do my current job alongside Mr Kiyota, and that I might also be working with the real-life Mrs Fujiko. I think, on some level, I wanted to believe that what they were saying was in fact the truth of the situation.

On the way home from dinner, it struck me that I was no longer feeling a deep sense of attachment to my work. Of course, I knew that it wasn't anything as vague as a 'sense of attachment' that I should be aiming towards – that I should be aspiring instead to go at work with determination, but frankly, I felt I didn't want to go at it in any way at all.

Then suddenly it came to me: I could just not renew my contract. I'd never intended to stay all that long in this company, and although the pay and other provisions were good, it was clear to me that things could get tough if I stayed on much longer. At some point after Ms Fujiko's Soy Sauce had gone on sale, there had been a shift in my working situation. When I thought about how many people there were in this world struggling for work, not to mention how I owed my ability to do this job and the previous one at the bus company almost entirely to those who'd walked the path ahead of me, my desire to quit felt like an impudent thing to be feeling – but there it was.

The next week, I had the news that Mr Kiyota's return would be slightly delayed. It wasn't that he was having second thoughts – rather, he'd decided that he wanted to see his psychiatrist first and discuss how best to approach this new phase of working life, so as to ensure he was properly prepared. The director readily consented. How generous of him, I thought. I was sure that plenty of bosses would have said something to the tune of 'You've caused us enough problems already, now hurry up and get your arse back in here!' It also gave me an understanding of just how much of a slot Mr Kiyota had carved out for himself at this company.

It had been decided at a meeting the previous Friday that the real-life Mrs Fujiko would serve as respondent for a limited-edition release of Ms Fujiko's Soy Sauce. At first it seemed to me peculiar that I hadn't been invited to that meeting, given I was in charge of writing the text for the packets, but it made more sense when I remembered that I was on a limited contract and my job was just that of a content writer – so I could hardly be expected to contribute my opinion about the company's sales policy.

And so, since Mr Kiyota wasn't back, I ended up meeting the real-life Mrs Fujiko. For the first time ever, I was shown into the reception room, where I found her waiting: a genteel old woman with fine features and youthful-looking skin that led me to imagine she had been a real beauty when she was younger. It was clear as soon as she started speaking that she was cheerful and spirited, and I could easily understand how she would quickly garner popularity among people.

'I so look forward to reading the backs of the rice cracker packets,' she said. 'I always assumed it was a very well-educated man writing them. I was most surprised to discover it was a woman!'

'Oh, I'm just taking over this job temporarily from someone who's off work at the moment. He's a man, and as far as I can work out, very well educated.'

'But it was you who wrote the back of the Ms Fujiko packets, wasn't it?'

'Yes, that was me.'

'Honestly, I can't tell you what you did for us! You saved my family. You know what they say, that the best way for husbands to be is healthy and not at home, but I would hate it if he died on me. He can't do anything without me, see, and that day he invited me to climb the mountain with him, but I didn't feel like going, and so I gave him those crackers as a substitute. You know, because they've got the same name as me! Fujiko! That cheered him up. And then he went and lost his way on the path … '

She went on, narrating the story I knew well already. So well did I know it, in fact, that even nodding along seemed bothersome to me, and I stared down instead at the tea leaves at the bottom of my cup.

'You look so tired,' she said suddenly, after she'd reached the end of her tale. 'You should rest! It doesn't do to be thinking about work all hours of the day, you know.'

From the angle of her head and the look of her eyes with their big irises, I understood that Mrs Fujiko could see that my soul had seized up and grown stiff. I felt a sudden urge to kick the coffee table away and hurl my teacup at the wall.

'So, we'll be asking you to select the questions to put to Mrs Fujiko and to edit her answers, okay?' said the director. I intended to nod, but found I couldn't move my head.

'When the time comes,' I replied in the end, a statement whose meaning wasn't clear even to me.

Yet it seemed that the two of them took my response as a form of consent, because they started thanking me, saying over and over, 'We're counting on you!'

Walking back down the corridor it occurred to me that 'We're counting on you!' and 'You should rest!' were actually contradictory messages, and a lump formed in my throat. Which did she really mean? Or did she mean neither? Maybe it was all just meaningless conversational fluff – or was this what they called a double bind?

I went back to my room behind the Rice Cracker Museum, sat down on my chair and for a little while, did absolutely nothing. When I came back to myself, it was starting to get dark outside so I turned on the lights, but I didn't boot up my computer, or make any notes, or drink any tea. I just sat there, unable to move.

After a while the phone rang and I picked it up. It was the director. 'I forgot to say, your contract is coming up for renewal, so we'll need you to fill in the form. Could you take your personal seal over to the admin office? It won't take very long – you just circle to say whether you want to extend or not. Oh, and we've heard from Mr Kiyota that he'll be returning on the first of next month.'

I looked at the calendar on my desk, and saw that I had four working days left in my current contract. Four days would give me enough time to create handover instructions while also seeing off my regular work. I started up my computer and began researching the damages that could be claimed for extramarital affairs, as I'd been doing before I met real-life Fujiko, but stopped after five minutes. I was sure Mr Kiyota would look into that on his first day back. Maybe, I thought, I could write into the company in secret: 'Someone has appeared to try and take over my job. What should I do? My boss hasn't noticed, and I'm unsure whether I'm just being paranoid … '

The Postering Job

'No, it definitely was a good job.' I had no idea how many times I'd said those words, but it must have been at least thirty. 'No, it definitely was a good job. All my colleagues were lovely, and I got the sense that my predecessor, who I'd have been working with if I stayed on, was talented and nice. I just couldn't really understand how they could get some outside person in to hand out life advice to people … But no, you're right, it definitely was a good job.'

Listening to the stream of complaints-cum-excuses pouring from my mouth with no perceptible end in sight, Mrs Masakado nodded from time to time.

The best explanation I could have given as to why I hadn't renewed my contract went as follows: I hadn't been able to get over the fear that my job would be stolen away from me by the type of person I had an intense aversion to, and so I'd run away. Of course, it wasn't like the person in question had actually announced her intention to steal my job, and in fact, what terrified me more than that eventuality was the gulf that would open up between me and the director and all the other employees when they refused – as I felt sure they would – to acknowledge the pernicious aspects of that woman and her meddling ways. If on top of having fallen into a love–hate relationship with my work I was also going to have to deal with that kind of dynamic then, it had seemed to me, I was best off escaping.

'So, what you're saying is that you felt like the job itself was very worthwhile, but there was some interference that prevented you from properly engaging and building a healthy relationship with your work.'

Adopting an attitude that said nobody would ever dream of questioning the reasonableness of either my judgement or my commitment, Mrs Masakado paraphrased my waffly self-justifications in clear language. I nodded repeatedly, as if doing so might free me from the sense of defeat that had enveloped me.

I felt convinced that Mrs Masakado was going to tell me I should have stuck it out a bit longer, but she didn't. At the start of the interview, she'd asked me what I hadn't liked about the company, which seemed to be her way of discovering my reasons for not renewing my contract, but it seemed that as I'd gone on speaking, she'd grasped that it wasn't a question of the job being suitable or otherwise, but rather about a difficult encounter which fate had served up to me.

'I'd like an easy job.'

I'd started to realise that offering up any more hazy explanations about why I hadn't stayed on would only strengthen the amorphous sense of oppression that had formed inside me, so I changed the topic. 'I'm sorry I've left so many of the jobs you've helped me find so far.'

'Don't apologise. They've all been limited-contract jobs anyway, and the rice cracker job didn't come through me but from your previous position.'

This was true. Which meant that, in total, I'd only left two of the jobs that Mrs Masakado had helped me find. Was that a lot, or not? I guessed it probably was.

'If I'm honest, at that last job I felt able to settle down a bit and devote myself to the work, and neither the people nor the environment were at all bad, and yet when something unexpected happened, it really threw me off balance, and I feel like it's shaken my confidence. I think I'm in a slightly different boat to your regular person who's "all set to work" or whatever.'

'I think it's hard to define what being "all set to work" means with any generality, but I agree with what you say about the unexpected developments.' Saying this Mrs Masakado opened up the file in front of her and began slowly leafing through its pages.

'I guess it'd be misleading to say I'll do anything, but what I mean is, I'm happy to do the kind of job that I haven't done in the past. It doesn't have to be desk work.'

'Right, right, yes, I see,' Mrs Masakado said, apparently just trying to fill the silence as she carefully examined the file, which I conjectured must contain a list of job vacancies.

'I've never done an outdoor job, but I'm happy to give it a try. That might actually be better.'

A job counting the number of sparrows sitting on telegraph cables, or the number of red cars passing through a crossing – I felt like if I listed those kinds of examples it would seem like I was joking, so I kept quiet, but in truth I was semi-serious. I wanted a job that was practically without substance, a job that sat on the borderline between being a job and not. The sort of job where there was no chance of a genteel old lady with more time on her hands than she knew how to deal with showing up out of the blue and saying, 'You look so tired!' and 'We're counting on you!' Above anything else, I wanted a job I could do alone. I knew that I'd need to leave that stipulation behind me at some point, but at least for the moment, that was how I felt.

'Outdoors,' said Mrs Masakado, adjusting her glasses, nodding and flicking through the file, then making a little noise. 'Ooh, this might be good.'

She handed the file to me, pointing to the job description and details.

'You'd be going around shops and houses replacing posters,' she told me, then explained that I'd be taking a cut in pay, and that the initial contract wasn't a very long one. Whether or not it would be renewable would depend on various factors, but health insurance was included. The company in question had been entrusted by a government agency to stick up posters promoting road safety awareness and so on.

'So, what do you think?' Mrs Masakado looked at me across the desk, her back rod-straight, her eyebrows slightly raised.

Without really thinking about it, I blinked and nodded.

I sent off my CV, and received a phone call asking me to come into the office so they could run through the details of the position. 'Will there not be an interview?' I asked, upon which the man on the other end of the line told me that there weren't any other applicants, and since the recommendation came through Mrs Masakado, he felt secure in taking me on without one. Realising once again how well trusted Mrs Masakado was, I wondered if I was really deserving of her patronage. Yes, I may have worked in the same company for a decade after graduating, but since leaving I'd flitted from one job to another, and had turned down two opportunities for renewing my contract. If I were Mrs Masakado, I would have started to feel suspicious of me at this point, and yet it seemed like I was going to be offered another job. Were standards lower for limited-contract jobs?

The address to which I was directed was on the outskirts of an old residential area, not far from my parents' home. The office occupied the ground floor of a converted house, its exterior covered in small cream-coloured pearlescent tiles which placed it as at least forty years old. The area of about eight tatami mats, the office was no larger than a regular house – about the size of my parents', in fact. A very thin man of indeterminate age came to greet me. He wore thick-framed glasses, his hair hung down to his chin and his face wore a dusting of stubble.

'Good to meet you. I'm Monaga.' Mr Monaga was the only person working in the office, and there was only one computer.

'I'll talk you through the job. Please take a seat,' he said, showing me towards a table in the corner of the tidy office space. The old wooden table had metal fixtures at the ends, suggesting it was foldable. The chair was small and old-looking, but strangely comfortable, and I guessed that both items were of some value. Having disappeared into the back, Mr Monaga now returned with a tray and set down a cup of steaming green tea on the table in front of me.

'As I imagine Mrs Masakado has told you, this is a postering job,' he said. He brought over some rolled-up posters and spread them out at the end of the table. 'They're not for commercial purposes, and we're not asking you to stick them up anywhere new, so it should be simple enough.'

At the moment, he explained, there were three types of posters concerning the following topics: traffic safety, tree planting and water conservation.

On hearing that the posters were commissioned by the government, I'd instantly envisaged something nondescript, but with their eye-catching compositions and bold yet simple colour palette, the examples Mr Monaga presented put me in mind of Eastern European or vintage Soviet poster design, and I wouldn't have hesitated to call them cool. The road safety poster was predominantly red, with what appeared to be a road cycle racer glancing back over his shoulder, accompanied by the slogan 'Check behind you when turning corners!' The tree planting poster was covered in a textile-inspired clover pattern, with copy that read 'Make Our Town Greener!' – while the water conservation one featured a slightly unnerving image of a human silhouette kneeling down creature-like on all fours to lap at a big drop of water coming out of a tap, with the slogan 'Water Belongs to Everyone' in a bold font.

'These are the newest posters, which we'll be asking people to keep up for about six months. Your job will be to swap these ones over with the previous set. We're not explicitly aiming to branch out into new territory, but I'd like you to go around all the buildings in the specified area, and if you do happen to find anybody who agrees to have our posters up for the first time, then please go ahead and put them up.'

The focus of the work might have been swapping over existing posters, but if Mr Monaga was already emphasising that, if I could, I should stick posters up in fresh territory, I imagined that the ideal scenario was one where I did, in fact, conquer pastures new.

'As you may be aware, most postering jobs pay per poster, but we pay by the hour. And actually, in addition to the postering, there's a bit of research work involved.'

Having rolled up the posters that he'd shown me, Mr Monaga set down the clipboard, which had been hanging by a strap from his shoulder, on the desk. There was a map pasted to its fold-over cover, and inside was a sheaf of A4 forms. 'It's just a simple checklist. As you go around, I'd like you to ask residents and shop owners the questions on this list, regardless of whether or not they agree to stick up the posters.'

On the forms were blank fields for address, name, gender, age, shop name or type of business (if applicable), followed by several questions:

How many people are there in your family?
Do you have any concerns?
Do you have anyone to talk to about your concerns?

The questions were inoffensive enough, but I sensed a certain darkness lurking behind them.

'In other words, as well as postering, I'd also like you to carry out a brief resident survey.'

Mr Monaga closed the cover on the clipboard to display the map, and turned it around to face me. The map didn't use official region names, instead dividing the territory into numbered blocks. 'This is where we are now', said Mr Monaga, pointing to the bottom right-hand corner of the map, which was labelled Block One. Underneath the map were a few sheets of lined paper labelled NOTES.

'The aim of these posters isn't profit-making, but the regularisation of society. As you're making your rounds, you'll encounter places with other kinds of posters stuck up, and I'd like you to check in with those houses too.'

'Just check in?' I asked. 'I shouldn't try and persuade them to take the other ones down?'

Mr Monaga shook his head. 'Just do what you can. There's no point trying to force people.'

And with that, I was sent out onto the streets. It was somehow clear to me that I wasn't supposed to come back until I was done for the day. I'd been told to return to the office at 5 p.m., but that wasn't a strict rule, and I didn't need to stick to it if it was going to present an impediment to my work.

I was assigned to call in at every building, so I made the house next to the office my first stop. Beside the door was a nameplate reading 'Tadokoro' and under-neath it the words: 'Ma Chaussure Rouge: Shoes Made Just for You', but when I pressed the intercom button there was no reply. Stuck up on the wall of the house was a poster that I guessed must have been from the last batch, reading 'Drink Plenty of Water to Prevent Heatstroke'. The picture showed a blue silhouette of a long-haired woman holding a cup to her mouth. One of the posters I was currently carrying with me was about saving water, and it occurred to me briefly to wonder if the two messages weren't actually contradictory, but maybe that was okay as long as none of the directives were actually harmful.

Next to the heatstroke poster was another one featuring a photo of a very pretty woman in a white dress and straw hat, extending a hand towards the viewer. The text read: 'Lonely No More!'

I cocked my head and stared fixedly at the poster. The lovely young woman certainly grabbed the attention, and I was also drawn by the phone number, Facebook details and Twitter handle listed at the bottom of the poster. It seemed that this organisation wasn't content with just transmitting their 'Lonely No More!' message; they wanted people to look at their social media accounts too – to follow and be in touch, and what have you.

Intrigued, I took out my smartphone and brought up the group's Facebook page. Lonely No More! turned out to be the actual name of the organisation, and their cover photo was set to the image of this same poster woman. Their latest post invited people to come along to the socials they were holding in a meeting hall in the area marked on Mr Monaga's map as Block Four. Older posts provided reports of gatherings and neighbourhood clean-ups, complete with pictures showing men and women of all ages smiling contentedly. Were all these people now lonely no more – was that the idea? According to their profile page, Lonely No More! were also conducting private home visits.

Compared to the neutral messaging of the posters I was charged with distributing, these others seemed to bring many additional layers of meanings to bear. My hand hovered above the house marked as Tadokoro in the Block One section of the map on my clipboard before I eventually wrote 'P' to signify the presence of a foreign poster. Then I pressed the intercom button again, just to make sure there wasn't anyone in, but it seemed as though the Tadokoros truly were out.

I was lingering in front of the posters, wondering if I'd done all I was supposed to, and if there wasn't something else I should be seeing to, when I saw a petite but apparently hale elderly lady with shopping bags in hand, entering the next-door property, an old-looking house whose nameplate read 'Ōmae'.

'Are you a poster person?' she addressed me. 'Are you looking for the Tadokoros?'

'Yes,' I nodded, finding it peculiar that she would know at first sight that I was a poster person – although a moment's reflection told me that the rolled-up tubes under my arm and the clipboard I was wearing must have given the game away.

'They're probably just pretending to be out. He's usually in, I think.'

'Is it a family living there?'

'A married couple. They don't have any children, as far as I know.'

'And where has the wife gone?'

'She works. The husband quit about a year ago.'

I peeled back the map and noted this information down on the memo pad. Then I remembered that the Ōmae house also fell within my purview, and looked up to investigate the poster situation: this one had just the heatstroke prevention one, and nothing from Lonely No More!

'Would you mind if I switched the one you've got there for a new one about road safety, or planting trees, or saving water?'

'Hm? I don't care what they say, but what colours have you got?'

Rather taken aback by the old lady's selection criteria, I answered, 'Red, green or pale blue.'

'I'll take green this time.'

I removed her heatstroke prevention poster and, flipping through the roll of new posters, pulled out a green one and stuck it up with tape. Mrs Ōmae stepped back a little to get a decent look at it, and said, 'Ooh, it's rather nice. Very fresh.'

'You may have answered something similar six months ago, but would it be alright to ask you a couple of questions?'

'Yes, of course.'

'How many people are living in your household?'

'Just me.'

The old lady went on to tell me that her husband had died twenty years ago, and her daughter had married and moved to Anchorage.

'And do you have any concerns?'

'Yokohama DeNA BayStars have been performing so badly recently,' she answered immediately, before adding, 'Oh, and my knee is playing up.'

'Is there anyone you can talk to about those things?'

'Well, there's someone working at the convenience store over there who I usually talk baseball with, and a man who's often in the cafe I go to in the evening. And about my knee, well, I talk to my doctor.'

As she spoke, Mrs Ōmae slotted her key into the door. Feeling slightly disappointed by her evident desire to get away, I made a note of her answers.

'The young man from Lonely No More! was around here yesterday,' she said to me over her shoulder as she opened the door. 'He says to me, "A lovely old lady like you needs somebody to rely upon! Your neighbour Mrs Imakawa has been coming to our socials – you should give it a try!" Well, I don't get on with Mrs Imakawa, and I don't need to rely on anyone, and what's more, I don't like being called "old lady" by someone I've just met!'

Feeling instantly bad for calling her something similar in my head, I asked, 'How would you prefer to be referred to?'

'Hmm, just "lady", I suppose.' She thought for a bit and said, 'Although maybe "lovely lady" is rather presumptuous as well. Anyhow, enjoy the rest of your day.' Saying that, she shut the door. Left standing there alone on the doorstep, I pondered this job that I'd suddenly found myself doing – and how it now seemed as though I was not the only one. Pinned up at the house beside Mrs Ōmae's, whose nameplate read 'Imakawa', was a poster with the drinking woman's blue silhouette and a Lonely No More! poster that featured a man in place of the young woman.

As I went walking around the neighbourhood, I noticed that although there were houses that exclusively featured Mr Monaga's posters, and houses with a combination of Mr Monaga's and the Lonely No More! ones, there were none that just had Lonely No More! posters.

Perhaps by virtue of the sheer number of houses with one of each, I found that the more I went on seeing Lonely No More! posters pinned up beside Mr Monaga's neutral ones, it started to seem as though they had been issued by the same organisation. The sensation reminded me of finding out for the first time that the cleaning company Duskin was run by the same firm as Mister Donut.

Yet with even more time spent looking at them, it became clear to me that the intentions behind the two posters were very different: one was straightforward and focused specifically on behaviour – *drink water to avoid heatstroke* – while the other was more psychological in its emphasis. The emotional weight behind them felt totally different. The young man and woman may have been very attractive, but the longer I stared into their eyes the more uncomfortable I began to feel.

The previous set of Monaga posters consisted of the heatstroke one in sky blue, a yellowish one that read 'Try Walking for Your Health' and one in a warm peach shade reading 'Remember to Greet Your Neighbours!'. I guessed they'd been designed to form a soft, comforting palette when put up in combination. As soon as there was a Lonely No More! poster in the mix, though, you'd be reminded that they were, after all, just regular posters stuck up around the town – although arguably that was less to do with anything specifically about the Lonely No More! poster campaign, and more about them taking away from the uniformity of the Monaga ones.

On the other side of the block to Mrs Ōmae's was a house labelled Terui, which boasted a 'Try Walking for Your Health' poster alongside the version of the Lonely No More! poster with the woman. As I stood there taking the pair in, an elderly man wearing a cap and jacket and carrying a cane stepped out of the front door.

'Mr Terui?' I hazarded. He nodded and lifted one corner of his mouth.

'I've come to change over this poster,' I said. 'I've got a red one about traffic safety, a green one about making the town greener and a blue one about saving water. Which would you like?'

'Whichever,' he said. He screwed up his face, adding, 'I don't care.'

'Let's try road safety, then,' I said, retrieving one from the roll and holding it up to him. He nodded.

'May I ask how you came to have this poster with the woman up?'

'It's because you lot came first,' he said.

'Sorry, what do you mean exactly?'

'You lot came and asked to put up one of your posters, so I said you could,' Mr Terui explained, with a face that suggested he'd rather not, his hand – the one that wasn't holding the cane – shaking.

'And then she turned up and asked to stick up one of hers. That woman on the poster,' he said, pointing.

'Oh, really!'

'Yours mark out the houses of people who aren't bothered about what posters they have up.'

'I see,' I said. His analysis made instant sense to me. Sensing from his words that it might be worth trying my luck, I said, 'How about having two of ours this time?'

'No, I'll keep the woman,' he said curtly, cutting short my little adventure.

'Well, if you change your mind … ' I smiled at him. I'd never done a job with a sales-like element to it before, but there was something I found enjoyable about behaving this shamelessly.

'Will you get out of the way? I'm off to play shōgi.'

'Oh, of course,' I said, stepping aside.

'Or maybe I'll go along to the social,' he deliberated aloud to himself. 'Yeah, maybe that's a better idea. There's girls there, and they serve tea.' With that, he disappeared around the corner.

Realising I'd made the stupid mistake of not asking him any of my survey questions, I shook my head. I made a note of Mr Terui's opinion that Mr Monaga's posters were courting the Lonely No More! ones, and then went for lunch.

In the space of three days, I progressed from Block One to Block Three on the map. There were a few places like the Tadokoros' whose inhabitants I couldn't get hold of, but the people who did open their doors answered my questions without complaints, and weren't bothered by my changing over the posters. There was even one woman who asked if she could keep the old water conservation poster because she wanted to pin it up in her room. She was apparently a freelance writer. In these three days, it had become clear to me that the posters were designed by Mr Monaga himself. Indeed, I had learned that Mr Monaga's main vocation was graphic design, and while I was making my way around the neighbourhood, he was working away on design jobs – not just for posters, but other jobs for other clients.

When I passed on to my boss Mr Terui's opinion that our posters were attracting the Lonely No More! people, it seemed to affect him.

'That must be right,' he replied. 'I was dimly aware of that, but hadn't really thought it through. Yes, that makes a lot of sense.'

I wanted to ask Mr Monaga if his true objective was in fact sticking up his posters, or rather, preventing other people from sticking up theirs – but I felt like that wasn't the best idea on my third day of work. Instead I asked, 'If we stopped sticking ours up, would all the houses switch over to the Lonely No More! ones, do you think?'

Mr Monaga considered this a while, then said, 'I don't think all of them would, but they'd probably snare the majority who weren't bothered either way.' His use of the word 'snare' suggested something less than peaceful in his conception of the whole affair.

On my fourth morning, Mr Monaga asked me where I'd been eating lunch so far. I told him that on the first day I'd eaten at a gyūdon restaurant, on the second I'd gone to a fast-food place, and yesterday I'd had gyūdon again – and that all of these places had been slightly out of the way. Anywhere with two of our posters stuck up offered us a twenty per cent discount, he told me.

'What kinds of places are there?' I asked, and Mr Monaga replied that there was a restaurant close by called Hulala that served nyūmen – sōmen noodles in hot soup – and a place called Sampo-ya, specialising in curry bread.

'Right,' I said, thinking internally that both places were oddly specific in what they offered, and that I'd probably leave it for today. In the end, I went back to the gyūdon place.

When I'd been around all the houses in Block Three, I returned to Block One and tried knocking again at those houses whose tenants I hadn't yet managed to catch. This had become something of a habit. I finished work at 5 p.m., but usually when it got to about 3.30, I'd give up on visiting new places and make my way back to Block One. The area where I was circulating was a quiet neighbourhood with a lot of elderly residents, and there was very little human traffic. In the morning you'd see the odd person about, but past three it was customary for me to be the only one on the street.

Today, however, was different: to my surprise, I happened to see someone going around pressing people's doorbells, just as I had been doing all day since I started working for Mr Monaga. I let out a little gasp of surprise, at which the figure promptly turned right and disappeared down an alley before I'd had the chance to work out if it was a man or a woman, and how old they were. Whoever it was must have been pressing Mrs Ōmae's bell, though, because she now emerged from her house, murmuring, 'Have they gone yet?'

Noticing me she said, 'They're just so persistent, aren't they!'

Feeling like her words could also be very reasonably applied to me, I was unable to say anything except, 'Are they?'

'You're just doing your job, so if a person doesn't come out by the tenth ring, you decide to come back another day and go on your way. Right?'

'Yes, that's true,' I said, noting how observant she was. I hadn't figured out whether or not she was on my side, but I was grateful that at the very least she didn't seem to think me the enemy.

'I pretend to be out when they come. I've got a friend in Block Five – a Hiroshima Carp fan – who's already got one of their posters up, and they came around to ask if she'd stick up another one. Apparently they were doing all they could to make their way into her house. It sounded awful!'

'Goodness!' Even I would never think of trying to muscle inside people's houses, I thought. Luckily I hadn't been instructed to do so by Mr Monaga, either.

'They don't give up. It's not a job with them, see – it's a dogma.' Mrs Ōmae folded her arms and looked down with a serious expression and then, as if she'd just remembered something very important, said, 'Ah! You should get an answer at the Tadokoros today.'

She told me that Mrs Tadokoro had taken the day off because she'd had something to do at the city hall, but was back home already.

'You're very well informed!' I said, trying to say what I was really thinking – *How on earth do you know all this stuff!* – in the politest way possible.

'She told me herself,' she said. 'We're both Yokohama fans, so we chat sometimes.'

'I see.' On the memo pad, I noted down the names Mrs Ōmae and Mrs Tadokoro, and drew brackets around them with arrows pointing to the word BAYSTARS – although, in truth, I didn't really know if this was the kind of information I needed to be jotting down. Mrs Ōmae said she'd already informed Mrs Tadokoro that I was going around switching over the posters, so I thanked her.

Mrs Ōmae now rang on the Tadokoros' door, and Mrs Tadokoro emerged immediately. She was fully made-up, presumably because of whatever she'd been doing that morning, but her long hair hung loose about her shoulders and she was dressed casually in a grey marl sweatshirt. She had a slight gloomy look about her, but her face lit up when she saw Mrs Ōmae, and she bowed in greeting.

'This is the person who's doing the posters,' Mrs Ōmae said, indicating at me, so I smiled and gave a low bow. In stark contrast to the very diminutive Mrs Ōmae, Mrs Tadokoro was fairly tall. I was five-foot-four and I had to look up when speaking to her, so she must have been at least five-seven.

'I've come to change over your poster,' I said.

'Oh, of course.'

I explained the choices, and she selected the red road safety poster, so I put it up right away. She complimented the design, so I decided to risk saying, 'Would you like me to put another one, here?' I pointed to the poster of the Lonely No More! woman in the white dress. Mrs Tadokoro's expression immediately darkened.

'You'd need to ask my husband's permission,' she said, looking down at the ground. I looked to Mrs Ōmae, thinking she might help me out, but she was staring at the floor also. I sensed something shady going on.

'Let's just try switching them, shall we? The 'Make Our Town Greener!' poster is lovely! And there's this water-saving one which, admittedly, looks a little threatening when you first see it, but is a very eye-catching design.'

I wasn't really intending to force her to go against her husband's wishes, but I tried pushing a little, just for the sake of it, with affected casualness. Mrs Tadokoro winced, as if genuinely pained by the situation, then shook her head, staring at the Lonely No More! poster with a troubled air.

'I better not. I don't like it, but I can't.' She sighed.

'You should tell this lady what happened,' said Mrs Ōmae.

'But … But … ' said Mrs Tadokoro.

Noting that there was something extremely ominous about this interchange, I adopted the attitude that I would gladly listen to anything so long as it pertained to my work, assuming a solemn facial expression and nodding encouragingly at Mrs Tadokoro in the hope that she might open up.

But despite my best efforts, Mrs Tadokoro remained silent, the expression on her face so pained that eventually I said, 'If it's difficult to talk about it here on the street, we could go for nyūmen.' I pointed in the direction of the restaurant that Mr Monaga had told me of. Mrs Ōmae and Mrs Tadokoro exchanged glances.

'Your husband's in?' Mrs Ōmae said in a hushed tone.

'Yes,' said Mrs Tadokoro, in a similar one.

'I'll go and get my purse.'

'Me too.'

'Don't worry, it's my treat!' What the hell was I saying! I thought, as the words spilled from my mouth. With all the switching of jobs I'd been doing, I was hardly in a position to be buying other people's meals. And yet it seemed like a necessary measure in getting a feel for this job, whose essence was still eluding my grasp in some way. The two women looked at each other, then assured me they'd pay me when we got back, and so the three of us headed over to the nyūmen restaurant.

Hulala, located in Block Five of the map I'd been given, was a small establishment seating about twelve people, whose sole employee was a woman in her mid-thirties. With its simple, tasteful interior in light beige that recalled the colour of noodles, and soft French music playing in the background, it seemed implausibly stylish for a neighbourhood like this one. Hanging on the walls were two of Mr Monaga's posters. I hadn't made it as far as Block Five yet, so they were still the old ones on heatstroke prevention and greeting your neighbours. Even in a spot as well designed as this, they didn't look out of place.

Mrs Ōmae and I ordered ume and shiso nyūmen, and Mrs Tadokoro went for the curry version. On my way back from the toilet, I introduced myself to the woman who I assumed was the owner, telling her I worked for Mr Monaga, and thanking her for sticking up our posters.

'Oh, not at all.'

'I heard from Mr Monaga that you offer a discount?'

'Yes, of course. I'll charge you the Mr Monaga rate.'

I resisted the urge to say, 'Huh … ?', and instead opened my eyes wide to create an expression that said, 'Oh yes, of course, the Mr Monaga rate!'

'I only started this week, so I'm very new to all this. I was wondering, does having the posters up help improve business in any way?'

'Hmm, I don't think so.' The woman shot a glance over her shoulder towards the kitchen, clearly itching to get back to work.

I shook my head. 'I'm sure you're very busy, so a short answer is fine!'

'With two of them up, the other lot don't come.' Having provided this truly very short answer, she took out some dry sōmen noodles from a tall thin tin, tossed them into a pan and began cooking. I returned to my seat, dipping my head respectfully at my companions. A stilted atmosphere reigned between the three of us, as though nobody quite knew what to say, so I ventured gently, 'So, what we were talking about before … ?'

But both women remained silent. 'If it's too difficult to discuss, of course,' I added, 'then don't worry about it.'

'No,' Mrs Tadokoro said, shaking her head. 'I'm happy to talk about it.' And so she began.

'We don't have children, me and my husband.'

'Right.'

'And they say that's because we're lonely.'

'Hm?'

'We're lonely, so we can't have children, and not having children makes you lonely. But if we join Lonely No More! we won't be lonely any more, and then we might be able to have children.'

Mrs Ōmae tutted.

'Do they also offer medical treatment?' I asked, aware it might be a dumb question but realising my priority was to grasp the basics. The women shook their heads.

'What exactly is Lonely No More! then?'

In perfect synchronicity, both women looked down and shrugged. They were very different ages and heights, so seeing them performing the exact same gesture made for a peculiar spectacle, but their demeanours were dead serious.

'Helping people feel less lonely doesn't seem like such a bad aim, but why do they have to go barging their way into people's lives like that?'

'Right …' I had no idea how to answer the question, so I just agreed.

'But my husband's always home, so he ended up talking with them a few times, and gradually started coming around to their way of thinking.'

Mrs Tadokoro drained the water from her cup and sighed. I brought over a jug of water from the counter and topped her up.

'Now he says all this stuff to me like, we're lonely even though there's two of us, two might seem okay at first but after a while it gets lonely, it's not good for our mental and physical health, and so on.'

Just as Mrs Tadokoro had drained another glass of water with an embittered expression on her face, the woman brought over our noodles. I had almost no interest in nyūmen so I'd opted for the plainest, cheapest version on the menu, but the curry nyūmen set down in front of Mrs Tadokoro gave off an incredibly appetising aroma and looked really delicious.

'Is it the people from the organisation who come to talk to you?' I asked.

Mrs Tadokoro nodded deeply. 'The woman from the poster.'

It seemed as though Mrs Ōmae was even more outraged by all this than Mrs Tadokoro herself, and here she let out a loud sigh.

'We've got that poster stuck up inside the house as well,' said Mrs Tadokoro.

'Can you believe it? She distributes her own posters herself!' Mrs Ōmae looked at me, her eyes open terrifically wide. It appeared it was the self-aggrandising element of Lonely No More! which stuck in her craw the most.

'She comes along and says, "Would you mind putting this up? It might not help, but it might at least make you feel a bit less lonely." Smiling that coy smile the whole time.' Mrs Tadokoro winced as if she couldn't bear to talk about it any longer, then looked down, her shoulders tensed. I got the impression she was squeezing her hands together in her lap. 'They always mention the socials at the meeting hall on Tuesdays, Thursdays and Saturdays, saying we should go and talk to them there.'

'And he goes on Tuesdays, Thursdays AND Saturdays! And comes back saying how much fun he had!'

Mrs Ōmae was angry. Mrs Tadokoro looked like she was about to burst into tears. I sat there idiotically repeating, 'Oh, really, oh goodness,' as I listened to the tale of how Mrs Tadokoro's domestic life was being eaten away little by little by Lonely No More!

'Which is more important, I wonder – not to be lonely, or to live the life you've chosen for yourself?' She sighed and brushed away her tears with the fingertips of her right hand. The fact that she didn't have a handkerchief with her suggested she hadn't been planning to cry. I was starting to understand why Mr Monaga had felt the need to make posters and shop them around.

'So is every house with a Lonely No More! poster involved with the organisation?' I asked. The women exchanged a look.

'There are different degrees of involvement,' Mrs Ōmae said, cocking her head and folding her arms as if choosing her words carefully. She was approaching the matter with the utmost seriousness. I felt tempted to tell Mrs Tadokoro that although her husband may have taken a funny turn, she should count herself lucky to have someone like Mrs Ōmae as a neighbour.

'I don't think you can necessarily say that everyone who's got Lonely No More! posters stuck on their walls is a member. There are people who go to the meetings because there are women there and they hand out free tea.'

I thought back to Mr Terui who I'd met on my first day. He didn't seem to have many scruples about anything, which was to say, he had a pretty simple outlook on life – but as with many of his age, he was the kind of person who would definitely not respond well to having that fact pointed out.

'My husband started out like that too!'

Apparently surrendering to the despair rising up in her, Mrs Tadokoro began fiercely slurping at her curry nyūmen. I thought the noodles might have got cold by now, but as she ate I saw a faint plume of steam coming off them. They looked as delicious as ever. I sipped the soup of my ume and shiso version, and was pleasantly surprised. Seeing me and Mrs Tadokoro tucking in, Mrs Ōmae also made a start on hers, as if she'd just remembered it was there.

'They came here a while ago too, the Lonely No More! lot,' the restaurant owner said, coming over to the table to refill our water glasses. 'They send the woman out to talk to men, and the man out to meet the women. The guy they sent invited me along to their meetings too, saying all this stuff like, "It must be so hard, running a shop on your own as a single woman."'

'Is it hard?' I asked.

'No, not really,' she replied without hesitation. 'But I figured out that with two of these up, they don't come here any more.' With this, she pointed to Mr Monaga posters.

I nodded, picked up my bowl to drain what remained of the soup, then looked up at the posters. So, having one would bring the Lonely No More! lot in, I thought, and having two would send them away – which made me wonder if the best option wouldn't be to do without posters of any description. But though it was all very well for me to think that, maybe for those with a real stake in the matter, that was gambling too much on the residents' inclinations. Most likely it was, and that was exactly why I was going around like this, trying to persuade people to put up posters.

We finished our noodles and our meal came to a natural end. Mrs Ōmae said she'd arranged to Skype with her daughter and Mrs Tadokoro had to take back a DVD she'd rented. It was an hour after I was supposed to finish work. The woman in the restaurant really did charge me the Mr Monaga rate, and our three dishes came to less than 1,500 yen.

I wandered a little dazedly through Block Four in the direction of the station. It was now properly dark and the LED street lights were on. I was tied up in pondering whether I should invoice Mr Monaga for the nyūmen or pay for the meal from my own pocket, when I heard a cheerful, youthful-sounding voice behind me.

'Good evening! Are you on your way home from work?'

It was a young man, easily ten years younger than me. He had a bit of a baby face, and was handsome without being intimidatingly so.

'That's right,' I said. I was about to beat a hasty retreat, but then it occurred to me that this young man quite feasibly had something to do with Lonely No More! and – seized by a strange sense of duty – I turned around again to face him. 'Why do you ask?'

'Oh, no particular reason. We run a social circle in this part of town, just a very casual thing. We get together and talk about our hobbies, and go places on our days off.' The man took a step closer and handed me a flyer. His face wore the kind of expression that only celebrities could be forgiven for making, where his face was smiling but his eyes were not. The flyer said in a cutesy, excessively rounded bubble font: 'ayudarte!'

'Do you work around here?'

'Yes, not far,' I responded vaguely. I knew I couldn't specify a place, but also recognised it wouldn't be good to brush off his question completely.

'Do you usually come home at this time?'

'Usually a little earlier.'

'And does your husband get home around the same time?'

'I don't have a husband. My work is really all-consuming.' Feeling a certain sense of exhilaration that his line of questioning had finally grown intrusive, I batted my eyes open wide and let my lips speak the truth: 'I feel ever so lonely when I get home.'

'Do you?' His tone was surprisingly cold, and I panicked, thinking maybe I'd made my trap too obvious.

'I really do feel ever so lonely.'

'And you're trying to comfort yourself by making light of it like that, aren't you?' The man took another half step closer. I didn't like him having him that close and instinctively took a step back. The man took another step forward. Remembering that this was my job, I forced myself to stay put.

'But it's okay,' he said. *What's okay about it*, I wanted to retort. Something cold and unpleasant rose up in my chest. My intention had been to learn about the tactics Lonely No More! used, but he'd managed to catch me off guard.

'Oh, it's definitely not okay,' I said.

'We hold socials in Block Four,' the young man said, and grinned, triumphant at being able to offer the promise of a cure for my woes. Again, his eyes did not smile. 'Please do come along and see us.'

'Yes,' I said, lifting the corners of my mouth into a smile, and the young man went away down the alley.

A shiver ran through me, so I pulled my shoulder bag in close, left the alley and walked towards the station. I was glad I was getting on a bit in age, that was for sure. I knew full well that if I'd been twenty-three or so, he might have got a hold on me. But unfortunately for him, I'd interacted with several of his sort in my old job – the kinds of people who wormed their way into the cracks in people's psyches, then poked their little needles in to create punctures. Their modus operandi was generally either to suddenly withdraw their support when it was most needed, or else to rely on people's desire for information they happened to possess. Either way, sometimes they themselves didn't have any awareness of what it was they were doing, so when they made their initial approach, you wouldn't have the faintest suspicion of their ill intentions.

Listen, pal, I addressed the young man in my mind, *if I want help, I'll consult a professional or someone I trust, not a stranger who tries to fabricate weakness in others for themselves to inhabit.* And as I thought this, I also acknowledged that there might be something appealingly straightforward about doing exactly as he suggested. At the moment, though, I was employed by Mr Monaga, so I had to deal with Lonely No More! from a different angle.

Ascending the stairs to the station, an image of Mrs Tadokoro's tear-streaked face suddenly flashed through my mind. I decided that the following day, I would make sure that I got at least one person to switch their Lonely No More! poster over to one of Mr Monaga's.

'If they come in, you have to serve them tea, you know? But I was using my kettle to brew maté, so I couldn't boil any water. I suppose I could have just served them maté and been done with it, but there're lots of people who really don't like the taste. I didn't particularly want to chat, either, and I was messaging my niece at the time. She was saying she wanted to borrow my *Il Divo: Live in Barcelona* DVD, and was asking when she could come by and collect it. She lives really close, and she likes maté, and I was all ready to tell her to come around right away, but the Lonely No More! man kept saying, "Oh, Ms Kohashi, next time we'd like you to bring Mrs Ōmae along to the socials," going on about how much fun we'd all have.'

'Have you taken people along to the meetings in the past?'

'Yes, I've taken Ms Kashima and Ms Muraki from Block Three, and Ms Asakura and Ms Shirota from Block Two, and then Mrs Togawa from opposite.'

'Did they ask you to bring them?'

On the NOTES page of my clipboard, I jotted down the name Kohashi and circled it, then scrawled the names Kashima, Muraki, Asakura, Shirota and Togawa, connecting them up to Kohashi's circle with arrows.

'They give you fancy cakes if you take people along. Do you want to see?'

I nodded. Ms Kohashi disappeared inside, and re-emerged with a cardboard box in a pretty shade of lavender. Inside were ten round parcels, individually wrapped in delicate Japanese paper. It appeared to have been a box of twelve, with two already eaten.

'Would you like one? If you don't mind washing it down with a cup of maté … '

It would be bad if they'd sneaked something strange inside the cakes, I thought, but at least that would mean something concrete to report back to Mr Monaga, and so I accepted the offer.

Ms Kohashi disappeared inside again, returning with a glass of cold maté and a small plate for me to place the Lonely No More! cake on. I peeled off the wrapping paper to see a white, round ball, like a steamed bun. Breaking it in two, I discovered a white cream filling. It looked good, and not in any way suspicious.

'They give you a dozen-box of these whenever you take a new person along to the socials.'

'Well, that's quite something.'

'I mean most people would agree to do it for that, right?'

No bloody way, I thought, but swallowed the words, and very hesitantly raised the steamed cake to my lips. It was not at all bad.

'But the thing is, I'm bored of it. I've taken along five people, and each time it's the same box of cakes, so I've got five of them now.'

'In that case, would you mind if I took another one?'

'Yes, of course. Take the whole box, if you like!'

'Oh no, that's okay. One is plenty.'

The extra one I wanted to take back and show Mr Monaga. The steamed cakes had a gentle sweetness that wasn't too cloying. Even if giving people boxes in return for bringing others along to meetings seemed rather pushy as a strategy, I could see how this was definitely the type of taste that would encourage people to go the extra mile.

'They all sit around and eat these as they chat. At first it's all small talk and smiles.' Ms Kohashi put the lid on the cake box and plunked it down beside her. 'But after a while, everyone starts coming out with all of this stuff about their home lives. Nobody talks about their hobbies or interests. I'm sick of it, to be frank with you. I got divorced when I was forty, and I've lived on my own since, so I've nothing to say about my family.'

'Oh, I can understand that. It's much more fun to talk about hobbies and so on, isn't it?'

'It really is. So, I've been thinking that maybe I should give up going, but just as I was about to tell them that, the man seemed to sense what I was thinking and started saying, "Please do come again, and bring Mrs Ōmae if you can!"'

Ms Kohashi seemed like a rather unscrupulous type: although she had a Lonely No More! poster stuck up outside her house, I got the sense she thought of the organisation as little more than a supplier of cakes. Yet it was clearly serving as a community hub in this neighbourhood, and was therefore a base worth covering as far as she was concerned.

'When the time comes for talking about problems at home, that Mrs Togawa from opposite suddenly comes to life, so to speak. It's as if there are all these things she's saved up and has just been waiting to talk about. But when you listen carefully, you start to realise that it's exactly the same stuff each time.'

'Oh ... ' I say and nod.

'Oh, there she is, just come out of her house now. Mrs Togawa!' Ms Kohashi said, and waved. I supposed that this was just an instinctive reaction to Mrs Togawa entering her field of vision, but I was still slightly astounded by how cheerfully she could wave at some-one about whom she'd been bitching until the previous second. I turned to look, smiled my best benevolent smile and bowed my head.

The woman living opposite whom Ms Kohashi had referred to as Mrs Togawa – who had, by the looks of things, come out of her house to check her letter box – was a strangely delicate-looking lady poised some-where between middle and old age. She bowed in a refined manner in my and Ms Kohashi's direction and headed over.

'This lady works with Mr Monaga,' Ms Kohashi introduced me.

'Oh!' Mrs Togawa said quietly, seeming surprised.

'Why don't you tell her what you're always telling people at the meets?'

Wasn't it a bit rude, I worried, to plunge straight into a person's problems like that? But Mrs Togawa seemed less fazed by that aspect of the situation, and more by Ms Kohashi's representation of the facts, because she now pulled a face and said, 'I'm not *always* telling people.'

'Your daughter is giving you the cold shoulder, no?'

'That's right,' she began.

It seemed to me that her story went on for quite some time – time enough for me to pour myself another cup of maté and take another of the Lonely No More! cakes. In summary, the tale went like this: Mrs Togawa had a daughter and a son. The son lived by himself locally, and Mrs Togawa did all of his housework. It was his words of gratitude – 'Thanks, Mum' – which he uttered about once a week, that gave her life its meaning. Her husband, who had retired five years ago, never thanked her for anything – and whenever Mrs Togawa called her daughter, the daughter would lecture her, telling her not to complain about Mr Togawa not carrying heavy shopping bags unless asked, and so on. Mrs Togawa admitted that she did do her fair share of complaining, but insisted that she phoned her daughter once every three days because she was worried about her. Despite reaching a decent age, her daughter wasn't married and still worked all the time. Mrs Togawa would tell her that women only became proper women when they had children, and that she wanted to have grandchildren and go shopping for baby things together, but the daughter would answer coldly that in that case, Mrs Togawa should get her son to have them instead. That wouldn't do at all, Mrs Togawa would say. Her son was only just recovering from his illness, doing his best to reacclimatise to society and – what was more – she still found him adorable, and he kept her company. In all honesty, she didn't want him to get married. Besides, the daughter had worked for such a long time! Wasn't it time to call it a day? But apparently when Mrs Togawa had said all this, her daughter had flown off the rails, and now refused to pick up the phone when Mrs Togawa called.

'I don't see what the problem is,' Mrs Togawa said. 'It's just a phone call. And to think I brought her up so well.' With this, she broke down into sobs.

'So cold of her,' said Ms Kohashi, in a tone that suggested that she had no thoughts or feelings on the matter whatsoever. I nodded, making appropriate noises, feeling that my brain was slowly festering.

'Why not try complaining about your husband to your son, and try to get him to have an arranged marriage?' I said, without really meaning to. 'I mean, why don't you try reversing your treatment of your children?'

At this Mrs Togawa let the lower half of her face fall strangely slack and opened her eyes wide into an expression of total incredulousness. I shook my head and turned my palms to her, saying, 'Uh, sorry, really, forget I said anything.'

It seemed as if the Lonely No More! socials were a breath of fresh air for Mrs Togawa, who lamented that she didn't 'see the point in having lived up until now.

'When you get to my age, there isn't anyone who'll properly listen to you. The people who go to the socials are all in a similar situation to me, or even worse off, and it cheers me up.'

I nodded hard, hoping that if I fostered a welcoming attitude towards this woman with my body the rest of me might follow.

'But I'm *always* listening to you, I don't do anything else,' said Ms Kohashi, with a roughness of tone that brought into clear relief the gap that yawned between 'listening' and 'actually taking in'. But Mrs Togawa seemed oblivious even to this, and she said, 'You haven't been coming to the socials of late, I've missed you.'

I realised very clearly that I was currently looking at two people who unquestioningly swallowed the idea that talking to someone face to face automatically entailed a lack of psychological distance between you. The very notion made me tremble in agitation. What on earth was that about? Did everyone from this generation feel like that? Surely that couldn't be?

Perhaps satisfied at having now imparted her story to me as well, Mrs Togawa told Ms Kohashi she'd pop back around five to see if she wanted to go to the shops, then disappeared back inside her house, across the alley.

'You see,' said Ms Kohashi, folding her arms across her chest and adopting a look that seemed slightly, but not really, put out. 'That's the spiel she gives every time at the socials.'

'In that case, why don't you change that poster there over to one of ours?' I said, having no idea of any relation between the two topics that might have warranted my saying 'in that case'. 'We don't have socials or anything like that, but if you switch your Lonely No More! poster to one of ours, we'd be delighted to present you with some edible treats.'

'Oh, well!' At the mention of 'edible treats', Ms Kohashi's eyes seemed to sparkle.

'We're considering implementing a system whereby each time you manage to convince one of your friends to switch over their posters to Mr Monaga's, we'll give you another batch.' The words came sliding out of my mouth ever so smoothly. I knew that if I said 'box' or 'dozen', I'd have been tied to providing a certain number, so I stuck with the more ambiguous 'batch'.

'What do you think? They're requiring you to take Mrs Ōmae along to the socials, whereas we're only asking that you switch over your poster.'

'Yes, great,' said Ms Kohashi, in exactly the same tone of voice she'd used with Mrs Togawa, before adding, 'Although it depends on what the treats are, of course.'

With the force of sheer pragmatism, Ms Kohashi landed me a meaty punch square in the jaw. Internally groaning *such a forceful opponent* ... I lifted up the corners of my mouth into a smile, and rather than pushing any further, moved off to another house.

When I returned to the office at the allotted time and told Mr Monaga about the incident, he scratched his plentiful head of hair and said, 'It's a bit problematic for us if you go making promises like that.' It seemed that he was under some deadline pressure recently. There were black bags under his eyes and two nutrition-drink bottles perched on his desk by his computer.

'But I feel that Ms Kohashi might be a really key player in all of this,' I said, thinking even as I did, who was I trying to kid by attempting to speak the lingo like that? In truth, though, I couldn't think of any other phrase to use instead. 'We can't underestimate the effect it might have if we do convince her to change her poster over to ours, and use her to convince others too.'

'We're not supposed to bribe people, that's the thing.'

'But this isn't bribery. It's just a thank you present.'

'Hmmmm.' Looking down at the various diagrams I'd sketched on the notes page, Mr Monaga shook his head. 'For the moment, we don't have a budget for thank you gifts. I'll talk to my boss and ask if there's any room for creating one. But if we can't get it in the budget, you'll be paying for them out of your own pocket. Are you prepared to do that?'

'Yes.'

Hold up a minute, I said to myself immediately. What did I mean, yes? And yet I had come out and said it. Why? Was this job really that gripping? Was it because I'd sat there and watched Mrs Tadokoro crying? Or was it rather because I wanted to erase the young man in the alley from my head?

'Okay, well, I have to deliver my report today and we've a meeting tomorrow, so I'll ask them then to consider it. I'll have an answer for you by the end of the day tomorrow.' Mr Monaga opened up his notebook and jotted something down, then suddenly pulled a serious face and went on: 'You do know there's no need for you to be making this much of an effort?'

'It's my job,' I answered offhandedly.

'Yes, and that's exactly why I'm saying it,' Mr Monaga said in a mumble, as if speaking to himself, dropping his gaze to his notebook. I wasn't sure exactly what he was trying to say, but I knew enough to grasp that he found my behaviour in some way distasteful. I was aware that I was acting strangely, but now I'd gone and promised Ms Kohashi a free gift, and given that she could reasonably be expected to yield results, I felt I had no choice but to uphold my promise.

We were assigned a budget for the thank you gift, but it was a borderline sort of sum, so I decided to get in touch with my previous workplace: the rice cracker company. Despite the fact that I'd practically fled, the company and I were unified in our desire not to acknowledge any rift between us, and so on the surface we interacted with each other with perfect equanimity. I could contact them and broach the subject of a reduced rate for buying up a certain number of crackers without any qualms.

The product I chose was Ms Fujiko's Soy Sauce. I hadn't been keeping track of its progress, and by now it had ceased to be featured in the media, but my former lunchmates from the factory informed me that sales were still very good. I also heard how, at first, the real-life Mrs Fujiko had been very enthusiastic about her duties in responding to people's requests for advice, coming in to the company twice weekly, but of late she'd been complaining of health problems and they were lucky if she showed up once a week. It seemed as though now there were no journalists around, she found the task of selecting a topic, doing the research and coming up with an answer too much like hard work. My predecessor Mr Kiyota was, by the sound of things, a scrupulous and earnest fellow. After dealing with the extramarital affair question I'd picked, he was now giving serious thought to enquiries such as 'Why should you take your work seriously?', 'Should we study hard as teenagers?' and 'What are the conditions for a sustainable, satisfying marriage?', which he would discuss over lunch with my former companions.

At an employee discount of twenty per cent, I procured a box worth of Ms Fujiko's Soy Sauce, which was still selling out as soon as it made it onto the shelves. From this, I took three packets, along with three of the Rice Cracker Selection Bags that the company had thoughtfully thrown in for free, and ventured with trepidation to Ms Kohashi's house.

'I've been looking everywhere for those!' she cried out when she saw the crackers. It seemed as though after such a surfeit of cakes, she was pleased to have something savoury for a change.

After we'd switched over her poster, Ms Kohashi was in high spirits. She offered to share some of her Ms Fujiko's with me, eulogising about how delicious they were and once again serving me a cup of maté. I noted that it was exactly this quality that had enabled her to entice so many people along to the Lonely No More! socials. The Ms Fujiko crackers were as good as I remembered them. It crossed my mind that if real-life Mrs Fujiko had stopped coming into work already, then there hadn't been any need for me to quit that job, but I shook my head as though to dislodge the thought.

'I got divorced,' Ms Kohashi began telling me, 'because my husband started seeing a younger woman. It was the second time it'd happened. I tried at first to think of it as just one of those things, you know? But then one day while walking around – I used to be an insurance salesperson so I was walking about selling insurance, see – I had this sudden revelation that he was going play me for a fool for the rest of my life. I didn't mind it for a year, and ten I could just about bear, but I didn't want that for the rest of my life. And so we split.'

As I nodded along to her story, I cast a glance out of the window, only to catch sight of Mrs Togawa standing by her door staring fixedly at me and Ms Kohashi. There was something about her expression that I found marginally terrifying. The lower part of her face hung utterly slack, and there was no light in her eyes.

'Come on over, Mrs Togawa!' Ms Kohashi called out, waving. 'I was just griping about my ex-husband!' But Mrs Togawa disappeared back inside.

'She must have things to do,' I said.

'I wonder. That's how she is whenever I talk to anybody else,' Ms Kohashi said. She bit into the last cracker from the first Ms Fujiko packet, took a sip of maté and smiled, 'Ahh, *so* good!'

'I understand it might be tricky with Mrs Togawa, but do you think you could talk to the other four women you took along to the socials, and ask them if they'd switch their posters over too? For each person you manage to convince, we'll give you three bags of Ms Fujiko.'

'Okay.'

'If possible, it'd be great if you could ask them not to go to the socials, either.'

'Okay, I'll give it a try.'

Ms Kohashi agreed to my request with the utmost casualness, then sent me on my way.

That day, I made it as far as Block Six. I hadn't yet managed to get anybody to switch their Lonely No More! posters to Mr Monaga's under my own steam, but the task of updating the existing posters was going well. These days, as I made my way back to Mr Monaga's office at the end of the day, I'd sometimes run into people from houses I'd visited and stop for a chat, and it had become a routine of mine to go for nyūmen for dinner in Hulala before heading home. Whenever the owner wished me luck, I'd emerge feeling galvan-ised in my quest.

Three days later, I heard from Ms Kohashi that four people – Ms Kashima, Ms Muraki, Ms Asakura and Ms Shirota – had all decided to change their posters over from the Lonely No More! ones to Mr Monaga's. Ms Kohashi had been to Spa Land the day before yesterday with Ms Kashima and Ms Muraki, and had managed to talk to them about it then; and yesterday she'd talked Ms Asakura around while queuing with her for ice cream at the Hokkaido Fair in the depart-ment store; earlier that same day, she'd changed Ms Shirota's mind as they ate their katsu bento boxes at the cleaning company where they both worked part-time. That morning, I'd made it to Block Seven, before returning to visit those in Block Six who'd been out the previous day. Standing in the road, looking down at the text message from Ms Kohashi, I let out an appreciative murmur. Truth be told, I felt exhilarated. Things were starting to get interesting. My predic-tion had been correct: if we could bring Ms Kohashi around, others would follow.

Without thinking, I put in a call to Mr Monaga's office. I'd never done such a thing before, and Mr Monaga sounded concerned as he asked, 'Are you okay? Are you feeling unwell?'

But when I conveyed to him the news about Ms Kohashi, his tone switched to one of excitement. 'Oh, that's great!'

'We did it!' I said, punching the air, indifferent to the fact that I was standing in the middle of a residential street.

I hadn't yet perfected the knack of bringing around those with Lonely No More! posters, but for the rest of the day I felt very high levels of professional commitment. Thinking that a better understanding of the people living in the neighbourhood would help with my work, I struck up conversations with everyone I met, listening to their complaints and concerns. Granted, there were the odd few who were having none of it, but I found that so long as you asked your questions earnestly, made it clear you weren't trying to exploit anyone in any way, and then hung on their every word with great interest, the majority of people would share something that was on their mind. Their concerns ran the gamut – from how expensive vegetables were of late, or how they had become addicted to a game on their smartphone, or how dull TV programmes were – to how their grandchild didn't seem to be warming to them, or how their husband had lost his job and was forever out playing pachinko, or how since being made redundant they'd noticed how wasteful their wife was with money, or how until now they'd been really content being single, but now the friends they went out drinking with were all sick and suddenly they were feeling quite alone. Leaving aside the question of whether said worries were reasonable concerns or had grown out of some kind of indolence on their part, there was nobody without anxieties of some kind. And so, Lonely No More! would muscle their way in and provide an explanation – 'the reason you're addicted to your smartphone is because you're lonely,' or 'your wife wastes so much money because she's lonely' – to which their organisation just happened to offer a seemingly perfect solution.

To believe that such tactics wouldn't work for most, because the bulk of people had managed to procure the relationships they needed in their lives, and wouldn't go leaping voluntarily into a connection that a strange young man or woman who'd popped up out of the blue tried to forge with them, was overly optimistic. In reality, when issued an invitation by a good-looking youngster who was sympathetic to their predicament, there were a lot of people who would fall for it.

Running out of space in the allocated memo section, I began jotting down notes about various people's issues in my own notebook. As I walked along, I wondered whether we were better to keep on as we were doing, attempting to halt Lonely No More!'s encroachment by swapping over their posters and preserving the feel of the town as it was, or whether we needed to try and combat the brand of 'connection' they'd offered by providing a rival bond of a different nature. Making my way down the alley, very dark now that dusk had descended, I was thinking that maybe I should try talking the matter over with Mr Monaga, when I felt something hard and light strike my shoulder. Looking up, I noticed I was right outside the Tadokoros' house. Thinking that the projectile must have been an insect of some sort, I continued in the direction of Mr Monaga's office when something of a similar mass and texture hit me again, this time on my forehead. It fell on the ground in front of me, so I bent over and picked it up. It was a scrunched-up ball of what looked like washi paper. I unpicked it with a fingernail and opened it out. Just as the realisation dawned that it was a wrapper of one of the steamed cakes Lonely No More! had been giving out, which I'd sampled at Ms Kohashi's house, I heard a voice from behind me.

'Hey, you!'

I looked up to see the first-floor window of the Tadokoros' house open, a man sticking his head out.

'Who the hell are you?'

The man's face was hidden in shadow so I couldn't make it out, but I could see he was wearing a sweat-shirt in a rather shocking shade of yellow.

'Nobody whose name you need to know.'

'I can see you're a crafty little so-and-so.'

Yep, that was about right, I thought. But for some-one who'd been working for over a decade, that was a compliment. Yes, I'd grown to be very crafty – and boy, had I worked for it.

'Why are you always traipsing around these parts? I'm sick of the sight of you.'

'It's my job to update the posters.'

'Stop it!! What are you doing!' Suddenly Mrs Tadokoro's voice cut in from somewhere behind the man, and then I heard the sound of someone inside clattering down the stairs. Not wanting to stay there a second longer, I set off running back down the alley in the direction I'd come until I reached Block Two. I felt relatively sure that the man who'd just spoken to me was Mr Tadokoro – he who was such a fan of the Lonely No More! socials.

'What's with him?' I mumbled to myself. To give me something to do as I crouched there in the shadows, I leafed through my notes, all the while glancing back towards his house. Or was the fault mine – had I been way out of line, as he seemed to be suggesting? Or else, if not way out of line, perhaps I was at least exercising an unnecessary degree of enthusiasm? But that couldn't be helped. It was pretty fun, this job.

I made my way out of the prescribed postering area, resolving to return to Mr Monaga's office via another route. Glancing back towards the neighbourhood in which I worked, I noticed it left a rather gloomy impression as night fell – was it something to do with the rows of low-roofed houses, and the lack of lights in the first-floor windows? In any case, I felt somewhat dispirited to realise that I'd been working in a neighbourhood that dark.

'DIE ALONE!'

So read the message directed at Mr Monaga – and me too, quite probably.

When I reached the office in the morning, Mr Monaga had the shutters down and appeared to be dabbing at them. Getting closer, I saw he wasn't touching them, but holding various small red cards up to them.

'Good morning,' I said.

'Morning,' he replied. Stepping away from the shutters, he gesticulated towards them to show me what was going on. DIE ALONE, said the lettering in red paint, besmirching the shutters. What the … ?

'That's vandalism!' I said.

'It is, isn't it?' Mr Monaga nodded. Plainly put, the graffiti looked really damn angry. It was the writing of someone who couldn't keep their feelings inside a moment longer – although it seemed highly questionable whether either of us had done anything to warrant such feelings. We were both just doing our jobs. It looked as though the cards Mr Monaga had been holding up were a set of colour cards, because he was muttering away to himself, 'Yes, it's got a Munsell value of 6.0R 5.0/18.3.'

'Did you take a photo?' I asked.

'Ah, that's a good idea,' he said, tucking the colour cards into his pocket. He stood back a little and captured the scene with his phone camera.

'Should we call the police, do you think?'

'No, we don't want to cause too much of a fuss, it might put them off. It's better to wait.'

Mr Monaga looked calm enough, but from the slightly strained quality of his voice, I could sense that the incident had shaken him.

'Let's leave the postering for today,' he told me, pulling up the shutters and going inside the office. There was essentially nothing for me to do in the office, so I asked if I should make some tea.

'No, that's okay. Have a seat,' he said, pointing me to a chair in the meeting space where I'd spoken with him on my first day on the job. Feeling something in my chest that closely resembled heart palpitations, I pulled from my bag the clipboard that I wore around my neck on my neighbourhood outings and flipped through it aimlessly.

It wasn't like I'd not experienced things of this nature before. In fact, my working life had contained its fair share of unexpected occurrences: I'd had to deal with defamatory documents and prank phone calls, not to mention being yelled at by people I was working with. Still, 'DIE ALONE' seemed to me a pretty singular sort of attack.

Usually, when on the receiving end of an unexpected strike from external sources that didn't directly impact my work, I'd find that even as I reeled a bit from the blow, I'd experience a species of thrill which would help me laugh the whole thing off. At first, I thought this occasion was the same. I even felt a kind of contempt as I said to myself that *now* the idiots had really gone and done it – this was proof they couldn't stand the heat. And yet, I could feel that phrase which I was trying to parse as pretty singular – 'DIE ALONE' – that phrase which seemed to have the power to seep into the cracks of my soul and wreak havoc there – had without doubt thrown me off balance.

Mr Monaga set a cup of hōjicha in front of me. I supposed he wasn't feeling much motivation to work either, because he sat down on a chair in the meeting space beside me and began sipping his tea.

'Have we really done anything that intolerable, I wonder?' I said.

'If that's how it seems to them, I guess we just have to swallow it.'

I wanted to laugh at their expense. I mean, come on! 'DIE ALONE' was such a ridiculously theatrical message. There was such an excessive amount of hatred packed into those two short words. Besides, I'd realised that its function as an insult depended on certain assumptions about its intended target. What if its recipient wasn't at all bothered about dying or being alone? It was branded all over with the value system of its author. You could practically hear them shriek: *I'D RATHER DIE THAN DIE ALONE!!!*

I tried raising the corners of my mouth into a smile, but it didn't go too well.

'It feels unfair, doesn't it?' Yes, I agreed with myself internally, it was damn unfair. The idea that we just had to take their words lying down without being given a chance to reply, it was terrifically unjust. 'I want to laugh at the fuckers for having done something so idiotic, but I can't get over the unfairness.' It really was a brutal thing to say to someone. I couldn't bear that it had affected me like this. I wasn't trying to draw any particular kind of response from Mr Monaga with my words, but eventually he looked up, glanced at the clock, turned to look at the alley behind him, then finally looked at me and nodded.

'I'm alone enough as it is,' he said.

An emotion rushed in on me that seemed to be made up of a confusing number of different parts. All I could say was, 'Oh.'

I drained the tea in my cup and reached for the teapot, saying, 'I'll make the next round.'

And so we drank another cup of tea, then Mr Monaga announced he was going to the barber, and asked me to keep an eye on the office while he was out.

'Oh, why the barber?' was not a question I felt I could ask.

With nothing in particular to do, I checked Lonely No More!'s social media accounts on my smartphone. As usual, there were lots of cheery posts about neighbourhood clean-up initiatives and socials and so on and so forth.

A little after twelve, some time after Mr Monaga had gone off to the barber, Mrs Ōmae stopped into the office. Seeing me sat alone at the meeting table, she said, 'Well, well! Are you not working today? Where's Mr Monaga?'

'At the barber's.'

'Is that so? When will he be back?'

'I don't know.'

'Oh! Well, it's lunchtime, so do you want some of these?'

Saying this, Mrs Ōmae set a large bento box down on the table. I peered at it with unbridled curiosity as she removed the lid, revealing twelve inari-zushi parcels packed tightly in rows.

'I made them yesterday, but I did too many.'

'That's quite an over-calculation!'

'Well, Mr Monaga's all on his own, you see.'

As I nodded, it struck me that I knew virtually nothing about Mr Monaga. Not that I needed to know anything, of course. I'd realised after my first two years of employment that, so long as your colleagues presented you with 'good interface' while they were at work, it didn't really matter what kind of people they were outside of it. The same was true of Mr Monaga. I didn't know what sort of person he was, but as colleagues went, he wasn't at all bad.

And yet, in the moment, my curiosity was piqued, and I began to try to elicit more information from Mrs Ōmae.

'You mean he doesn't have any family?'

'He told me he lived alone.'

'How long has he been in this office?'

'Six months,' said Mrs Ōmae, handing me a pair of disposable chopsticks. I sheepishly accepted them, moved one of the inari-zushi on to the bento box lid, then bit into it. It was outrageously delicious. There were sesame seeds inside, and the faint taste of wasabi cut through the sweetness of the deep-fried tofu. 'Are you not having any?' I asked.

'No, I ate before I came,' she replied, so I brought her over a teacup and brewed some more hōjicha.

'I guess it must have opened about two months after Lonely No More! turned up. At that time, everyone was accepting their pamphlets and going along to their socials, just like they suggested. I guess you could say they were all pretty lonely. That was when Mr Monaga set up the office. At the start, it was him who went around putting up posters and asking people questions. He passed along the information he gleaned further up the chain, and then occasionally people from the town hall would come out to the area. The situation's already a lot better than how it used to be.'

'What is it that Lonely No More! want, ultimately?'

I could hardly believe that I'd managed to get to this point without grasping the answer to such a crucial question, but I'd been so absorbed in the nitty-gritty of my job that I hadn't even thought it through properly. Mrs Ōmae shook her head as she raised her cup to her lips.

'Oh, lots of things. They get you to confess your worries at their free socials, and then they ask you along to different, more serious socials. Those you have to pay for. From there, they sift out the people who are willing to pay whatever it takes to avoid being lonely, and invite them to dinner parties. Of course, those also cost money. They also list information about everyone who comes to their meets, including all their worries, and then they send around whichever Lonely No More! member they think a particular individual would be most likely to trust, and have them try to gain access to their house. I've heard that people rewrite their wills so as to leave the organisation all their possessions.'

'I see,' I said, nodding. I didn't feel particularly angry. It struck me that these kinds of things happened every-where. If old age found you lonely, maybe you'd want to leave your possessions to someone who'd made you feel less so, even if just for a little while.

'Lonely No More! recruits some members especially to do that kind of fundraising, and others to slither their way into people's personal affairs. Apparently, someone from Mr Monaga's family has ended up with them. As a member, I mean.'

Cutting an inari-zushi in two with her chopsticks, Mrs Ōmae stopped speaking and a look of panic shot across her face, as if she were shocked by what had slipped out of her mouth. I nodded casually, making vague noises and pretending that I'd not really been paying what she said any mind.

'And that's really all I know.' It sounded like exactly the sort of thing someone would say when they realised they'd said more than they were supposed to, but I guessed that in this case it actually was the truth. Mrs Ōmae ate her inari-zushi, drank a sip of tea and said, 'There's a bit too much wasabi, isn't there! Sorry.'

Surmising that she didn't want to talk about Lonely No More! any longer, and that she preferred to talk about the inari-zushi, I asked, 'Are those mustard greens you've mixed in with the rice?'

'No, wasabi leaves,' she said.

Mrs Ōmae and I ate three inari-zushi and drank two cups of hōjicha apiece before she headed off home, asking me to pass on the remaining six inari-zushi to Mr Monaga. It occurred to me to wonder if Mrs Ōmae wasn't also rather lonely herself, and if that was why she was bringing Mr Monaga his lunch, but I tried not to think too much about it. Nobody's life was untouched by loneliness; it was just a question of whether or not you were able to accept that loneliness for what it was. Put another way, everyone was lonely, and it was up to them whether they chose to bury that loneliness through relationships with other people, and if so, of what sort of intensity and depth.

Soon after Mrs Ōmae had left, a stranger with a crew cut strode into the office. I stood up in a bid to stall him, saying, 'Umm, er, I, um, err, I ... ' But as I was doing so I realised that his clothes were the same ones that Mr Monaga had been wearing earlier. Mr Monaga had had his hair cut, his beard shaved off, and was wearing the contact lenses he apparently carried with him in his bag. Compared with the Mr Monaga I'd previously known, who, in the manner of so many graphic designers, had an unkempt quality which stopped just short of being out-and-out messy, this version was so fresh and clean-looking that I had literally failed to recognise him.

'What happened? What are you doing?'

'I thought I'd try and infiltrate one of the socials.'

Oh yes, I noted to myself, it was Thursday today. Nonetheless, what he was saying seemed to me downright crazy, so I went on, 'Don't you think we'd be better off just reporting them to the police?'

But Mr Monaga shook his head. 'At the moment, we don't have proof of who did it. Besides, don't you want to know what they're gonna do to us next?' In the space of just a few hours, his tone seemed to have grown coarser and more urgent.

'Okay, I'll come along too. I'll go get my hair cut.' Before I knew it, these words were out of my mouth. Mrs Masakado's face floated up before me. I hadn't been asked to go to the social, and here I was volunteering. This was what was known as an inappropriate relationship with one's work.

Still, I couldn't back out now. Who knows, maybe this could even be passed off as a perfectly reasonable reaction to being told to die alone. I pointed Mr Monaga to the inari-zushi that Mrs Ōmae had brought, and asked him to draw me a map to the closest hairdresser.

I had my hair cut, put on the glasses I usually kept in my bag in case there was a problem with my contact lenses, took off my make-up and went along with Mr Monaga. I was feeling quite excited, and indeed had suggested setting out as soon as I'd got back from my haircut, but Mr Monaga had advised that since we looked like working people, we'd be safer going to the evening social as opposed to the afternoon one. The meeting hall welcomed visitors all day, but the socials took place at 2 p.m. and 6 p.m. Feeling in something of an argumentative mood, I countered with a suggestion that we go under the guise of siblings who were both unemployed, but he put the kibosh on my plan, saying that though it wasn't unthinkable in theory, he had a feeling we'd probably be found out. Compared with the desperate nature of what he was intending to do, his judgement seemed relatively unclouded.

I managed to get into the Lonely No More! meeting hall in Block Four easily enough by presenting the flyer I'd been given by the man in the alley. From outside, the meeting hall looked like a private house that had been converted into a rather stylish cafe space, the sort of place which passers-by might easily drop into, oblivious of the building's true identity – although, of course, I couldn't be sure that attracting such unsuspecting visitors wasn't in fact the building's implicit intention.

For safety's sake, Mr Monaga and I had decided to pretend not to know each other, and so I went in ahead. Mr Monaga came in a little afterwards, adopting an idiotic whiny voice and saying, 'I just came across the page on Facebook … ' Then he sat down at a table alongside Mr Tadokoro, the man who had just a few days ago thrown balled-up cake wrappers at me.

The socials were not, as I'd initially imagined, a staged, whiteboard-and-rows-of-folding-metal-chairs kind of affair. Instead, participants sat with people they knew around one of several tables, chatting reservedly or unreservedly as they waited for the young people from Lonely No More! to come around and talk to them. The woman from the poster was there, wearing the same white dress, as was the man who'd stopped me in the alley. There was also a girl with a faltering, childish way of speaking who couldn't have been more than twenty, and an older man of about my age wearing wire-framed glasses. They seemed friendly and nice, yet looking at their faces more closely, I noticed that all of them had strangely large pupils that seemed to bleed over into their irises, making their eyes seem either out of focus, or weirdly well in focus – but in either case, not exactly as they should be.

I chose a table, doing my utmost to avoid any of the people I'd come into contact with during my postering adventures, but I ended up on a table with Mrs

Togawa, who came in exclaiming, 'Ooh, I'm late, I'm late!' She seemed not to recognise me now I was wearing glasses and my previously shoulder-length hair had been shorn back to an undercut, asking with a smile, 'Are you married?'

'No, I'm not,' I mumbled.

'Well, you'd better start making an effort to be more feminine, then,' she said, rather presumptuously.

'My mother said that can also bring its own problems,' I said, baiting her.

'That's very true,' she said with a sigh. 'But you've got to at least try it, otherwise you won't have even made it to the threshold of life.'

'Absolutely,' I agreed good-naturedly.

Sitting at the table beside Mrs Togawa and me were a grey-faced young man and an immaculately made-up young woman. These two would exchange a few remarks with each other, then abruptly break off their conversation, leaving it a little while before restarting this cycle. Both seemed very distracted – the grey-faced man was following the poster woman with his eyes the entire time, while the made-up woman was continually darting glances at the man who'd spoken to me in the alley. In the centre of the table was a basket heaped with the washi-wrapped steamed cakes I'd sampled at Ms Kohashi's house. The girl with the babyish way of speaking came over and began handing out cups of tea that smelled like ginger hōjicha. I decided not to drink any, just in case.

'This is my first time here,' I said to nobody in particular, in the interests of research, or maybe just out of personal curiosity. 'My work is taking over my life, and I really need someone I can talk to.'

It was, after all, the truth.

'You poor thing!' said Mrs Togawa, and the young man echoed, 'You poor thing.'

'That must be really tough,' the young woman said.

Amazingly, I felt my mood improve slightly. So, I thought, I've been wanting sympathy, have I? So far, the only person who'd offered me straightforward sympathy about the inappropriate relationship I'd formed with my work was Mrs Masakado. I should probably have talked to my friends about it, but they were almost all of a similar age to me, and were also just gritting their teeth and clinging on as best they could, so it hardly felt right to drone on about my problems. Besides, I didn't want to worry them. I had one friend who was currently enduring a situation even worse than the one I'd encountered in my old workplace. Whereas I'd ended up quitting with burn-out syndrome, she was still hanging on in there. Even in the past, when my friends had been kind enough to say that what I was going through sounded tough, I'd always felt morally indebted to them in some way, because what they were going through was, in point of fact, tougher. In contrast, the sympathy I got here may have been superficial, but at least it came without fetters, and thus felt easy to accept.

'You must be tired,' said a voice at my back. I turned around to see the man in wire-framed glasses of about my age, who had something of a teacherly air to him.

'Are you working too hard?'

'Yes, possibly.'

'Tell us all about it. You'll feel better afterwards.' He smiled gently as he said this. I was torn between a desire to scream, *There's no way you could ever understand!* and a desire to get everything off my chest right then and there, in a ratio of approximately four parts to one. In view of this disorderly emotional state which showed no signs of resolving itself, I decided for the time being to say simply, 'Maybe one day.'

'Of course! Whenever you want to talk, we'll be here,' he said, his eyes glinting. The way he said it reminded me of a shop person saying, 'Have a nice day, please come again!' and I felt glad I hadn't shared my worries with him.

I glanced around in Mr Monaga's direction to see him speaking stiffly to the young girl, who looked as if she might not even be out of high school, yet his gaze was fixed on the poster woman in the white dress. She was at another table, shaking hands with an old man. Looking closer I saw it was Mr Terui, who had brushed me off on my first day on the job. I could see that he was trying to maintain a stern expression, but the corners of his mouth were raised and he was clearly enjoying the whole performance. Each time he folded his arms and came out with some new bravado-filled statement, the woman would nod, or laugh, or clap her hands in mirth. He seemed to be in a very good mood.

As he spoke to the girl attending to him, Mr Monaga would glance over sporadically at the woman, his eyes muddied with distress. It crossed my mind to wonder if he hadn't developed a dubious sort of attachment to her, and whether that was the driving force behind all his efforts to put an end to Lonely No More! – but I immediately thought better of it. The emotion in his eyes was pain, pure and simple – a mountain of pain bordered by a sadness that stretched on without end. He was sad that the woman in the white dress was here. Yet whenever she made her way over to his table, Mr Monaga stood up and walked away. Instead, I heard Mr Tadokoro's voice telling her flirtatiously, 'You get prettier every time I see you!'

'I had an awful experience at my last workplace,' said the grey-faced man hesitantly, presumably addressing me. 'When I tell my parents about it, they just ask me why I quit, or say I'm stupid for not staying. And when I go for job interviews, they ask me my reasons for giving up. I can hardly tell them I quit because my boss yelled at me every day, can I? But while I'm thinking about what to say instead, I get tongue-tied, and then nobody wants to employ me.'

'Right, I see,' I said, nodding along as I listened to the man.

'But quite honestly, as a parent,' said Mrs Togawa, 'if one of my children were in that situation, I'd probably say the same.'

The temptation was very strong in me to pipe up and say, *Wait, isn't that exactly what did happen with your son?* but of course I knew that would be a very bad idea right now.

'Actually, a similar thing happened to a friend,' I told the man, 'and at an interview, they said they'd quit because they didn't feel properly valued, and the interviewer replied, "In other words, you were just very young and naive," but in the end they got the job regardless.'

The man narrowed his eyes and looked at me in a way that seemed to signify that he found my story highly dubious, before eventually saying in a voice so quiet it was barely audible, 'Really.'

Mr Monaga entered the room again from a corridor at the back of the room. The very young girl who'd been at his table came over to ours and stood next to the grey-faced man.

'Are you feeling any better since we last spoke?' she asked.

The man shook his head with affected solemnity. Feeling suddenly restless, I asked the woman where the toilets were. 'They're through there,' she said, indicating the corridor Mr Monaga had come from.

'I'll be back in a minute,' I said, standing up and heading in the direction of the toilet. I didn't particularly need to go, but I wanted a moment to hone my strategy about what to say, and what information to try and draw out of the others at the table.

To go down the corridor, you had to take your shoes off and put on slippers. The thought of using the communal slippers in this building didn't appeal at all, so I shuffled down the corridor in my socks. The low door, with its sign showing not the standard word for toilet but the lesser-used character for 'privy', helped generate the feel of a charming little cafe set up in a renovated old building. There were so many different ways of garnering people's trust, I reflected. Not needing to avail myself of its services, I walked past the door and peered down a dark corridor leading off to the left. Some way down stood a three-tier wire shelving unit, whose middle shelf was stacked high with the same boxes of steamed cakes of which Ms Kohashi had managed to earn so many.

They probably owned a factory somewhere that produced them for cheap, I thought as I drew closer, pulling my phone out of my pocket to illuminate the rack. On the bottom shelf were stacks of the 'ayudarte!' flyers, the same one I'd been handed in the alley, and on the top shelf was a row of unmarked ring binders neatly sandwiched between two bookends. What was inside? I wondered, standing on tiptoe and trying to get a glimpse of their contents. The nearest one was full of slightly battered pieces of printer paper. The next but one along held a number of clear pockets, which contained what looked like share certificates. I recoiled instinctively. What the hell were those? Had they swindled them from the people who came along to the socials, or were they just investments that the organisation had to begin with?

I was stretching my head towards the back of the rack, intending to check if there was anything behind the bookends, when I spotted a tin of paint. In lieu of a torch, I moved my smartphone closer to check the colour, and saw that it looked like the same shade that had been used for the graffiti. Feeling my breath catch in my throat, I recalled that Mr Monaga had identified the shade of paint on the shutters using his colour sample chart.

'Are you looking for something?' Quite unexpectedly, I heard a voice from behind me, which I recognised instantly as that of the man who had spoken to me in the alley. I hurriedly rotated my head to an angle at which I imagined my face would be just about obscured from view, thinking furiously about what I could say that wouldn't give the game away.

'Yes, I was looking for the toilet.'

'It's here.' I heard a knock-knock as he rapped on the door. 'Just behind you.'

'Oh! I couldn't read the character on the door, and I thought it was a storeroom or something!'

'It says "privy". It means toilet.' The man's voice was cheery, but laden with a spine-tingling tension. 'Come back and join us soon, won't you!'

I nodded with exaggerated enthusiasm so he'd would be sure to see without my having to turn my head and reveal myself. When I judged that he'd returned to the space where the social was being held, I moved from the dark passageway towards the toilet. I pushed the door beneath the 'privy' sign and scoped out the inside. There was a small sink with a door next to it, which I opened to reveal a cubicle with a western-style toilet and a small window to one side. I went into the cubicle, opened the window and peered out. The adjacent building was extremely close, but I had a feeling that the gap in-between would just about accommodate me. I wouldn't have very far to jump, either.

I ripped off a length of toilet paper and took it in hand before leaving the privy and moving back to the wire shelving. Lifting up the handle of the paint tin and wrapping it in the paper, I picked up the whole thing and shuffled back. I collected my shoes from the entrance, then returned again to the privy.

In the cubicle, hardly daring to breathe, I opened the window as far as it would go and first dropped my shoes down the crack between the two buildings, and they landed with a soft thump. Then I closed the toilet lid, wedged the paint tin under my arm and rested my other arm on the window frame. Beneath my socks, the toilet lid was so slippery that for a moment I felt genuinely scared I might take a tumble – but things got easier once I rested my weight on the window frame. I adopted a position as though I was about to do a bar spin, and lowered the paint tin down onto the ground below. From there, holding on to the window frame with both hands, I extracted one leg at a time, then slid down in the gap between the two buildings.

I wedged my feet into my shoes, picked up the paint tin and – moving sideways like a crab – made my way along the dark crevice between the two buildings in the direction of goodness knew where. I was aware that what I was doing was ridiculous, but I overrode that awareness with another thought: *Take this, you fuckers! If you can tell me to die alone, I at least get to do this to you.*

The paint in the tin had a Munsell value of 6.0R 5.0/18.3, which matched the paint used for the graffiti. 'But doesn't carrying the paint out of the building render it inadmissible as evidence?' Mr Monaga said, as if he'd found himself a part on *CSI*.

'I see what you mean,' I replied, 'but surely carrying it out is better than them disposing of it?'

Although I wasn't really conscious of it, everything about my behaviour towards Mr Monaga suggested that I didn't really conceive of him as a boss or my employer. He didn't behave much like my employer, either, which might have been because he'd worked out that we were roughly the same age.

He was putting in calls to what I guessed were printing companies, asking them a lot of questions like 'What's the minimum number of days you could do it in?' and 'What would be the extra charge for that kind of turnaround?' I had nothing in particular to do, so I got up several times to make tea, taking detailed notes on the computer of everything that had happened since that morning's graffiti discovery and writing them up in timeline format.

'I'm going to work through the night, and the day after tomorrow I'll be asking you to swap around the posters again. You can go home now and take tomorrow off.'

Such were Mr Monaga's words after wrapping up his negotiations with the printers – but I wanted to see how things would pan out here so I answered that if I wasn't bothering him, I'd stay a bit longer. I imported the photos Mr Monaga had taken of the graffiti into my word file. However many times I looked at them, something about the hate spilling from those letters made me wonder if we'd done anything to deserve it.

A little while later, Mrs Ōmae and Mrs Tadokoro came into the office. Mrs Ōmae was carrying a tiered bento box wrapped in a furoshiki. Mrs Tadokoro was wearing a trouser suit and was fully made-up, but her face looked gaunt and she was gripping her phone in one hand.

'I made too much chirashi-zushi so I thought I'd bring some by. And Mrs Tadokoro has something she wants to talk to you about,' Mrs Ōmae said.

At this, Mrs Tadokoro nodded, and asked Mr Monaga, 'Is it okay to sit down?'

'Of course,' said Mr Monaga, gesturing towards the meeting table. The two women pulled out chairs and seated themselves. Mrs Ōmae unknotted the furoshiki, took out four paper plates and served us all portions of chirashi-zushi. I made some more tea, wondering how many times I'd made tea in the course of the day.

'They graffitied your shutters, didn't they?' Saying this, Mrs Tadokoro – who I guessed must have been on her way home from work – blinked in concentration as she jabbed away at her phone. 'I woke up early today, about four or something, and as I was brushing my teeth, I saw someone walking by. It spooked me slightly, so I had a look to see who it was, and realised I recognised the man. So I followed him.'

Mrs Tadokoro laid her smartphone down in the middle of the table and pressed play on a video. Holding what looked like a paint tin in his hand, the young man who had approached me in the alley – and then had tried to herd me back inside the Lonely No More! social – walked past the camera lens. There was a rustling sound as the camera moved, and then the next shot, taken through a gap between two bushes, showed the man painting the shutters with a paintbrush.

'Will this be of any use to you?' Mrs Tadokoro said, looking up.

Mr Monaga nodded. 'I believe so.'

Mrs Tadokoro slurped two mouthfuls of tea, then hung her head and let out a great sigh. 'How pathetic my husband is, hanging around with those kinds of people!'

Unexpectedly, Mr Monaga shook his head. 'That's not true,' he said.

'It's not,' I chimed in with Mr Monaga while internally disagreeing, and ate the chirashi-zushi Mrs Ōmae had made. Once again, it was very tasty.

The following day, I stayed home and slept. Maybe because the previous day had involved such unfamiliar behaviour and strange places, I felt utterly wiped out and found myself unable to get out of bed until evening. Mr Monaga had seen me off the previous day with the words, 'Rest well, because the day after tomorrow will be busy.' Quite without intending to, I'd followed his advice.

He'd told me that he was planning to close the office for the day and gather together everything that might constitute evidence of vandalism, such as the paint tin, Mrs Tadokoro's video, the timeline I'd created and so on. According to what he'd gleaned at the social,

'the design office on the outskirts of town' – our office
– was a much-loathed presence in Lonely No More!
circles, much as we'd guessed. People had said all kinds
of things about us: that feeble messages like ours were
a waste of the paper they were printed on, that we had
a cheek to be so pushy when nobody even knew what
we were about and that the owner was on his own as
a punishment for his actions in life up until that point.
'I mean, nothing they said was untrue,' Mr Monaga
told me, unfazed. I had made a note of their insults in
the document where I'd recorded everything about the
graffiti.

When I went into work the morning after my day
off – a day that more or less hadn't existed as far as I
was concerned – there was a pile of posters sitting on
top of the meeting desk, curling at the ends. Sitting
on top was a protective sheet of brown paper, conceal-
ing their design from view.

'These have just been printed.'

'Right.'

'I'm sorry to do this when you've only just changed
them over, but I'd like you to go out and put these ones
up in place of the last batch. Is that okay? I'll be helping.' As he spoke, Mr Monaga peeled back the brown
paper, revealing the design of the poster that he had
stayed up all night to send to print.

'No More Graffiti!' read the slogan. A picture showed
our office depicted in simple lines, its proportions
slightly exaggerated and its distinctive pearlescent

tiles reproduced in pale rainbow tones. Across the shutters of the building were scrawled the words: 'DIE ALONE!'

For three days straight, Mr Monaga and I traipsed around every house in the neighbourhood, swapping over all the water-saving and tree-planting and road-safety posters for the 'No More Graffiti!' ones. Those who knew about the graffiti incident sympathised with our plight, and many of those who didn't had their curiosity piqued by the new design, asking us what it was all about. Even those who were at first reluctant to put up the graffiti posters – believing they'd attract too much attention from Lonely No More! – changed their minds one after another when we listed our supporters and made it clear that they held an easy majority.

Moreover, the uniformed policemen who came to investigate the crime scene had a big role to play. It was debatable whether the tin of paint I'd smuggled out of the meeting hall was admissible as evidence, but apparently the fingerprints did match up with those on the flyer I'd received from the young man. They also said that Mrs Tadokoro's video alone was substantial enough to corroborate our account.

That week, Lonely No More!'s activities were cancelled. Their members were nowhere to be seen around town, and their meeting hall was shut. Thanks to a bout of low pressure, it drizzled the entire time Mr Monaga and I were going around switching over the posters, so Ms Kohashi rewarded me for my services by inviting me in for some maté, telling me while I was there that, without the socials, Mrs Togawa had been coming around to her house every day, staying for hours on end. And Mr Terui came up and asked what we'd done to put an end to the socials. But that was about the extent of the backlash towards us.

Around the time that most of the posters had been swapped over to the 'No More Graffiti!' ones, the police paid a visit to the Lonely No More! meeting hall, but found it deserted. Nobody was answering the phone, and the group hadn't posted on social media for a while, either. The police said there had been several reports of suspicious activity in other neighbourhoods; on the back of the vandalism accusation, they were planning to try and infiltrate the organisation and get a better grasp of what was going on.

The day we finished swapping over the old posters for the graffiti ones, Mr Monaga and I were invited by Mrs Tadokoro and Mrs Ōmae to Hulala. Mrs Tadokoro and I ordered curry nyūmen, while Mr Monaga and Mrs Ōmae opted for ume and wakame. Mrs Tadokoro footed the bill, saying she'd just been paid, and the owner was good enough to charge her the Mr Monaga rate.

'I'm thinking about separating from my husband,' announced Mrs Tadokoro as we were sat round the table. It wasn't that her affection for him had cooled, but she felt it was a good idea to put some distance between them to think things over. Neither Mrs Ōmae nor Mr Monaga – nor even I, needless to say – could express a view about whether that was a good or bad thing. But after a little silence, Mrs Ōmae said, 'Keep in touch, won't you, if you move? Let's have tea from time to time.' Mrs Tadokoro nodded and said that she would.

Then Mr Monaga's phone rang and he excused himself, slipping outside. He didn't come back, which meant he didn't get to taste the almond tofu dessert that the owner brought over on the house for us all, saying that it was 'a celebration, after all'. Just as the three of us had finished ours, Mr Monaga quietly slid open the door, and said, 'Excuse me, something urgent has come up, I'm going to have to go. Thank you very much for everything.' Then he shut the door again.

When I got to work the following day, the office shutters were down. They had been entirely repainted and there was no longer any trace of the graffiti.

Attached to the shutters was a Post-it with my name on it and a message from Mr Monaga thanking me for my wonderful work. He apologised for not saying goodbye properly, notified me of the date he would transfer my salary, informed me that my job was now over and wished me the best of luck with the next one.

I put my hand to the shutter handle and tried to hoist it, but it wouldn't budge. Mr Monaga had always been in the office – to the point that I had to wonder if he'd actually lived there – so I'd never been given a key.

For quite some while I stood still, staring dumbly up at the building in front of me. The nine o'clock morning light reflected off the white pearlescent tiles, making the building shimmer like a mirage.

The Easy Job in the Hut in the Big Forest

'When I went into work in the morning, the office had just disappeared!'

'I see,' said Mrs Masakado, unfazed.

'This might sound strange, but I felt like that position really suited me. It came as a real shock, you know?'

'Right, yes, I see. Mr Monaga mentioned in his report that you'd done a very good job.'

Mrs Masakado flipped through the file on her desk, staring at it hard. 'Yes, he says here that you provided insightful new ideas, and that you approached your work with great diligence.'

'Did I do something wrong in some way?'

Don't get ahead of yourself, I counselled myself in my head. *There's no way that Mr Monaga's disappearance could have anything to do with an underling like you.*

'No, no, not at all!' As expected, Mrs Masakado widened her eyes slightly and cocked her head as if to enquire what on earth I was talking about. 'He just moved on to the next job. Apparently they needed a replacement urgently.'

'A replacement?'

'Yes, the previous employee was suffering from mental fatigue and became unable to work, so Mr Monaga was sent in to fill their place.' Dropping her eyes to her file, Mrs Masakado traced the relevant line in the document with her finger. 'The person he stepped in to replace also had a member of their family taken away by Lonely No More!, like Mr Monaga himself. But battling an organisation that actively involved a family member was apparently accruing more psychological damage than expected.'

Staring at Mrs Masakado's right hand where it rested on the table, I fell silent. Oh, I thought. I couldn't rustle up a reaction with any more content than that, so I just came out and said it: 'Oh.' Feeling a sense of futility I probably didn't need to feel, I squeezed together my hands in my lap.

'With Mr Monaga, they took his younger sister first, and then his parents,' said Mrs Masakado. 'His sister has risen high in the ranks of the organisation. You sometimes see her on the posters.' I immediately thought of the poster of the woman in the white dress that I'd encountered so often on my rounds.

'Is Mr Monaga's job not graphic design?'

'No, it is,' said Mrs Masakado, shooting me a slightly unsettled glance. 'I believe he does his design jobs while also keeping an eye on Lonely No More! But I'm afraid I don't know any more than that.' With characteristic gentleness, Mrs Masakado hammered the nail in the coffin of that conversation. I nodded. Unsure how to reply, I gazed at the file by Mrs Masakado's hands. I had no idea what was in there, so I simply stared at the binding of the paper.

After what felt like a long time, I finally came back to myself. Seeing this, Mrs Masakado said tentatively, 'Would it be okay to discuss your next post now?'

Thinking that there was no point in obsessing about Mr Monaga, I assented.

'Do you have any particular requirements? Did you enjoy working outdoors, or do you feel you'd rather do desk work?'

'I don't have any particular preferences. But this job definitely proved to me that an outdoor job isn't out of the question.'

Really and truly, I didn't care. At this moment in time, I wasn't sure if I wanted to work at all. Were I to be told there weren't any jobs available, I'd probably just nod and quietly make my way back home. Equally, if I was asked if I was available to go and work for a construction company in Dubai, I was likely to say, quite offhand, that I was up for it.

'I see, right. Well, there's a position here that seems to combine both of those elements. Shall I give you a rundown?'

I nodded.

'It's a little difficult to explain. It might end up having a bit of an odd-jobs feel to it.'

'Really, anything will do.' I was aware that this made me sound desperate, but I didn't say anything to amend it. For no reason I properly understood, talking with Mrs Masakado here today, I felt that a hole had opened up in my heart. If being busy would prevent me from having to look at that hole, I could probably handle any kind of job.

'The posting comes from a park maintenance office.' Mrs Masakado tilted her head as she peered down at the advert. '"An easy desk job in a hut in a big forest," it says. It just came in this morning, so I haven't had much time to get my head around it.'

Even for someone who had previously been thinking they might accept a job in a construction company in Dubai, there was something about this sequence of words that made me frown and look up. Mrs Masakado read on a bit further, then shrugged and said, 'But it's under the jurisdiction of the Ministry of Agriculture, Forestry and Fisheries, so it must be a proper organisation. There hasn't been a single report filed of harassment or failure to pay wages, and they provide health insurance. Hm, and what about the pay? Oh, it's not that high, 850 per hour, nine to five, with paid overtime. The hourly rate for overtime goes up to 1,000 yen per hour.'

'Long hours and cheap wages … '

'It does emphasise how easy it is, though. "Really a very easy job!" There's an exclamation mark and everything. What do you think?' Mrs Masakado straightened herself up and looked me right in the eye. It seemed that the job had roused her curiosity, and she wanted to send me in.

I owed a lot to Mrs Masakado, I thought, and however strange a job it might have been, it was better to act while people still had high expectations for you, and so I nodded. 'Okay, sure, I'll give it a go.'

I'd been to Ōbayashi Daishinrin Park several times on school trips, when I'd loved visiting the park's museum, but I'd never been back as an adult. Leaving aside the time it had made the news when a fossil of an early human had been discovered on its grounds during the preparatory work for a scheduled museum extension, it was basically a tranquil sort of place where time flowed by peacefully.

Mr Hakota from the admin office, the man I'd arranged an interview with, was waiting for me by the park entrance gate. He looked to be in his mid-sixties, and was wearing a green boiler suit with the letters ODP embroidered on it. He beamed as he greeted me in a voice with a distinct Kansai twang: 'Thanks so much for coming!' He gave the impression of being a genuinely pleasant person, and I prayed to myself that this impression bore out, and that this benevolent exterior didn't conceal a highly problematic personality. I bowed to him and said, 'Mrs Masakado sent me.'

'You know,' he said, 'it's the first time I've placed one of those ads, and I don't know if what I wrote wasn't up to par or what, but you were the only applicant we had! Are you happy to start right away?'

Not again, I thought. As late in the day as it was, I felt a sense of suspicion towards Mrs Masakado surface in me, although I assured myself quickly that I was overthinking. The job she'd steered me towards may not have had any other applicants, but that wasn't the same as landing me at the mercy of a boss known for emotionally blackmailing his employees or giving unfair workloads.

'Yes, that would be perfect.'

'Excellent. That's a tremendous help,' he said. 'Your predecessor, who came to us through one of our employees, decided she couldn't hack the place any more.' Mr Hakota smiled knowingly as he raised his eyebrows and touched an index finger to his temple.

'Hah!' I laughed along, thinking that I'd almost certainly landed myself in a bad situation.

'I don't think she was suited to it. The neurotic type. You know, the kind who gets jumpy if it's too quiet. Are you okay with silence?'

'Yes, fine,' I said, smiling composedly.

'Oh, that's good to hear!' Mr Hakota nodded repeatedly. Climbing into what looked like a golf buggy parked beside the gate, he gestured for me to get in the back. The buggy was painted with a Japanese spider crab, the logo of the Cangrejo Ōbayashi football club. I had very little interest in football, so this observation elicited very little in me other than the recollection that Cangrejo Stadium was located right beside the park, and the thought that there was something kind of creepy about spider crabs. Allegedly Cangrejo had chosen the spider crab as their emblem because they'd uncovered a load of spider crab fossils while the stadium was being constructed, but since the discovery of the early human fossil, the spider crabs had been relegated to the realm of the far less interesting and promptly forgotten about. I remembered hearing people talk over lunch at a previous workplace about how the early human from whom the fossil had come was referred to as 'the Ōbayashi hominin'.

'Is the office not walkable?' I asked now.

'It's not *not* walkable, but it takes about twenty minutes from the main entrance.'

This took me aback. It seemed to say a lot about the size of the park, for a start.

'How long does it take to walk from one side of the park to the other?'

'One side to the other?' Mr Hakota repeated my words to me curiously, as if he'd never even thought about such a thing. I started to acclimatise to the idea that the size of the park far exceeded my estimation.

'From the west side to the east, for example.'

'Hmm, let's see ... ' Mr Hakota nodded his head thoughtfully as he drove along the park's paved road. The leaves falling from the tall ginkgo trees lining the sides of the path made for a beautiful sight.

'I guess about three hours? Although I've never done west to east, so it's hard to say.' He chuckled good-naturedly. I kept my mouth shut. Just how many people did you need to maintain a park of that size? Was it even possible to 'maintain' such a place? What kind of crazy workload could I expect to be assigned at the very bottom of the pecking order in a place this big? Although, I reminded myself, the advert had stated it was a desk job, so maybe I wouldn't be doing anything maintenance-related.

'It's a great place.' Apparently oblivious to my worries, Mr Hakota was still beaming to himself as he drove along. His cheerfulness and his affection for the park didn't seem fake – I got the sense he really did like this place. As he drove, he answered whatever questions I put to him, but didn't speak needlessly or pry in any way, maintaining instead a comfortable distance.

Our journey was a smooth one, and we made it to the office in ten minutes. Still, I thought, the fact that it was a ten-minute drive even inside the grounds made this a unique situation. The maintenance office proved to be a single-storey building about the size of a school classroom. According to Mr Hakota, this was the headquarters for the 'Gifts of the Forest' section, of which he was in charge. There were five other maintenance offices dotted around the park, one for each section. Inside the office was a man called Mr Nojima, about ten years Mr Hakota's junior, and a young woman wearing glasses called Miss Kudō, who didn't even look twenty. Both were introduced to me as Gifts of the Forest employees. Like Mr Hakota, Mr Nojima sported a boiler suit with ODP embroidered on it, while Miss Kudō wore an ODP blouson-style jacket over jeans. All three of them seemed like good sorts, which eased my anxiety a bit.

Once the introductions were over, Mr Hakota handed me a jacket in a plastic bag, saying, 'For you.'

Strangely enough, the jacket wasn't green but orange. I put it on, as I was encouraged to, wondering if all the lower-ranking employees wore orange. Miss Kudō clapped her hands together in delight, saying, 'Oh, it really suits you!'

Did the colour have any relation to the orange of the Cangrejo Ōbayashi kit? The jacket, made of a stiff fabric, seemed sturdy, and like it would keep out the cold well. I was rather taken with it.

'Right then,' Mr Hakota said, when that was over with, 'let's hop back in the buggy, and I'll show you where you're going to be working.'

I looked at him uncomprehendingly. 'Will I not be working here, then?'

'No, this is the headquarters for the Gifts of the Forest section. You'll be stationed further in.'

Now I recalled the words of the job posting: 'An easy desk job in a hut in a big forest.' This building might have been single-storeyed and a bit cramped, but it definitely wasn't a hut.

'Follow me,' said Mr Hakota, leading me around the back of the building, where the forest spread off into the distance. There were three buggies parked up there. The one that he'd driven me here in was still parked at the front of the building, which meant there were at least four in total.

'Can you drive this one around to the front of the building?'

'Ah, no, no, I've never driven one of those before.'

Mr Hakota's eyes widened. 'But the woman at the agency said you had a driving licence?'

Unable to argue with this, I said nothing.

'It's easier than driving a car,' Mr Hakota said, coaxing me into the driver's seat and then indicating various controls: 'That's the side brake, and that turns the warning sound on. Try moving now, and see how you get on.'

With great trepidation, I put my foot on the accelerator and the buggy began to trundle forwards.

'That's it, keep going and come around to the front of the building,' he said, disappearing back inside. I drove carefully, steering clear of the trees, listening to the tyres crunching over the fallen leaves, before finally showing up outside the Gifts of the Forest headquarters. I'd been sufficiently slow that Mr Hakota had already emerged from the front of the office. He now handed me a thick pamphlet.

'Here you are!' he said. 'This explains about the Gifts of the Forest section. You don't have to memorise everything in here, but take a look through when you have a minute.'

'Right,' I said, setting the pamphlet down on the passenger seat.

'Okay, follow me,' he called out, getting into his own buggy, and we set off in convoy.

Mr Hakota took us down a small path leading off from the back of the headquarters into the trees. The forest around here was clustered with fruits and berries – these, I thought, must be the 'gifts' which the section name alluded to. I wasn't an expert in botany by any means, but I could see what looked to be persimmon trees. The forest was quiet – quiet enough that I could understand why my predecessor's getting 'jumpy' might have been chalked up to the silence – and the only sounds I could hear were the engines, the leaves crackling beneath the tyres and various bird calls. Driving the buggy was good fun, but the thought of being left all alone somewhere as quiet as this did make me feel slightly uneasy.

Where the path ended was a hut. With its pointed roof, it was maybe one and a half times the size of a standard police box, sitting amid the quietude of the forest as if someone had left it there by mistake.

'This is it here,' Mr Hakota called as he parked up, so I did the same and got out of my buggy.

'Don't worry, there's a toilet inside. It has electricity, and there's a stove you can cook on.'

'Oh, right,' I nodded. Was this a good thing or not? Judging by Mr Hakota's tone, it was probably a good thing.

'We'd like you to stay here throughout the day,' he said. Very hesitantly I nodded, then immediately wondered if I'd regret doing so. 'Essentially, we just need someone to be here. But we thought doing nothing might actually be a strain, so we've given you an easy task to complete at the desk.' He picked up a cardboard box from the back seat of his buggy, unwound the wire that was looped around the clasp lock and carried the box inside. I followed after him into the hut to find a smallish space, into which you could have fit three tatami mats, but probably not four, complete with a small desk. There were windows on three sides, and the door had a clear glass panel, so there was a view in all four directions.

'These are tickets for the Scandinavia Exhibition that'll be opening at the museum here in two months' time. The company that was supposed to be perforating them has done a runner, so we're asking you to do it instead.'

Mr Hakota took out a stack of tickets from the box and placed it on the desk. 'You'll be using these,' he said, handing me a rotary cutter with a blade like a cogwheel, a stainless steel ruler and an A4 cutting mat.

'When you get bored of doing that, we'd like you to explore the area on foot. If you find anything, you can note it down on the map.' Saying this, he took out a square of tightly folded paper from the breast pocket of his boiler suit and spread it out on the desk. As maps went, it was on the sketchy side – in fact, most of it was blank. The markings that immediately jumped out at me were the Gifts of the Forest office and the path leading to this hut, as well as a few illustrations of trees dotted here and there. There was something with a pointed roof which I assumed to be this hut, and a little further along from that, another drawing that caught my eye: what looked like an item of clothing labelled 'Away kit, rain jacket (yellow)'. Even further in was a note reading 'Isaguirre towel (in tatters)' alongside a picture of what I could only assume was a towel.

'Erm …'

'Yes?'

Mr Hakota opened his eyes wide and looked at me receptively, which made it somehow harder to come out with what I wanted to say, but knowing I had to move the situation on somehow, I pointed in turn at the rain jacket and the towel.

'What are these, exactly?'

'Ah, those. Yes, they're landmarks.'

'A rain jacket and a ragged towel?'

'Yes, they somehow got caught up in the branches of the trees. Nobody's sure where they came from.' Mr Hakota went on, unfazed. Hold up a moment, I thought, did that not strike you as slightly creepy? For items of clothing to be found inside the park, and nobody to have any idea where they came from? The path ended with this hut, after all.

I recognised the name from the local evening news: Koldobika Isaguirre was a player for Cangrejo Ōbayashi, who came from San Sebastián in the Basque Country. A devoted Catholic, he'd developed an interest in Japan after learning about Francis Xavier, a fellow Basque who had come over here as a missionary back in the sixteenth century – and Isaguirre had then ended up tracing the missionary's footsteps. He was a petite, fleet-footed forward, the news had said. I didn't know much about football, but something about his unusual name in combination with his distinctive appearance – his big dark eyes, exceedingly thick eyebrows and very pale skin – had left quite an impression on me. Come to think of it, the news item I'd seen had featured shots taken in this very park, claiming that this was one of Isaguirre's favourite spots and that he often visited. They had related the story of an incident when Isaguirre had got lost in the park and stayed on past closing time, eventually being rescued by a member of the museum staff. More than anything, I remembered his childlike grin, which looked like the smile of someone unburdened by any pangs of conscience.

Subsequently, I'd seen online that when Cangrejo Ōbayashi were relegated, Isaguirre hadn't renewed his contract, but had instead returned to Spain, citing family reasons. In the comments at the bottom of the news piece, people had exchanged all kinds of opinions and speculations: 'I can't believe he'd just do a runner as soon as his team was down,' and 'He's just as much to blame for this mess as anyone else,' and 'I think Isaguirre really did his best for the team,' and 'Don't you guys care that his father's really sick?' Six months later, Isaguirre had returned to Japan, recontracted with Cangrejo Ōbayashi, and was still playing for them to this day. Last week I'd seen on the news that Cangrejo Ōbayashi were to be promoted again.

'Are you not tempted to try returning them to their owners?' I said to Mr Hakota now, abandoning the 'this is obviously creepy' tack and attempting to bring him around with a more peaceable approach.

'They're both in tatters, though! If they were in a slightly better condition, I might think about it,' said Mr Hakota, scratching his head. Surely it wasn't a question of their condition, I made to say, then thought again.

'How did they come to be caught on trees so deep inside the forest?'

'I guess they were carried by the wind?' he suggested. 'I mean, when Cangrejo were relegated last year, there were all kinds of things flying around the park. Not just towels, either, but bits of kit and men's underpants and everything.'

'What did you do with it all?'

'Anything in a decent state we saved. For a while, we ran a special lost property office by the entrance gates for anyone who dropped by to collect their items. Everything that hadn't been claimed at the end, we handed over to the museum, and they're continuing to return things to people still. Especially now that Cangrejo are being promoted again – we're seeing a surge in people wanting their lost items back.'

'Don't you think the owners of this towel and rain jacket might want them back too?'

'Oh, but they really are in *shreds*!' he said, screwing up his face in distaste and shaking his head. 'They're in such a bad state you have wonder what on earth could have happened to them. It's like they've passed through a mile-long stretch of bushes, or been repeatedly trampled on or something.'

Both of those hypotheses were profoundly disturbing, I noted internally – but, in any case, it was clear that for Mr Hakota, the towel's and the rain jacket's state of disrepair marked them out as things that didn't merit being returned.

'Anyway, leaving Isaguirre aside, when you've time then fill in the map. If you can, try and get out for an hour in the morning and an hour after lunch. If you see something noteworthy, mark it down on the map and let us know. Oh, and you should have these,' he said, handing over a compass and a walkie-talkie. 'I recommend taking the compass with you whenever you leave the hut. And there's no phone signal out here, so if anything happens you can use the walkie-talkie to contact us.'

'What sort of thing are you thinking of?'

'Oh, anything! If you feel like you're coming down with a cold, or you spot an animal you don't recognise.' Mr Hakota sounded so laid-back that I guessed he really meant what he said and it was okay to contact him about anything, but thinking of how the silence had allegedly sent my predecessor loopy, I imagined it wouldn't do to be in touch just for an idle chat.

'Is it okay to use it if I get lost?'

'Of course. Although there are signs dotted around, so you're unlikely to.'

And yet he averted his eyes as he said this, clasping his hands behind him, jiggling around and generally acting in the sort of suspicious way that cast his previous statement in doubt. So people do get lost here, I noted internally. The idea made me reel, slightly.

'If you're worried, you can use these.' From his bumbag, Mr Hakota pulled out a bunch of the small white plastic markers used for sticking in flower beds, and handed them to me. 'You can mark your way with these when you're map-making. We've loads, so if you run out, then let me know.'

'Okay,' I said, accepting the white markers and resolving to use them like crazy. I didn't want to get lost. Not here, not this late into autumn.

'As for lunch, today either me or Mr Nojima or Miss Kudō will bring you a bento box. From tomorrow, we'd like you to bring your own.'

'Sure.'

'As long as you're careful not to set fire to anything, you're welcome to boil the kettle, and otherwise use the place as you see fit. The door can't be locked from the inside, and we only seal it from the outside with wire, so if you're worried, then take your valuables with you when you go out. If you ever feel unsafe by yourself, then be in touch via the walkie-talkie.'

Looking around him he said, 'I think that's about all there is to say.'

'If you think of anything else, let me know on the walkie-talkie,' I said.

'Right you are!' he said. As he left the hut, I noticed him putting his hands to the small of his back, as if to protect it.

'I have troubles with my back too,' I said.

At this Mr Hakota turned to look at me, screwing up his face and shaking his head. 'I'm fed up with it, honestly,' he said. Stepping into his buggy, he went on, as if to himself, 'I used to be able to walk around this park. Go wherever I wanted to go.' Then, snapping out of it, 'Well, if anything happens then be in touch. At five, drive back down the path to the office.' With that, his buggy pulled away.

When he was out of sight, I moved over to the desk in the hut and took out a stack of the tickets he'd left. Their simple design, with just the words 'SCANDINAVIA EXHIBITION' printed in Gothic font on paper of a standard thickness, announced quite clearly that the museum had no intentions of spending much money on such things as tickets. And yet, the Ōbayashi Daishinrin Park Museum was a rather stately looking building, which attracted not only local visitors, and those on school trips, but those from other prefectures as well. I imagined it must be their philosophy not to get too caught up in extraneous details like ticket design and printing and what have you, and that they'd rather go straight in for the kill with the strength of their exhibition content.

I sat down on the chair and placed three Scandinavia Exhibition tickets in a pile on the cutting mat. After lining up the rotary cutter against the ruler, which I held along the dotted line printed on the paper, I rolled its perforating blade across the ticket. It was, just as promised, a very easy job. The line on the first three tickets came out a little bit warped, but by my next go I'd nailed the art of cutting in a straight line. And so, surrounded on all sides by trees and only trees, I sat there quietly perforating tickets. The task required no brainpower whatsoever. In fact, it was nigh on meditative. I'd only been doing this job for several hours, and while I felt it was overly rash to be thinking such thoughts, I couldn't help feeling I was well suited to it. Why on earth had my predecessor walked away from a peaceful, easy position like this?

I was aware it was something of a bad habit of mine to feel, after a very short time on a job, that I had grasped its essence, but when the bento box that Miss Kudō delivered at midday was genuinely delicious, I couldn't shake off the exhilarated sensation rising up inside me. The bento was one that they sold in the park shop, and all of its elements – tofu burger, salt-and-pepper flavoured breadfruit crisps, a salad of kale, quinoa and nuts, and slices of persimmon for dessert – had reportedly been harvested from the park. Miss Kudō explained that one of the issues brought up consistently at annual policy meetings was a sense of frustration with the falling rates of self-sustainability in Japan, and so the park made a concerted effort to grow edible plants. All the elements to the bento were great, but I was particularly partial to the breadfruit crisps, and I resolved to buy some at the shop to eat at home.

When Miss Kudō had gone, and I'd finished my bento, I allowed myself to zone out for a while. So silent were the surroundings, all I could hear were the birds, and the sound of the leaves rustling in the wind. I folded my hands behind my head and closed my eyes. I felt peaceful. As I sat there, I thought about all the jobs Mrs Masakado had found me. I'd made my way through four already. None of them had been particularly awful, but it hadn't been the most settled of times.

I wasn't holding out any particularly high expectations for this job, but I did hope it would serve as a foothold in locating something better afterwards. The low hourly rate meant my thoughts automatically moved to what lay next on the horizon. Although, it struck me now, I could always wait until they were recruiting for permanent-contract employees, and reapply.

Partly thanks to my full stomach, I began to feel quite drowsy sitting there with my eyes closed, and so, summoning my resolve, I stretched and got up from my chair, promptly giving myself a head rush.

To clear the haze that had descended over me, I picked up the map, compass, walkie-talkie and markers that Mr Hakota had given me, and left the hut, fastening the door behind me with the wire. There was no path extending from the back of the hut, only uninterrupted forestland, carpeted in fallen leaves. The terrain wasn't in a bad condition, and it seemed I would have no problems walking in the trainers I was wearing. As far as I could tell, all the trees were of the same type, and the only thing that seemed like it would serve as a landmark was the hut from which I'd emerged.

I went around to the back of the hut, stuck a white plastic marker into the ground, and moved off. I planted another every twenty paces or so, continually turning around to check that the markers were visible, and that they led back to the hut. So doing, I made my way further into the forest, but nothing worthy of marking on the map presented itself. The only thing of note was how the leaves on the trees were all turning red and yellow at their own pace and rhythm, and looked very beautiful. Also, there were lots of chestnut burrs strewn about on the ground, and persimmons growing on the trees. Feeling rather excited by the thought that maybe a day would come when I could take some chestnuts home with me to eat, I picked up a burr. Thinking it strangely light, I turned it over, only to find it split in two, its insides empty. I picked up a few others and checked them as well, but they too were split in half and devoid of chestnuts. All the burrs in the area, it seemed, were empty.

Were the birds eating the nuts or what? I wondered, making a note in the corner of the map: 'Lots of chestnut burrs on floor but none have any chestnuts inside.' I supposed that I couldn't rule out the fact that there were park visitors who made it this far in. It was a park, after all; it figured that people would feel comfortable walking without a path to guide them.

I stuck a marker in the middle of the chestnut patch, ready to forge ahead when I spotted a piece of yellow cloth caught up in the branches of a tall tree. I opened up Mr Hakota's map again. Could this be the legendary 'Away kit, rain jacket (yellow)'?

Standing there, I squinted up at the piece of yellow cloth. The sleeves had green lines running their length. I'd never seen a single Cangrejo game – in fact, I never watched football at all – but I imagined the players wore this kit, green stripes on a yellow background, when on enemy turf.

I heard a rustling from far away, drawing closer. It was the sound of the wind passing through the trees, oddly leisurely in its encroach. Feeling an unbearable chill on my neck and my legs, on which I wore only a pair of chinos, I looked up at the rain jacket on the tree. It fluttered jubilantly in the wind like the flag of a ship.

Since sampling them in my bento box on the first day, I'd begun to buy breadfruit crisps from the gift shop beside the park gates to take home with me almost every day. It'd become a ritual of mine to open a packet after dinner and eat them in front of the TV. I found their subtle flavour suited my taste buds curiously well. My mother asked to try them, so I let her, but her only comment was, 'What on earth are these?'

It seemed that not everybody found them as delicious as I did.

For the time being, my sole concern was that these packets of breadfruit crisps I was so enamoured by cost 280 yen for a 50-gram bag, making them considerably more expensive than a standard packet of crisps. As far as the easy job in the small hut in the big forest went, things were going smoothly, although the job was so lacking in complications it was probably impossible for it to go any other way.

Mr Hakota, Mr Nojima and Miss Kudō were all good sorts, although my only contact with them was the ten seconds when I said good morning to them at the headquarters, so I couldn't rule out the possibility that they were actually bad sorts just pretending to be good. In any case, they provided me with more markers when I asked for them, and they didn't complain that I was making slow progress with perforating the Scandinavia Exhibition tickets. Mr Hakota would ask if everything was okay, to which I'd reply, 'Yesterday I made it as far as the Koldobika Isaguirre towel, and it was still there,' and he'd nod, and that would be the end of that. I told him about the empty chestnut shells, and was told it was probably animals that carried them off.

And so, my worrying mind settled for its fodder on the price of the breadfruit crisps I was eating on a daily basis. All day long, as I perforated the tickets, I thought about how I could try and get the unit price down to 200 yen, or at the very least, 230 yen. I tried entering the search term 'breadfruit crisps' into a mail-order portal site, and I even attempted to find the fresh fruit, thinking that deep-frying them myself might work out cheaper, but neither search yielded a single hit.

First thing the next morning, I mentioned to Mr Hakota that I was looking to buy some breadfruit, and asked if they sold them anywhere in the park.

'Ahh, you can just take home the ones growing here,' he said casually.

'What? Is it okay for employees to do that?' I was genuinely surprised.

'Yes, within reason it's fine,' he said, repeating, 'within reason.'

'You mean like one or two?' I pressed him.

He nodded, and said, 'Yes, that'd be fine.'

And so, looking between the pamphlet and the map that I'd received on the first day, I decided to go out straight after lunch on a breadfruit-harvesting mission. According to Mr Hakota, if I headed north-east from the back of the hut, I would find the sign that read 'Breadfruit Patch', and all I needed to do, then, was walk in the direction it pointed. So I set out valiantly in a north-easterly direction, laying markers as I went, and found the sign soon enough: a brown wooden number, with an arrow and the words 'Breadfruit Patch, 300m straight ahead' painted in white. The sign also featured an illustration of a breadfruit, its pimpled skin recreated in strangely realistic detail. Was it Mr Hakota who'd painted it, or Mr Nojima? Or Miss Kudō?

Three hundred metres was super close, I'd thought when I saw the sign, and yet, however far I walked, I could see no indication of any breadfruit. I looked about me voraciously, expecting to see a breadfruit tree at any moment, but the only trees in sight were chestnuts and persimmons. Not that these were bad in and of themselves, but what I really wanted to encounter was a breadfruit tree, and I felt my facial expression growing

more and more embittered. The fact that, in my unwill-
ingness to get lost, I'd been laying down plenty of
markers meant that at least I was assured of finding my
way back, which I supposed was a kind of silver lining,
but even when I got down to my last marker, there was
still no sign of any breadfruit-tree patch.

I decided to beat a gracious retreat. I couldn't run
the risk of getting lost just to get my claws on some
free breadfruit. Maybe I would have done if I'd been
younger, but I was now at an age where I was supposedly in possession of a mature faculty of judgement.
Instead, I decided to tell Mr Hakota about the matter,
and resolved to leave the markers in the ground rather
than pull them out. To make up for the breadfruit I
hadn't managed to find, I took six persimmons back
with me, but I still couldn't get the breadfruit out of my
head. Back in the hut, I peeled a persimmon and ate it. It
wasn't desperately delicious, but it wasn't offensive. One
was plenty, though – I had no need for the other five.

The following day when I went into work, Mr
Hakota enquired about the success of my mission.

'Well, actually,' I said, 'I followed the sign, but I
couldn't find the patch.'

'I wonder why?' he said, cocking his head and looking puzzled.

'The sign said 300 metres ahead, but I kept walking
and walking and I couldn't find it. I just kept going
further and further into the forest. I took some persimmons back with me instead.'

'How many?'

'Three,' I lied. I was aware that six was on the cusp of being not 'within reason', but maybe my disappointment at not finding any breadfruit had been sizeable enough to necessitate taking that many.

'Did you eat them?'

'I ate one.'

'I'm not so keen on persimmons myself. Every year my wife says she's going to dry some, then never does it. Though that's by the by.' He opened up the map and traced the location of the signpost with his finger, saying, 'Let's see … Right … Okay, I'll pop over after lunch today and check. This morning I've got to make some holes in the wire fencing.'

'Make holes, rather than repair them?' His pronouncement seemed unusual so I decided to quiz him on it, unrelated as it was to the signpost issue. Mr Hakota screwed up his face and nodded. 'This is off the record,' he began, 'but we actually create escape holes for people who don't manage to make it out before closing time.'

'Wow.'

'The best thing for them to do in that situation is make their way to the museum and get help from someone still working there, but some people set off walking in the wrong direction and just keep going. At some point, they'll reach the outskirts of the park. It's part of my job to make enough holes in the external fencing so they can get out.'

'Gosh, there's so much going on in this park!'

'Well, that's what happens with a place this vast.' Mr Hakota shrugged his shoulders as if to say, honestly, what can you do! But there was a familiarity to his tone which reminded me of a parent grumbling about their child. This guy really did like this park, I thought.

Mr Hakota had said he'd be along in the afternoon, so in the morning I did my usual ticket-perforating duties and walked around. At lunchtime, I was eating onigiri and drinking instant miso soup that I'd bought at my local convenience store, when a message came through from Mr Hakota on the walkie-talkie.

'What is it?' I asked.

'We've got a lost person. It seems like they're in your area, over.'

'What kind of person?'

'A middle-aged woman in a red anorak. Apparently she went missing when she was gathering chestnuts with her companion, over.'

'Okay. Should I try and look for her?'

'Yes, please. According to her companion, the last time they saw her she was near something yellow in a tree, which I think must be the Cangrejo rain jacket, over.'

Aha, I thought, secretly impressed that the creepy tattered garment was actually fulfilling its purported role as a landmark.

'Okay, I'll make my way as quick as I can towards the rain jacket, over.'

'Thank you!' With that, Mr Hakota's voice cut off.

I pushed what remained of my onigiri inside my mouth, ate up the bits from my miso soup, then went around to the back of the hut and got into the buggy. The markers that led to the rain jacket – which I'd stuck in the ground on my first day – were still there. Since starting this job, I'd had the feeling that using the buggy would carry me too far afield, so I'd been moving around mostly by foot, but of late I'd got a bit more used to driving the buggy as far as set landmarks.

I found the woman in the red anorak soon enough.

'Hello there!' I called out.

'Ah, you've come at just the right time,' she said, her eyes glinting. 'My friend's got lost.'

It seemed that the woman had no conception of herself as being lost. When I told her that it was in fact her friend who'd asked us to come out and look for her, she slumped her shoulders and said, 'Oh, how embarrassing! I'm so sorry for putting you out.'

'Not at all!' I shook my head, and beckoned her into the back of the buggy.

'I read on the website that there's lots of chestnuts to be gathered around here.'

'Oh yes?'

'And it's true that there are lots of the shells scattered on the ground, but they're all empty.'

This woman has the exact same suspicions as me, I thought, but tried to not show it, saying instead, 'Yes, they think the animals eat them.'

'Really? Are the animals around here dextrous enough to break the shells in half and take out the chestnuts inside?'

I couldn't help but agree with her scepticism. In a bid to smooth things over I told her that they sold chestnuts in the shop, all the while musing on what she'd said. A monkey might be able to crack one if it could use stone tools and so on, I thought, but it seemed doubtful that the squirrels who lived here could take hold of chestnut burrs and pull them apart with their bare paws.

When I took the woman back to the Gifts of the Forest office, her companion thanked me profusely. I shook my head, saying, 'Oh no, it was nothing,' but as she took her leave, she gave me a pack of burdock teabags. She'd apparently bought them in the souvenir section of the office while waiting for her friend to be rescued. I shot glances at Miss Kudō and Mr Nojima who were standing nearby, wordlessly asking if it was okay to take the teabags, but when both of them nodded as if to say, I guess so?, I thanked the woman as politely as I could and accepted the gift.

I returned to the hut in the buggy and was just parking up when I caught sight of Mr Hakota walking towards me from the trees. It seemed as though while I'd been finding the lost woman and returning her to the office, Mr Hakota had been to check out the signpost.

'You'd not skimped on the markers so I found my way soon enough, but the signpost was no darned good!'

'What do you mean by "no darned good", exactly?'

'Well, it was pointing in the totally wrong direction! There's no chance of getting to the breadfruit patch that way.'

'Is that so?'

'I imagine it must be one of the visitors, playing pranks. Terrible! I pulled it out and stuck it back, pointing in the right direction, but it was flipping heavy, and my back isn't half sore now.'

Mr Hakota folded his arms into a mock sulk. I was just thinking that I could hardly let him go straight back to the office after that ordeal when I remembered the burdock tea I'd received.

'Can I offer you a cup of tea before you go back?'

'Oh, are you sure?' He looked up at me.

'The friend of the lost woman bought it at the souvenir shop and gave it to me as a thank you.'

'Oh, the burdock! That's really good, that is.'

From the breadfruit that we were allowed to take home, to what would appear to be a redirection of tea supplies, it seemed as though the park took a relaxed attitude to employees sampling their wares. I put water in the kettle and moved it over to the ring to light it when I noticed that the hob was strangely warm. I had boiled water earlier today to make my instant miso, so maybe it wasn't that bizarre. I went back to turning on the gas, but found that it was still bothering me, so I set the kettle down in the sink instead.

It must have been at least an hour ago that I'd made the miso soup. I checked the display on the walkie-talkie in my pocket to find it was now half one, which made it ninety minutes since my lunch at noon. Would the hob have retained that much heat from boiling the kettle once? I turned around to mention it to Mr Hakota, but when I saw him sat at the desk with his head resting in his hands and his eyes closed, looking genuinely tired, I thought better of it. I returned the kettle to the hob and turned on the gas.

Maybe it was just one of those things. Maybe this hob was particularly slow to cool down. Without thinking, I shook my head slowly.

In time, I made my way through the box of tickets that I'd been perforating since my first day on the job. When I informed Mr Hakota, he instructed me to take the finished tickets along to the museum and pick up a fresh lot, so straight after lunch I loaded the box into the buggy and set out.

When I told the woman at reception what I'd come for, she led me to the museum office and introduced me to the PR department. Mr Hamanaka, the man in charge, asked if I'd mind taking another one. He retreated into the storeroom at the back and emerged wheeling a trolley with a cardboard box on it. It was

a weekday lunchtime, and the museum was practically deserted. In the entrance lobby was the skeleton
of a giant ground sloth that the museum had been
gifted by Uruguay, a life-sized recreation of a sabre-
toothed tiger, a stuffed wandering albatross with its
wings spread and a model of the Ōbayashi hominin
who'd been dug up in the park. The hominin, who
was staring off into the distance with a gaze that
seemed somehow sorrowful, looked decidedly warm
in his cape made of the skin of a bear or some other
animal.

I stopped pushing the trolley and was staring up at
the wandering albatross, impressed by its size, when I
heard a hesitant voice at my back say, 'Um, excuse me?'

I turned around to see a woman of about my age
or slightly older. I rifled through my recent memories
for a moment when we might have met, but remained
none the wiser as to who she was.

'Are you the person working in the hut in the Gifts
of the Forest section?'

I nodded, but having no clue as to how she'd be able
to tell such a thing, I asked, 'How did you know?'

'Your jacket,' the woman said. 'I was doing that
same job until a few weeks ago. I've just come in today
to pick up my separation notice.'

'Oh,' I nodded, as everything fell into place. It
figured that my predecessor would be able to work out
who I was.

'Is it going okay?'

'Yes, thanks,' I nodded again. The woman was thin and pale-skinned, and her face had a slightly neurotic cast to it, but I could see no trace there of the abject distress I'd imagined when Mr Hakota had spoken about her taking a funny turn. She just looked like the kind of person you had to handle with caution.

Our interchange could well have finished there, but the woman went on hesitantly.

'Erm ...'

'Yes?'

She seemed to want the conversation to continue, but was struggling for words, so I relaxed my shoulders, inclined my head, generally adopting a posture that indicated I was waiting patiently. The woman shook her head, glanced at the wandering albatross then, as if finally summoning up the resolve, looked straight at me and said, 'Have you noticed anything strange?'

It wasn't that I hadn't noticed anything strange, but only of a chestnut-burrs-split-in-two-without-any-chestnuts-inside kind, and I imagined that wasn't what she was getting at, so I repeated the words back to her. 'Anything ... strange?'

The woman frowned. 'Like, things moving about in the hut?'

'No, I haven't.'

'That happened, to me. I would always leave my compact mirror facing down on the desk, but when I came back from walking around outside it would be lying there face up, and the wire would've been wound around the lock in a different direction. Things like that.'

My compact mirror stays stuffed away inside my work rucksack I thought, but I decided not to tell her that. I'd never even considered in which direction the wire was wound, but up until this point, there hadn't been anything that made me feel uncomfortable. Although the hob thing from yesterday did bother me a little.

'Now you mention it, I went out for about an hour after using the hob, and when I came back it was still warm. That was a bit … I dunno.'

'I never used the hob, so … ' The woman looked down. What a waste, I wanted to say. Surely that was one of the best things about working in that hut? But I kept my mouth shut, thinking that since she'd never work there again, there wasn't much point in making her feel regretful.

In any case, the woman went on to tell me, weird things happened at a weekly rate, and even when she spoke to Mr Hakota about them, he'd just say, 'Let's keep an eye on it,' and never actually do anything. I wasn't sure how I felt about her criticising my boss to me when I was still working with him, but I listened and nodded.

'It was freaking me out so much that I stopped being able to sleep, and so I ended up going to see a psychiatrist who told me I had to give up working here. I love forests, and this park, so I wanted to carry on.'

'Right ... '

There was a lull in the conversation for a moment, so I asked whether she'd found another job, and she told me she was now working in the warehouse of a relatively major company. I knew that talking to her for just a few minutes probably didn't put me in a great place to judge, but the fact that she'd been re-employed so soon after leaving seemed to say that she wasn't an out-and-out weirdo, or too neurotic to hold down a job.

'I think it might be a ghost,' she said now with a pained expression. She turned around and glanced at the Ōbayashi hominin, trembling as if in terror, then faced me again.

'Sorry?'

I felt like I couldn't let it go. I knew that this was exactly the sort of remark I should have let pass, but instead I asked her to repeat herself. She snuck another look at the hominin, quivered, and then stared at me as if she was searching for a way to answer.

'I feel like it might have been a ghost.'

'What sort of—'

'The ghost of the Ōbayashi hominin. I mean, you know they found the bones, right?' she said, then squeezed her eyes shut and quivered again. This was clearly a serious situation and she seemed genuinely petrified, but there was a part of me that wanted to burst out laughing. I stepped away from the wandering albatross and stared up at the Ōbayashi hominin. His long straggly mane and beard, the dense hair covering his entire body, and the stone implement held in his hand, all tallied with the vague image I had of an early human – but his eyes were strangely sad and seemed to testify to all the hardships he'd endured. Even if, hypothetically speaking, it had been a ghost who'd been playing tricks on this woman, would this guy's ghost really do such a thing? But then I remembered: no, this was just an artist's impression. The real Ōbayashi hominin may well have been barbarity itself, embodying his eat-or-be-eaten lifestyle so completely that it left him no time for sadness, or any emotion of the sort.

'Please be careful!' the woman said, reaching out a hand to touch the sleeve of my orange jacket, then practically running off in the direction of the office. Looking between her retreating form and the Ōbayashi hominin, I tilted my head pensively. She wasn't odd enough to make me feel like I needed to exercise caution or anything, but I did sense that she struggled to separate fantasy from reality – that she was slightly too neurotic for her own good. You came across such people from time to time. Mostly they weren't bad sorts, but as you talked with them, they would gradually reveal their particular hang-ups and fixations. They didn't seek to impose those fixations on others, and in that sense they were harmless, but they themselves were incapable of stepping free of their anxiety, even if provided with material that should by rights have assuaged it.

I pushed the trolley over to the buggy and loaded the box into the back. It was as heavy as one might imagine a box packed full of tickets to be, and I felt simple gratitude washing over me at having a task to fill my time. Returning the trolley to the office, I crossed paths again with the woman who was my predecessor as she emerged from the office, a thermos flask printed with the words 'Ōbayashi Daishinrin Park Museum' clutched to her chest. Seeing me, she went striding off quickly and somewhat awkwardly in the direction of the museum hall. It was never particularly comfortable to encounter a stranger to whom you'd said too much, and I imagined this was especially true when you'd just divulged your fear of ghosts.

Driving the buggy back towards the hut, I mulled over what the woman had been saying. The chestnut shells came to mind, and then there was the hob incident – but then again, the hob was directly in front of a window, so it wasn't unthinkable that the sun could have heated it.

I got back to the hut and, remembering what the woman had said about the wire and the items on her desk, checked both carefully – but nothing struck me as out of order. If the woman hadn't been mistaken and her mirror really had been turned over and the door wire wound the wrong way, maybe the intruder had been a park visitor. Maybe they'd ventured this far inside the park – just as the chestnut-gathering woman in the red anorak had done the other day – entered the hut out of curiosity, touched the mirror, and then wound the wire in the other direction before leaving. Such an interpretation could allow both that my predecessor wasn't a liar, and that her ghost hypothesis was mistaken.

'Hello, hello, can you hear me, over?'

Mr Hakota's voice burst from the walkie-talkie, so I answered, 'I can hear you, over.'

It turned out there was another lost person. The last few days, they'd been cropping up at a rate of at least one per day. That was how huge a park, how vast a forest it was. I looked around the hut with a beady eye, imprinting the scene in my head so that I'd be able to tell if something had changed when I returned. The fact that I didn't go as far as taking a picture on my phone suggested that, maybe somewhere in my mind, I wanted to leave open the possibility of not totally losing it if something weird really did happen.

When the fluid level in my bottle of noodle sauce concentrate went down without my using it, though, I couldn't resist anxiety's clutches any longer.

On days when I was pushed for time on my way to work and couldn't stop to buy a bento, I would bring in a pack of frozen noodles from home, which I'd boil along with the noodle sauce, then I'd sprinkle some freeze-dried spring onion on top. Until yesterday I'd had enough concentrate for three servings, but now there were only two left in the bottle. The bottle had a gauge down its side, showing how much sauce you needed for one serving, how much for two and so on, which made it very easy to tell how much had disappeared.

Deciding to check my other ingredients, I brought out the selection of rice vinegar, chilli oil, herb salt and other condiments I kept in the hut, and arranged them in a line on my desk so I could scrutinise them – but I couldn't see anything out of the ordinary. I decided the noodle sauce must have been some kind of a mistake on my part, but I couldn't silence yesterday's self who was violently objecting in my head: *No, I'm telling you, there really were three servings left!*

In a bid to calm myself down, I returned to my perforating job, but I found myself incapable of concentrating, and the lines I created came out crooked, the perforations not deep enough. There I sat in my small hut in the big forest, my face contorted with rage. At least there was nobody else around to see me.

I tried to tell myself that it was okay, that at least the breadfruit crisps were now on offer. It seemed that aside from my compulsive purchasing, they weren't selling all that well and were now half price. I'd buy three packets whenever I spotted them in the shop, which meant the urgent necessity of locating the park's breadfruit supply had evaporated. And yet, now I'd acclimatised to the map-making job and was steadily filling in the blank areas, marking down that this patch was chestnut trees and those were persimmons and so forth, I'd started wanting to fill in the location of the breadfruit patch. So it was that, of late, I'd found myself in the strange predicament of searching for the breadfruit trees not for my own gain, but for purely professional motives – and still, I hadn't managed to find them. I could get to the sign without a problem, but when I followed in the direction it pointed, all I discovered were the usual culprits: chestnuts and persimmons. At first, I'd spoken of the issue to Mr Hakota, but his solution was always to offer to go and check the sign – and I felt I couldn't in good faith have him do that, given his back problems. After a while, I stopped reporting my failure to find the breadfruit.

Between my morning and my afternoon excursions, the map-creation task was gradually coming together. In addition to the Cangrejo Ōbayashi rain jacket and towel, I also found a tattered flag and scarf in the trees. Given the sheer prevalence of abandoned clothing in this park, I figured there was a good chance of encountering garments that had nothing to do with Cangrejo, but for some reason everything I found was Cangrejo merchandise. The scarf, too, had Koldobika Isaguirre's name on it. Why was it only Isaguirre items I was finding? Was there that much of a trend for Isaguirre merch? I put this question to a few people, both those who knew a lot about football and those who didn't, and received answers like, 'Well, he's skilful, tenacious, and a real team player, all of which means he's generally well liked, but there are other, better-looking players who are far more popular than him,' and 'Isaguirre? Is that his real name?' The sound of the Basque name, apparently, struck many as very unusual.

The area where I found the flag was full of almond trees, while the scarf was in a fig patch. I took photos of the flag and Isaguirre scarf and showed them to Mr Hakota, and he seemed impressed, saying, 'Wow, I've never seen those.'

'Shall I hand them in to the museum?' I asked.

'Ahh, no, don't worry,' he said, glancing at the photos again.

'But with so many fruit trees, there must be lots of gardeners coming to take care of them. Won't these get in their way?'

'We do have people in, but they're from a subcontractor, so they're not here that much. Most of the trees growing in the park can do without much help. And besides, the gardeners' instructions are to leave all personal property as is.'

It seemed as though the fate of the Cangrejo clothes scattered about the park was to be determined one-sidedly by Mr Hakota.

'They're good landmarks, after all. If you're sitting there in the hut thinking you fancy a fig, you know where to go.'

'That's true.' I didn't know if I should be agreeing or not, but it seemed as though, to Mr Hakota's mind, what he was saying was the most natural thing in the world, and so I nodded.

'We've got two kinds of figs growing here: those that bear fruit in June or July, and those that bear fruit from August through to October.'

Saying this, Mr Hakota puffed out his chest a little. It struck me for the umpteenth time how much he loved this park.

At the station on my way home, I came across another Isaguirre-related artefact. It was in a bimonthly free publication called *ODP Magazine*, issued by the company that ran the monorail servicing the park. It mostly featured articles about restaurants positioned along the route or events happening in the park museum, but from time to time there would be an article about Cangrejo Ōbayashi. On the cover of the latest edition, across the lower reaches of a photograph of a persimmon tree, danced the large headline: 'Koldobika Isaguirre: Long Interview (Part I)'. I looked at the editing credits, and was met with the unexpected revelation that the magazine was edited by Hanabatake Ads. That was Ms Eriguchi's company.

In the end, though, I didn't read the magazine on my train ride home. It had been a very busy day – in addition to three lost people, I'd also had to deal with a man who'd buried his wedding ring on impulse in the forest, then decided he wanted it back and asked me to search for it with him. Frankly, I was exhausted. When I told Mr Hakota about the ring man, he calmly informed me that they got quite a few such people. Unable to bring themselves to throw away or sell their rings, not even fully convinced they were ready to get rid of them, they would come to bury them in the forest.

Nodding along as the man told me that he'd figured he'd probably need his wife when he got old, I had thought back fondly to the days when I'd sat in my hut, quietly perforating tickets.

The following day, I took the magazine with me into the hut and read the Isaguirre interview thoroughly in the peace and quiet of the forest. As expected, the credit for the article read Mari Eriguchi. Had her name always been Mari, I asked myself, as I remembered her and the air of serenity she'd always exuded.

The interview contained nothing particularly sensational. I learned the following things: for the six months after relegation, Isaguirre had been in the Basque Country, giving a bone marrow transplant to his father; while over there, unsigned and caring for his father, he had enlisted the cooperation of a local team and begun training hard with them, which also helped him take his mind off things from time to time; and his interests weren't limited to Francis Xavier but extended also to ancient times, and he was most keen on meeting the Ōbayashi hominin. In the photos featured, his big, innocent grin remained unaltered, but it seemed to me that since his father's illness, his face had taken on a slightly more adult air.

When I'd read to the end of the interview, I decided to head out on a walk. In the forest, I bumped into the wedding ring man again, who informed me he'd decided to bury the ring after all, and I ended up listening to him for half an hour. The man had allegedly returned home and told his wife he'd figured out he'd need her in his old age, and she'd silently shaken her head then walked out of the house. 'Don't you think she could have at least said something?' the man asked, a question I struggled to answer. He was, after all, a park visitor, which meant I had to show him the politeness one was supposed to offer customers. I swallowed back what I was tempted to say, which was: *In that case, may I suggest you either sell it or dispose of it some other way?* And instead, handed him one of my markers, saying 'Why don't you use this, in case you feel like digging it up again?'

'Well, if you're sure,' he replied, writing 'RING' on the plastic and then sticking it in the ground where he'd done his burying.

As I stood there talking to the man and suppressing my yawns, I was seized by a strong desire to read the

Isaguirre interview again. I knew it was cheesy, but the fact that he'd donated bone marrow to his father had really impressed me.

I gave the ring man a ride on my buggy, dropped him off at the office on the edge of the forest and returned to my hut. There, I encountered the next strange occurrence after the disappearing noodle sauce: the magazine I'd left on the desk was now open at the Isaguirre page. I definitely closed it before I left, and the hut's windows were shut, so there was no way that the wind could have riffled the pages.

I dashed out of the door and looked around. In retrospect, that strikes me as a dangerous thing to have done, but at the time, even as a cold sweat formed down my back, under my arms and on the backs of my legs, I couldn't help myself. Hearing the rustling sound of footfalls moving further and further away, I squinted in the direction from where they were coming. I thought I could see a human figure in a big coat running off between the persimmon trees. I felt the blood drain from my body.

'Oh, there's a deer you sometimes see in the Gifts of the Forest section,' said Mr Hakota when I spoke to him about the magazine and the retreating figure. 'It's scared of people, so it scarpers like anything.'

'Nobody told me about any deer,' I said, lashing out slightly. 'It doesn't mention it in the pamphlet you gave me.'

Mr Hakota waved a hand as if to say, calm down, and spoke in a hushed voice.

'What I'm about to say is off the record,' he began.

There's a lot of off-record stuff with you, I came very close to saying – but I clamped my mouth shut.

'There was an incident a while back where a baby deer escaped from the zoo, and it still hasn't been found. They say that it came over this way and just started living here.'

'Are you not going to try and catch it?'

'I feel sorry for the poor thing,' Mr Hakota said and shrugged his shoulders, apparently feeling not an iota of guilt. 'We've not received any reports of it doing any harm, and we decided in a meeting that there's really no need to tie ourselves up in knots about it. I think we need to prioritise the deer's quality of life,' he said. Hmm, I thought. Quality of life was all very well, but this park was really pretty lax about a lot of things. I was gradually moving away from conceiving of this place as a regular park, the kind that was thoroughly patrolled and managed, and coming to think of it more along the lines of the Serengeti or Yosemite National Park, where the borderline between controlled public space and nature left to its own devices was somewhat blurred.

'But what do you make of the pages being turned?'

'I'd guess that was the wind's doing.'

'The windows were closed.'

'Ah, but the breeze gets in through the cracks in that hut. I worked there for a time myself, so I know.'

Mr Hakota clasped his arms to his chest, staging a pantomime of how freezing it was. 'Besides, you said it was the *ODP Magazine* you were reading, right? That's very flimsy. Don't get me wrong, I'm a big fan and I never miss an issue, but sometimes at home, it goes flying when I so much as close the sliding screen doors.'

There was something I found overwhelming about this little speech of Mr Hakota's, crammed full as it was of convincing detail. He wasn't a bad person – in fact he was on the good side of personhood. He loved his job, and he loved this park. But he was rather force-ful in his opinions.

'Don't worry about it! You're safe!' he said, giving me a thumbs up.

'Okay,' I began, as the tip of my thumb started to lift itself up in imitation, but at the last second I decided that I wasn't that much of a pushover and instead added, 'If anything else happens, I'll be in touch on the walkie-talkie.'

'Any time!' he said, thumping his lower back.

What an odd interaction, I reflected. The words we were saying sounded so even-tempered, but I had felt a fierce tension running between us. It was clear to me: I had lost to Mr Hakota.

Stricken by a sense of defeat resembling a chill to the skin, I buttoned up my orange jacket and went out to the front of the building, only to find Miss Kudō running after me.

'The markers we ordered came really quickly, so I'll give them to you now,' she said, handing me a card-board box with the name of a gardening mail-order site printed on it. Once I'd grown used to walking around in the forest, it had started bothering me that the markers I stuck in the ground were bright white, so I'd suggested that maybe we should go for a more natural shade that would be less noticeable to park visitors, if such a thing existed. 'They've got wooden ones,' Mr Hakota had said, 'so let's use those.' When it came to things like that, he showed real consideration, which made it hard to form a holistic assessment of his personality.

'The deer thing is funny, isn't it!' Miss Kudō said as she loaded the box of markers onto the buggy's back seat.

'This place is very lenient about a lot of things,' I said. Miss Kudō raised her shoulders and giggled with evident glee.

'The people in this section don't get on well with the zoo section. Although don't mention that to anyone,' she said, raising a finger to her lips. 'Mr Hakota and the zoo director joined the company one year apart, and it seems the zoo director treated Mr Hakota rather badly when he was just starting out.'

'How many years ago are we talking about?'

'I'd guess about forty?'

So Mr Hakota was dragging around a grudge from forty years ago? The thought stunned me, although it wasn't like I couldn't understand it.

'He's on really good terms with the museum director though,' Miss Kudō added. The museum director had joined a year after Mr Hakota. Apparently, Mr Hakota had told her all of this quite openly at her first end-of-year party.

Standing there outside the office, I told Miss Kudō about my experiences with the magazine and the retreating shadow. About the shadow, she said that it was hard to say anything for sure – if it wasn't a deer, it could have been just a park visitor – but she admitted that the magazine thing was weird.

'I mean, if it had been the wind, surely the whole thing would have been blown off the desk? And even if the wind did blow so as riffle the pages, it's odd that it would land on the Isaguirre page. I mean, that's near the end, right?'

'Right,' I said. When I remarked that she was clearly well versed on the magazine, she turned to me, her eyes sparkling slightly.

'I'm a Cangrejo supporter, so I read every issue. They often have interviews with the players. I became a fan when I saw the centre-half – his name's Jun Yurioka – in an U-21s match, scoring a header with blood dripping down his face. That was in the autumn of my last year of high school. After that I decided to apply for a job here.'

'Oh!'

I could see how a park right next to the stadium would be a desirable place to work for a Cangrejo supporter. I'd never heard of or seen Jun Yurioka but Miss Kudō explained that he was big and bald, and although his technique wasn't up to much, he had plenty of fight in him.

'I'm always hoping that the players will come into the park while I'm here, but that hasn't happened yet. I suppose they don't have the time to be visiting a huge park like this. And if anybody does get lost, it'll probably be Isaguirre again,' she said, then added, strangely flustered, 'Not to say that I'd mind Isaguirre, of course! I really like him too. I'd just have preferred Yurioka, that's all.'

I nodded as she offered this justification, though I hadn't reproached her in any way for what she'd said. She evidently felt some need to counterbalance her disappointment that it had been Isaguirre who'd got lost in the park, and not Yurioka.

'I don't know anything about football, but I read that Isaguirre went back to Spain after Cangrejo were relegated, and then came back six months later and recontracted when the team was being promoted,' I said to Miss Kudō, recalling that both the towel and the scarf on the trees were Isaguirre's. I wasn't at all sure that this had anything to do with the ghost of the Ōbayashi hominin that my predecessor feared so intensely, or the fleeing form I'd seen, but the fact that the magazine had been left open on the Isaguirre page was niggling at me. Yet how Isaguirre, with that butter-wouldn't-melt smile of his, could possibly have been connected with such events was totally beyond me.

'Yes, that's right. For the first month or so he couldn't recover his previous form and was on the bench a lot, but then there was this match where he came on in the seventy-ninth minute and took this amazing free kick. That seemed to shift something for him, and after that he returned to the starting line-up and scored – how many goals was it? I feel like he was the fourth-highest scorer in the whole league. And he only played half a season, so it was really something.'

'What do the supporters make of him?'

'People like him. He still does a lot of aimless running about, and even though he's coming up to thirty, he's still very hit-and-miss, and far from the finished article. He never gives up, though, no matter how badly things are going. As for him going back to Spain when they got relegated, I think a lot of people misunderstood the situation. I tell everyone it was because his dad was sick, but I know someone who's stopped coming to the stadium because of it. He used to adore Isaguirre, and now he's not even a Cangrejo supporter any more, and I can't get in touch with him.'

'Isaguirre's clearly a very influential player, then?'

'I think this guy's the only one who took things that far.'

'What kind of person is he?' I asked.

'A guy in his mid-thirties who lives in the next town along,' she explained. 'He was having a really hard time at work. I don't know what his actual role was, but he kept using the words "emotional labour". He said that when he saw Isaguirre in front of the goal, pulling everything he possibly could out of the bag to try and score, it'd cheer him up.'

Isaguirre had returned to Spain without any explanation, she told me, and the real reason for his return wasn't publicised immediately. It was only after he'd been gone for some time that reports began to appear over here about his father, so many people simply didn't know. For the three months until the truth got out, the supporters treated him like a traitor.

Miss Kudō clearly could have gone on forever about Cangrejo, but apparently sensing that she'd talked too much, she glanced at her watch, apologised for going on for so long, then hurried back towards the office as if she'd just returned to earth.

'I'd like to hear more about Cangrejo some time,' I said, and she nodded and waved.

Back at the hut, I made a note of a few things Miss Kudō had told me about Isaguirre. On one piece of paper I wrote down things about Isaguirre himself – about his father and his playing style – and on another I noted things that had a less obvious link – like the person who'd given up supporting the club, and the towel and the scarf in the trees, and finding the magazine open on the Isaguirre page. I set the sheets of paper down on the desk and let my eyes roam over them for a while, but although it was clear that there were plenty of bits of information about Isaguirre floating around, I couldn't see what it was that connected the dots. Maybe there was no connection between all these facts, or maybe they were connected in a way that signified nothing whatsoever.

I turned to look outside the window, but the forest was as tranquil as ever. Nothing moved. I felt rather dissatisfied but then, as I suddenly realised, I always felt like that of late. With that thought, I opened up the box of wooden markers that Miss Kudō had given me.

And with that, I was once again visited by a period of total uneventfulness, just as things had been when I'd first started out on the job. My condiments weren't tampered with, there was no sign of any objects in the hut moving, I didn't notice any change in the direction of the wire wound around the door and I didn't spy anybody fleeing the hut. I started to think that all the strange occurrences of the previous days must have been a product of my overactive imagination.

The task of replacing the white markers I'd stuck into the ground with the more discreet wooden ones was going well. From a distance, the markers I'd been using initially looked like little white stains on the brown forest floor, and when I swapped them over for the new wooden ones, the forest scene looked more natural than it had before. Yes, the wooden ones were harder to spot than the white ones, but I'd got to the point where I could move about in the vicinity of the hut without needing to follow the trails, so that wasn't much of a problem for me.

Everything was very peaceful, but that didn't alter the fact that I still hadn't found the breadfruit-tree patch. By now I'd more or less given up hope, and it wasn't taking up as much of my mental energy as it had at one point, but what I did find slightly troubling was the little heap of earth at the base of the sign, which seemed to suggest it had been pulled up and its direction changed. Still, I told myself, it could well date back to the time when Mr Hakota had changed the direction of the sign, and taken the decision not to report it.

I was making good progress with both the ticket-perforating and the map-creation, to the point where I'd filled in about four-fifths of the map I'd been given on my first day. I now had a firm grasp of where the chestnuts, persimmons, almonds and figs were in the Gifts of the Forest section, so that if my mother asked me to bring her back some figs, I could go out, pick a couple and find my way back to the hut without getting lost. I'd apparently made better progress with the map than Mr Hakota had envisaged, because when I showed him he would say things like, 'What a relief, to have someone capable working for us for a change!' Each time he said something like this I'd try and brush it off as flattery, but when I saw him calling the other two over and pointing out specifically what he liked about the map as I'd done it, I couldn't avoid the sense that he was being genuine. As he quizzed me for more detailed accounts of what lay in this or that spot, it occurred to me that maybe he'd wanted to fill in the map himself, but his bad back had prevented him. I knew that I was stupid for being so forgiving, but I'd now got to the point that even when Mr Hakota wouldn't listen to me for love nor money, I would make allowances for him, reminding myself that he really loved this job and he had problems with his health, so I shouldn't be too hard on him. I liked this job quite a lot, but I ended up feeling unconditional respect for anybody who engaged in their work with such passion. I was all too aware that such a trait was destined to cause me a lot of hardship in my working life.

Sometime around this point I began thinking about my old job – my first job. I didn't believe for a second I could ever do anything like that specific role again, but I could sense the unshakeable feeling I'd had when I'd quit – of not wanting to work ever again and especially not in that field – gradually receding from my body.

It was also about this time that I found something else in the forest that definitely shouldn't have been there. For once, it wasn't related to Cangrejo Ōbayashi – it was a book. The book was entitled *Deconstructing and Rebuilding Care*, and it was wedged face down in the branch of a tree, at a height I could just about reach if I jumped. By some bizarre coincidence, it was a book I'd heard of though I'd not read it. A colleague at my former workplace had recommended it to me. It had come out the year before last and hadn't sold at all well, but had made waves among those in my former field of work. As far as I could see from looking up at it from below, the book was well thumbed, and there were lots of little paper tags poking out of it. I looked around to see if there was anything of note in the vicinity, and saw a big patch of wild shiitake growing at the base of a nearby tree. I pulled out the map, and in the blank space, wrote 'Tree with shiitake (book)'.

I could have turned back at that point, but I had the distinct sense that I might be able to tie things together in some more coherent way from this position, and so, standing there, stock-still in the middle of the forest, I began to think. Up until now, all the items I'd found had been Cangrejo Ōbayashi merchandise and this was not, but there was no doubting that it still counted as an object left behind in the forest. I opened up my map and checked each of the locations featuring Cangrejo merchandise, finally looking at the note I'd just written, when suddenly it came to me that all the found objects had something edible growing nearby.

Holding the almost-complete map in my hands, I stared at the only remaining blank section to the north-east of the hut. What could be there, I wondered, in this territory I'd not yet set foot in? Was there any significance to the way all the Cangrejo merchandise was Isaguirre-related, or to the *Deconstructing and Rebuilding Care* book, or to the fact that all of these things were located near some kind of foodstuff? And was there any connection between all of this and the shadowy figure in the forest, be it the ghost of the Ōbayashi hominin, or the deer that had escaped from the zoo?

I removed my water bottle from my rucksack, took a sip of burdock tea and then walked in the direction of the last uncharted place on the map. My body felt like it was moving of its own accord. A rational part of me tried several times to keep myself in check, saying that I should take Mr Hakota, or at least Miss Kudō or Mr Nojima along with me, but the desire to find out what was there superseded it.

Fastidiously poking markers into the ground by my feet, I moved away from the tree with the book stuck in its branches, finally emerging into a clearing-like space where no trees grew. This section, apparently the north-east corner of the park, contained a huge rock-mountain the height of two human adults, and near it, a tree stump covered in moss and a big sculpture-type object surrounded by a stone circle. I smelled a faint burning smell. Approaching, I could see what seemed to be the remains of a bonfire with a pile of charred branches in the centre of the stone circle.

It wasn't immediately apparent from a distance, but now I was up close I could make out a gap in the rocks. There seemed to be some kind of cave inside the mountain. I stepped in, finding a space that would accommodate a 36-year-old, medium-built woman like myself, so long as I minded my head. The cave was about the size of four tatami mats, or a little smaller. Light filtered in through the cracks in the rocks overhead, illuminating the blue vinyl sheet spread out at my feet. In the spots where the rays of light struck the ground directly, I could see an ocean of chestnut shells. Now I thought about it, I realised that the damp air carried at its base the nostalgic, sweet aroma of roasted chestnuts. Shifting my gaze, my eyes lighted on a pile of the breadfruit whose pictures I'd seen several times online.

I stopped myself from trembling long enough to step outside, so nervous I felt like I could retch at any moment. Staring down at the remains of the bonfire, I noticed a small shiitake lying off to one side. From the back of my tongue rose up the powerful premonition of a taste: grilled shiitake with noodle sauce.

This was no hominin, I thought. There was a modern-day person living here. The modern-day person was using Cangrejo merchandise to mark out the places where food grew, gathering up chestnuts and breadfruit, grilling shiitake and eating them. It was hard to explain what the constituent parts were of the emotion that ran through me: there was awe there, and anger, and something that felt like those two things combined in equal parts, and then an oh-come-off-it! sort of feeling, a strange sense of respect, some astonishment, not to mention an awareness that I was still terrified and wanted fuck all to do with this affair. All of these combined to form a dirty-green-coloured feeling that filled my chest as I walked away from the rock.

What the hell was going on?

For no reason, I kicked at the ground hard, saying to myself that today, I would pick as many shiitake as I could carry and take them home. I saw a shadowy figure cut between the trees and move off into the distance. This time, I got a clear enough sighting to know what it was without any trace of a doubt. It was a deer.

– I've heard you had offers from clubs in Spain and other Japanese clubs, so why did you choose to return to Cangrejo Ōbayashi?

Isaguirre: I still had things left to do here, you know? My weakness as a player was one of the reasons we were relegated. Because of the unfortunate timing of my father getting sick, I had to return to Spain when that happened, but all the time I was over there, I was thinking that I wanted to get back to Cangrejo as quickly as possible.

– Do you ever think about returning to Spain permanently?

Isaguirre: Yes, for sure, sometimes I do think that I want to go back home and settle down. But for the moment, I want to see other parts of the world. I love my family and my friends so much, and if I spend too much time with them, I start to feel like I never want to leave again. But I think all that can wait for a little bit.

– Well, your choice to return paid off, and you became the force driving the team's promotion.

Isaguirre: It's so nice of you to say that, but really it was the whole team's doing. I was only there for the last few months, anyway. I'm just happy to have contributed in some way.

– Here at Ōbayashi Daishinrin Park, we're all delighted you're back.

Isaguirre: Thank you so much! I really like the park and the museum, and the model of the Ōbayashi hominin is so well done, I could look at it forever. I visited recently with Yurioka's family, actually, to gather fruit. Yurioka himself had a cold and couldn't come, unfortunately. Anyway, while we were there, his mother got lost in the forest! I've got lost there before, too. I was reminded of how enormous it is. I hear you've got an exhibition about Scandinavia coming up? I'm really looking forward to it. I'll come and check it out.

(*ODP Magazine*, Vol. 20)

After work, I got on the Albatross and went to visit Ms Eriguchi at Hanabatake Ads, offerings of shiitake and persimmons in hand. She was working away in her usual unruffled manner.

'You've had a haircut,' she said, 'I didn't recognise you at first.' But she made us tea and brought out some biscuits, introducing me to her colleagues and generally seeming more pleased than I'd imagined she might be at my visit. Working together at the bus company, I'd felt like a constant source of bother to her, so I was really happy to be treated like someone with whom she was on friendly terms.

After a bit of small talk, I broached the topic of the Isaguirre interview.

'Oh, he was a lovely guy,' she answered immediately. 'Are you a fan?'

'No, I'm not personally, but I know someone who adores him, and was over the moon about your interview.'

Strictly speaking, I didn't actually *know* the person who adored Isaguirre, but it appeared that he had enjoyed the interview I'd taken in with me to the hut.

'Oh, really? If they like him that much then I can print you out some of the shots we didn't use in the interview, if you keep it to yourself.'

She brought over the digital camera sitting at the side of her desk and showed me the screen. There were about ten photos of Isaguirre in a flannel shirt and a sleeveless hoody, and ten in his orange Cangrejo kit. The flannel-shirt shots hadn't been used in the first part of the interview. I asked when they'd been taken, and Ms Eriguchi answered that both sets of photos had been taken at the time of the interview.

'We're using the plain clothes ones in the second part, which will come out the day after tomorrow. He gets his clothes from Zara, apparently.'

'Because it's a Spanish brand?'

'He said that having Zara makes it easier to be in Japan.'

Looking at the pictures of Isaguirre in his own clothes, it struck me that although the photograph offer was of course a generous one, it wasn't exactly what was required.

'Um, I don't suppose I could have a copy of the magazine with the second part of the interview?'

'Yes, of course! I've got samples.'

Saying that, Ms Eriguchi fetched two copies of the magazine from the back room.

'Are you sure? Just one is fine.'

'No, take them both,' she told me. 'It's quite a good issue. There's a special feature on buses, so we covered the Albatross.' Saying this, she showed me a page showcasing various restaurants from the areas on the Albatross route. 'What with the Far East Flamenco Centre starting up a proper cafe and everything.'

Someone from the Far East Flamenco Centre had stepped in to interpret for the Isaguirre interview, Ms Eriguchi told me. The pictures of the churros and Basque-inspired roll cake had been artfully shot, and looked very appetising.

'Why don't we try it out some time?' I suggested.

'Sure!' said Ms Eriguchi. We swapped phone numbers and email addresses before I left.

The following day, I headed to the hut in the buggy. Using the wooden markers and the map that was by now almost complete, I found my way to the *Deconstructing and Rebuilding Care* tree and put the copy of *ODP Magazine* that Ms Eriguchi had given me at its base, placing a rock on top of it to make sure the wind wouldn't blow it away. After repositioning it to make sure that the words 'Koldobika Isaguirre: Long Interview (Part II)' were plainly, yet not too obviously, visible, I scurried away.

That day, I worked very hard on tasks that were entirely extracurricular. By rights you should be sitting in your hut busily perforating tickets, I told myself as I set out in the direction of the museum.

I deliberated hard about whether to tell Mr Hakota that someone was living in the forest, but decided to wait for the moment until I felt more certain. Part of my reasoning for this was that if news got out and a big fuss was made, the person might move to a different part of the park, which would mean a lot more work for me. I pondered the question of whether my judgement in this was a rational one or if I was getting overinvested again, but I couldn't arrive at an answer. When I reflected that the person was using my noodle sauce and reading the Isaguirre article, it did seem to me that they were preparing to return to the world of civilisation.

At the museum, I asked Ms Tsuchiya on reception if the person in charge of the lost property section was in. 'That's me,' she said, so I asked if there had been any enquiries about missing persons in the park.

'You mean people who've got lost?' she asked dubiously.

'Yes, I suppose so,' I said with a nod.

'We do receive police reports about people from time to time, but I think they've all been found. This park might be large, but it's not that large,' she said, bringing over a file. 'We had lots last year with the relegation, but they've all gone home now. People fell into a state of shock and got lost, you see. Cangrejo were fighting until the bitter end, and apparently a lot of people thought they'd pull through. In the end they were relegated on goal difference. It was December and fiercely cold, but we had people falling asleep in the park, dead drunk and stark naked, who had to be taken to hospital.' Ms Tsuchiya shook her head at this recollection, then opened up the file and looked for the page relevant to my query.

'Here we are. But this isn't limited to what's going on inside this park. I imagine this indicates missing people from this region as a whole.'

Mrs Tsuchiya spun the file around so I could see it. There were four missing person notices, of the kind you often saw stuck up around town. I was aware that I was straying into territory for which I needed a certain amount of mental preparation to enter, but although all the cases were grave enough – someone had run off with the monthly earnings of all their employees, another had been tricked by their fiancée, yet another person had asked their ex-husband for more child support and then run away – I was relieved to see that there was nothing truly awful there.

Thinking that the forest dweller could feasibly be any of these people, I flipped over the final page to find a missing persons report filed by a healthcare facility for the elderly in the next town along. Yoshiaki Sugai was thirty-six, and had been working at said facility as a medical social worker. A note said he was unmarried and had no contact with his parents who lived in Okinawa, which was why the report had been filed so late. For a few days before he went missing, something had clearly been the matter, and he had been losing his temper and suddenly bursting into tears at his workplace. His job was that of team leader, a position carrying some responsibility, and he was forever listening to the worries of those in the facility and their families, not to mention those of his colleagues. It seemed he was under a lot of stress, but for confidentiality reasons, he couldn't divulge the details of his worries to anyone else. As of March last year, he had stopped going into work and didn't seem to have been home either, so his workplace had filed a missing persons report.

The image of *Deconstructing and Rebuilding Care* lodged in the tree branches flashed through my mind. Then I remembered what Miss Kudō had said about the person who had stopped supporting Cangrejo after Isaguirre had gone back to Spain, and that he was no longer contactable. Was that not because he'd given up supporting Cangrejo, but rather because he'd given up life in society?

I made a note of the facility's phone number and thanked Mrs Tsuchiya, then left the museum and walked around to the back of the building. Looking at the plot of land where they'd uncovered the Ōbayashi hominin, and the construction site for the museum extension whose progress had been stalled since the fossil's discovery, I put in a call to the facility where Mr Yoshiaki Sugai had worked.

The woman who came on the line introduced herself as Ms Adachi. In a tremulous voice she asked me if there had been any further news about Mr Sugai. No, I said, I didn't know anything definite, but we had had some leads.

'We may have found some of his possessions. Could I ask you to confirm whether any of these sound familiar?'

'Of course.'

'There's a book called *Deconstructing and Rebuilding Care*.'

'Yes, I know that book. I borrowed it from him about a year and half ago,' Ms Adachi said.

'And then there's some Cangrejo Ōbayashi gear – a Koldobika Isaguirre towel and a rain jacket.'

'Isagi? Isn't that a kind of fish?' she asked. It seemed she knew even less about football than I did. But after thinking a bit she said, 'Now you mention it, though, I did hear him talk about sitting behind the goal each week. But even so, if someone at work had something they wanted to talk about, he'd always pick up his phone, and he'd sometimes stop by the facility on his way home.'

Then I heard her say to someone in the background, 'Huh, what's that about Isaguirre, Mr Ashida? You went with him to watch? And Hirokawa did too?' Then she came back on and said, 'My colleague would like to have a word with you, so I'll pass her over.' There was a muffled sound as she handed the receiver over.

'Hello, this is Hirokawa. We really hope you find Mr Sugai.'

'He's a great guy,' I then heard a man's voice say in the background. That must have been Mr Ashida.

'He's still alive, isn't he? He's going to be okay, right?' Ms Hirokawa's voice was subdued but you could sense her anxiety. I immediately understood how well loved Mr Sugai had been at work. I also saw how, thanks to his colleagues' valiant efforts, his disappearance had been smoothed over so it appeared as just a slight ripple on the surface – but underneath that surface it was causing profound panic. The realisation made me fume. What are you playing at, Sugai? I berated him internally, despite never having met the guy.

'We still haven't got any definite proof, but what you've told me has been really helpful,' I said. The receiver was passed back to Ms Adachi, and she went on, 'If you find him, please tell him that we understand he must have a lot on his mind, but we're eagerly awaiting his return.'

'Okay,' I said, 'I'll be in touch if we have any more news,' and hung up.

The Ōbayashi hominin was in fact a human living inside a rocky cave deep in the forest, whose name was Yoshiaki Sugai – however circumspectly I assessed the situation, I now felt at least seventy per cent certain of that.

Emerging from behind the museum, I began to wonder whether Sugai had fallen for my trap yet, so I headed to the spot where I'd left the *ODP Magazine* Ms Eriguchi had given me. Arriving at the tree, I saw the magazine was gone. 'That's right, mister,' I said, nodding. 'I'm going to stick even more wooden markers along the route to your place, so I can make my way there at any time. Also, I'm guessing that you've probably figured this out already, but I should tell you officially that Koldobika Isaguirre has returned and Cangrejo have been safely promoted. And not only that, but Isaguirre came to this very forest with Yurioka's family!'

You've got a cheek telling him that, I heckled my own inner monologue as I went about fortifying the path with my markers, *when you don't even know what Jun Yurioka looks like.*

Right before I reached the clearing where Sugai lived, I turned back and made my way to the hut.

If I was Yoshiaki Sugai, I asked myself as I walked back along the marker trail, would I choose to go on living in the park, or would I be feeling it was time to emerge? Autumn – the harvest season – was coming to an end, and the park would only grow colder from now on. Yet having taken unannounced absence for this long, Sugai would probably be out of a job, so there was that to consider. Also, he was single, and had broken off contact with his family in Okinawa.

Maybe he was just sick and tired of everything, and there was nothing to tether him to the real world. The only things he'd lost out on by going AWOL were the trust of society and a roof to live under. I remembered what Miss Kudō had said about the man who I imagined was Mr Sugai: he was having a tough time at work, and kept using the words 'emotional labour'. The kind of pressure he had experienced at work was not difficult for me to imagine, yet the high esteem he was held in by his colleagues suggested that it wasn't just sadness he'd got from his work, but joy, also. I could understand how that made it all the more unbearable. He had carried on with his job, trying to balance those two things, but Cangrejo's relegation and Isaguirre's subsequent return to Spain had been the final straw, breaking the delicate balance he'd been maintaining until then.

I shook my head at my knowing tone, even if it was purely internal. All of this was no more than projection, based on my own experiences. It wasn't even certain that the Ōbayashi hominin who lived in the forest eating shiitake, chestnuts and breadfruit was in fact Sugai. Maybe there really was a ghost, and it had a penchant for shiitake.

Thinking solely about how I might persuade the man in the forest to leave, I followed the trail of wooden markers back to the hut and immediately sensed something awry. Through the window, I could faintly see a black figure moving about inside. I swallowed hard and looked around me. After standing beside the hob for a little while, the figure lowered its head and then stood up again. I was pretty sure it was opening the fridge. Damn you, I thought. It was stealing my noodle soup again. And what was with this stealing one portion at a time? Did it have a vessel to transport ingredients in? A moment's thought, however, revealed how easy it would have been to rummage through the park litter bins and find some suitable container. I stood there, barely breathing as I stared at the hut, my thoughts inexplicably fixated on my noodle soup, then I reached a hand for the walkie-talkie in my jacket pocket. In a whisper, I spoke to Mr Hakota.

'There's an intruder in the hut. Can you come out here? Over.'

'Huh? Can you say that again?' Perhaps Mr Hakota was a bit hard of hearing, or maybe my voice was too quiet and wavering. In the end I had to repeat the same thing about three times.

'An intruder! Oh, heavens!' he said when he finally understood. 'I'll come right away.' I heard a bustling noise on the other end as he broke into a run.

'Quietly, quietly,' I remonstrated into the walkie-talkie, not knowing if he was listening or not.

Each time there was a movement inside the hut, I would silently entreat the figure: *Don't come out, I'm begging you, not until Mr Hakota arrives.* And perhaps my prayers had an effect, for after a little while I saw Mr Hakota come flying along the forest path in his buggy. The path was really very winding, consisting of the kind of S-curves I'd been made to practise in driving school, one after another, but the driving technique Mr Hakota unleashed that day was truly something to behold. With such skills, I thought, he could have conquered not only S-curves, but R- and G- and M-curves too.

'What's happened to the intruder?' he called out in a loud voice the moment he saw me, so I put my finger to my lips, bared my teeth and shook my head.

'Oh, right, yes,' Mr Hakota said, covering his mouth with a hand.

'He's in the hut. Going through my stuff.'

'What! That's unforgivable!'

Having left all my credit cards and everything at home, my purse only contained about 2,000 yen in cash, and the only other possessions of mine inside the hut were the rotary cutter, cutting mat and my seasonings, so the situation hardly merited an 'unforgivable!'-grade reaction, but Mr Hakota obliged me with one nonetheless.

'*Please* be quiet,' I urged Mr Hakota again.

'Oh, he's coming out!'

The intruder appeared at the door to the hut. It was my first clear sighting of him, and with his long straggly hair and beard, and the black coat that stretched down to his ankles, he definitely did give off a similar vibe to the Ōbayashi hominin for which my predecessor had mistaken him. But on closer inspection, there was no doubt that he wasn't some kind of primitive man. Sewn on the breast of his coat was a big Cangrejo Ōbayashi logo.

'Hey!'

Mr Hakota's buggy shot towards the hut with fearsome speed. 'Mr Hakota, you're going to run him over!' I almost shouted, as I too lunged forward. But the buggy drew to a sudden halt, and Mr Hakota jumped out yelling, 'It's over! Give it up!' When I came out from behind his buggy and moved around to the front to see what was going on, the intruder was curled up on the ground, cradling his head in his hands.

'You're Mr Sugai, aren't you?' At my words, the intruder dipped his head twice. 'Your colleagues at the elderly care facility filed a missing persons report for you.'

The Ōbayashi hominin, or rather, Yoshiaki Sugai lifted his face slowly and shook his head.

'I'm so sorry for all the trouble I've caused.' He gave us a long, deep bow. I was all ready to say, 'No, no, no trouble at all,' but when I looked over at Mr Hakota, I saw he had his arms folded across his chest and his head cocked, apparently astonished at how docile our interloper had proven to be. In Mr Sugai's right hand was one of the paper popcorn containers they sold in the park, and inside it, what looked like one serving of noodle soup concentrate.

Mr Hakota said that he would take Mr Sugai to the office, so I went along with them. I was feeling so exhausted that I didn't feel capable of driving, and I asked Mr Hakota if it was alright to ride with them, saying that I'd walk to the hut the following day.

'That's fine. I'll give you a lift to the hut tomorrow,' he said. And so I got into the back of Mr Hakota's buggy alongside Mr Sugai, and was driven to the office.

With the hood of his long bench coat trailing down his back, Mr Sugai sat staring fixedly down. His beard reached to his chest, but his hairline was receding and his hair was tied at the back, which made him look surprisingly sleek, considering. The Ōbayashi hominin in the museum wore a leather hood-type thing, making it impossible to work out precisely what was going on with his head, but his look wasn't so dissimilar to Mr Sugai's.

Maybe he'd managed to bathe in one of the many streams flowing through the park, because despite supposedly living rough in the forest, he didn't smell too bad. Clenching his papery dry hands on his thighs and stared fixedly down at them, he resembled a religious ascetic, although the Cangrejo logo on his coat, so very clearly of this world, served to counteract that impression.

'I'm thirty-six too,' I blurted out, with no idea why I was confessing something like that at this juncture. Mr Sugai looked at me, tilted his head slightly and said, 'You look younger than that.'

Those were the sole words we exchanged in the back of the buggy.

Inside the office, Mr Nojima came by and informed us that the police were planning to send someone over, but the person in question was tied up with something else right now, so we had been asked to find out as much as we could from the man before they arrived. Mr Sugai seemed to cower at the mention of the police. Miss Kudō brought over some tea that she'd made, circling Mr Sugai two or three times while he sat there at the table before suddenly shouting, 'It's Mr Sugai! My gosh! I didn't recognise you at first with the hair and the beard!'

Mr Sugai looked up at her and said, his eyes widening slightly, 'Yukey?' Miss Kudō's first name was Miyuki, and I guessed she was known as Yukey in the fan community.

'How is Jun? Has he been playing well?'

'I don't know, he seems to have a bit of a short fuse recently. Last week he got a yellow card during injury time, and now he can't play in the final match.'

Miss Kudō seemed like she wanted to carry on talking, but Mr Hakota appeared with some documents in hand and so she disappeared into the kitchen with the now-empty tray, casting several backwards glances behind her on the way.

In the end, I sat in for the interview with Mr Sugai. I did suggest to Mr Hakota that I might be better helping out Mr Nojima and Miss Kudō, but he replied that no, there were parts of the story he didn't really understand, and he'd prefer me to be there. It seemed he struggled with taking notes as he talked, so from a certain point I adopted the role of secretary.

Somewhat falteringly, but without any notable linguistic difficulty, Mr Sugai spoke of how it was that he had come to be living in the Gifts of the Forest section of the park. It was, as suspected, Koldobika Isaguirre's decision to return to Spain, coinciding with the team's relegation that had pushed him over the edge – although it transpired that in fact, he'd managed to stick it out for three months. On relegation day itself, he'd taken ill but had returned straight home and slept, never even setting foot inside the park. But in the time between when the relegation was announced and Cangrejo's first match of the season in the league below, the ever-growing public enmity towards Isaguirre and the general lack of information about the matter, together with his already challenging workload, had all conspired to make Mr Sugai feel that he was slowly reaching the bottom of his psychic energy reserves. He had even taken up studying Spanish in the hope of attaining some information about Isaguirre from the local Spanish newspapers, but all he could glean was that Isaguirre was back in the Basque Country with his parents. In the opening game of the season, Cangrejo suffered a humiliating 4–0 defeat at home. Just two days previous to that, Mr Sugai had finally glimpsed a solution for a difficult case he'd been struggling with. He had been feeling like perhaps things were on the up, but on the way home on the day of the match, he scaled the fence and snuck into the park, and had lived there ever since.

'I think if I'd really been at rock bottom, I'd probably just have become a straightforward recluse,' he said. 'It wasn't that simple, though. My job was really tough, but I'd always manage to get through the challenges it posed. And yet, I had the sense that another thing would always be following close on its heels. As soon as I'd crossed one mountain, another would appear, even higher than the first. I think to a certain extent, I'd accepted that was just the way it was, and I was banking on the fact that Cangrejo would be promoted again to see me through – but then suddenly it looked like they were in an even worse way than I was. And as a fan, of course, there's literally nothing I can do to influence the outcome of the matches. It was just this the whole time—'

Saying this, Mr Sugai held up a hand and swam his fingers through the air in a wave-like motion, before finally lifting them in a high arc and plunging them down.

'I just felt like I didn't understand a thing any more. I didn't know what the hell I was doing, what I was living for.'

'So when you found your way into the park, your thinking was, so long as I'm here I won't have to think about anything other than making it through the day?' said Mr Hakota, repeating back to Mr Sugai his reason

for being in the park, which he'd stated at the beginning of the interview.

'Yes, that's right.'

Mr Hakota scratched his head with his pen and
turned to look at me. I nodded several times and said
quietly, 'I can understand.'

Living inside a forest in a man-made park was not
so difficult, Mr Sugai went on to tell us. He'd made
use of the park toilets. He'd picked up lighters left in
the smoking areas and used them to make fires, cooking mainly in the evening so that the smoke wouldn't
attract attention. When it seemed as though the hut
was empty, and nobody was likely to return for a while,
he'd unfasten the wire and go inside, occasionally using
the stove. Since I'd showed up, the ground had been
peppered with markers, which had made it really easy
for Mr Sugai to find his way there. When the white
ones were replaced by wooden ones, it got a bit trick-
ier, but he soon acclimatised.

To wash, he would use the fountains and streams,
of which there were many, bathing once every day or
two. At first, he rummaged through the leftovers from
the cafes to find food, but after settling down in the
Gifts of the Forest section, he realised that the area
was so named because you could get by on eating the
plants that grew there. He climbed the trees and left
his possessions there to serve as landmarks, walking around during the day and collecting food. The
breadfruit was a very useful plant, and he wanted to

keep it to himself as much as possible, so he frequently changed the direction of the sign. (At this Mr Hakota, who had kept quiet for most of Mr Sugai's account, cut in with irritation in his voice: 'But what about the visitors who come especially for the breadfruit? What are they supposed to do?')

This way of life – where the day was spent procuring food, preparing and eating it in a labour-intensive way, with Stone Age-style tools, and where, when the sun went down, you would curl up and sleep in the rock cave – was an extremely simple one. Indeed, it was apparently not taxing enough to elicit assent to the question that both Mr Hakota and I asked: 'It must have been tough, no?' He also had his wallet with him, he said. There were no ATMs in the park, but his plan was to slip outside and withdraw some cash if he really needed anything. That day hadn't come, although he confided in us with a peculiar earnestness that he'd been thinking he'd probably have to go and buy some proper protective gear now that winter was coming.

'Of late, though, I was trying to get by on things just made within the park. I gave up collecting lighters, and tried using flints instead to create fire, and so on.'

'How long did you intend to keep up that way of life?'

At my question, Mr Sugai lowered his gaze and shook his head slowly. 'I really don't know. Until somebody found me.' He breathed a very deep sigh, then looked at me and Mr Hakota in turn. 'I'm sorry. I'm really and truly sorry. You must have been wishing you could go AWOL yourselves with all the stress.'

Neither of us nodded.

'I was so relieved when I found out that Isaguirre had come back and Cangrejo had been promoted. It made me feel glad to be alive still,' he went on, adding, 'I know that must sound strange.'

'Did you not think about returning when you found out about Isaguirre, though? About leaving the park?' I asked. Mr Sugai raised an eyebrow and seemed to fall into thought before answering.

'I knew that even if I left, I'd have nowhere to go back to. I've no family or partner, I don't speak to any of my relatives and of course I don't have a job any more.'

'If we pretended we'd never found you, and let you return to the forest, would you choose to go?'

It was a presumptuous question, and I had a feeling that Mr Hakota might be angry with me for asking it, but he said nothing, just stared at Mr Sugai, with his arms folded across his chest.

'I might do, but first of all I'd want to say thanks to all my old colleagues, and apologise for having run out and left them in the lurch.' When he finished speaking, Mr Sugai looked down. Nr Nojima called out, 'Mr Hakota, it's a call from the park director,' and Mr Hakota stood up and went over to the phone.

'I got in touch with your former workplace,' I said, and Mr Sugai looked up. 'They asked me to do my best to find you. They said that they understand you must have a lot on your mind, but they're eagerly awaiting your return.'

Mr Sugai closed his eyes for a while. Then he looked down again and seemed to squeeze out the words, 'Did they say that?' He shook his head several times. The only sound was Mr Hakota's voice, ringing out across the office floor: 'Oh, really? Yes, we're almost done with him. Yes, well, he's just a regular homeless person, he says he hasn't stolen anything. No, there's no evidence that he has, no. The police? They should be arriving soon. They said they're leaving it more or less to us. Ah, that's nice of you to say! "Old hand" with the emphasis on the "old", ha ha!' Mr Hakota laughed somewhat ostentatiously, then said goodbye to the museum director. At about the same time as he rested the receiver, a uniformed policeman appeared at the office door. Miss Kudō went over to let him in, saying, 'Oh, hello, we've been expecting you.'

Mr Sugai stood up from his chair and gave a low bow. I walked away, with no real idea of where I should go, so I decided to join Miss Kudō who was preparing more tea.

'He won't be arrested or anything, will he?' Miss Kudō said, staring with concern at the policeman's back as she brewed the burdock tea.

'I don't know,' I said, sipping from the cup that she handed me, 'but I'd guess it's up to Mr Hakota.'

Preparations for the Scandinavia Exhibition were finally complete, and those of us working in the Gifts of the Forest section were invited along to the opening event held for members of the press and affiliated parties. Mr Hakota and Mr Nojima said that they'd go once the exhibition was on and sent me and Miss Kudō in their stead, even though it took place during working hours.

Mr Hakota had been asked by the police if he wanted to file a damage report, but he'd said he wouldn't, since there hadn't been any real damages. After receiving a 'severe warning' from both the police and Mr Hakota in his capacity as representative for the park, Mr Sugai returned home that same day.

You would think that, after enduring an escapade of that sort, most people would be in no hurry to return to the place where it had occurred, but this appeared not to be the case for Mr Sugai, as two days later he showed up at the Gifts of the Forest office. His stated purpose for being there was to clear up the mess he'd left in the forest, but then he kept coming every other day or so, his reasons always slightly different: he wanted to check that he'd cleared up properly, or he'd inconvenienced us so he wanted to offer his services, and so on. I was still working in the hut, so I wasn't privy to the details, but the next thing I knew Mr Sugai was coming in to supply the park with information about how he'd got by in terms of food in the Gifts of the Forest section. Given that the park regarded a drop in the food self-sufficiency rate as one of its concerns, his testimony was of service. As it turned out, the breadfruit were, in fact, very useful.

Miss Kudō told me that Mr Hakota had made it very clear to Mr Sugai that the park wouldn't be paying him, but that didn't seem to bother him in the slightest and he helped out in the office good-naturedly, just like a regular employee. As a fellow Cangrejo supporter, Miss Kudō was concerned about what was going to happen to Mr Sugai now he was out, and so she found his visits reassuring.

'My other football pals want to see him too, and were saying that we should have a welcome back party, but he refuses to come. He says he's not good with that stuff. I mean, I do understand, but still.'

At the opening event, the organisers handed out packets of breadfruit crisps branded with the vague claim 'Now Even More Delicious!', but it seemed as though in this more delicious formulation, nobody apart from me really liked them that much. After eating three of hers, Miss Kudō said to me, 'I've opened these, but do you want them?' and gave me the rest of her bag. I thought the newly added rosemary worked exceedingly well with the breadfruit's plain, simple flavour, but I'd accepted this was a minority opinion.

As it turned out, I found myself in a predicament that prevented me from enjoying the Now Even More Delicious! crisps to my heart's content. A little while back, I'd mentioned to Mr Hakota that I had a runny nose and kept sneezing, and that I couldn't understand it because it didn't seem to be a cold, and he'd suggested that maybe I had hay fever. 'No way,' I'd replied, I'd got to the age of thirty-six and had never once been affected by hay fever. It was then that Mr Hakota told me about the alders: in a section on the other side of the park called the Swaying of the Forest – whose emphasis was on ambience, and which was sometimes used for TV shoots – was a swamp surrounded by alders. He added that park employees would sometimes complain of hay fever symptoms in the middle of winter.

I went to the hospital to be tested, and it transpired that although I was fine with well-known types of pollen like cedar, cypress, rice and ragweed, I had a severe allergy to alder and silver birch pollen. I reported this to Mr Hakota, and he told me that there were lots of silver birches in the Swaying of the Forest section too. Meanwhile, my runny nose and sneezing seemed to get worse by the day. If I was like this now, when the trees still weren't really in bloom, then it scared me to think how bad my symptoms might get as spring drew nearer.

It was the same at the opening of the Scandinavia Exhibition. While the people from the local TV station were having fun draping the hominin in Sámi shawls,

I sneezed so loudly and violently that they had to re-record the section. I also had an unusual sensation in my throat. The doctor had warned me about something called oral allergy syndrome, which was brought on by certain fruits and vegetables. It was a type of allergy whose existence I'd never considered before.

Listening to an announcement about a live performance of yoik, traditional Sámi songs, which would be taking place the Saturday after the exhibition opened on the park's outdoor stage, I pondered whether or not to stay on in this job. In all honesty, since I'd finished perforating the tickets and solved the Mr Sugai mystery, I had more time on my hands than I knew what to do with. It didn't help that it was now winter, and the number of park visitors had dropped off. I guessed having nothing to do was okay, but my sense of anxiety about the pay was mounting. I liked this job, and Mr Hakota said that if I kept it up for a few years, there was the chance of my becoming a permanent-contract employee, but this allergy I'd developed ruled out such a prospect. According to the doctor, being this close to a pollen source as spring arrived was likely to exacerbate my symptoms even more.

In fact, although I had no positive desire to leave the job, I had started to feel like my time had come. Maybe when you experienced four changes of jobs within the course of a year, you started to sense when the moment of transition was approaching.

As the male presenter told the assembled crowd about the stuffed reindeer and moose that would be added to the lobby, an image flashed before my mind of *Deconstructing and Rebuilding Care* wedged in the branches of the tree, and I immediately felt my stomach cramp, my body grow tense. Come to think of it, I now realised, I'd felt a certain tension when I'd first discovered the book. It felt like someone had unexpectedly called me out. 'Look at you,' they'd said, 'frittering your time away in the forest!' When I'd called up Mr Sugai's former workplace, I'd felt myself seizing up in a similar way. Having turned my back on the job that I'd decided to spend the majority of my life doing, unexpected encounters with those who were still in that same profession made me feel not just awkward, but envious as well.

I felt, now, that the time had come for me to return to the line of work I'd been in for over fourteen years after graduating university – to my first occupation. I knew this feeling was purely about what I wanted, and I was under no delusions that I'd be able to find such a job easily again, but at the very least, it seemed time for me to move in that direction.

Now the presenter led on a petite woman dressed in a baggy white outfit, and explained that this was a detailed replica of what Finnish snipers had worn in the Winter War to camouflage themselves in the snow. If visitors wanted, he said, they could have their photos taken wearing the sniper outfit. As the people around me all stirred, oohing and ahhing and making various other noises that left it unclear as to whether or not they really understood what had been said, I heard the sound of someone approaching at a run, and then sensed them drawing to a halt behind me. I turned around to see Mr Sugai standing there. He'd come from his home, so unsurprisingly he looked rather cleaner than when we'd first found him in the park, but he still hadn't shaved or cut his hair. Despite not working here, he was wearing a jacket with ODP embroidered on it, which suited him.

'So now, ladies and gentlemen, it's time to introduce our special guests!' The presenter turned around to address someone standing behind him. 'What do you think, Isaguirre? Would you like to wear this suit?' The interpreter standing next to Isaguirre whispered something in his ear and he laughed heartily, then said in a high-pitched voice, 'Sì, sì!' It was the first time I'd seen Isaguirre in the flesh, and he was shorter than I'd expected, but his eyebrows weren't quite as thick as they were in photos.

'That's right, Koldobika Isaguirre and Jun Yurioka from Cangrejo have come over to join us especially,' the presenter said. In matching orange tracksuits, Isaguirre and Yurioka came forward, each with an arm raised. Next to me, Miss Kudō inhaled, dropped her shoulders, opened her eyes wide and then screamed at top volume, 'JUUUN!!!' The yell seemed decidedly out of place in this setting and yet, when a second cry went up from behind me, this time 'ISAGUIRREEEE!!!', the people standing around seemed to conclude that this was the appropriate way to behave, and calls began to fly out from all around me. Unlike Isaguirre, Yurioka was taller than I'd expected – he must have been at least six-foot-two.

'I was supposed to visit to the park last month, but I caught a cold, so Isaguirre went gathering fruit with my family. They all had great fun.' Yurioka's voice was very deep, and he mumbled in a decidedly morose-sounding way, but his facial expression looked sanguine enough so I guessed that must just have been how he spoke. 'After you visit the exhibition, come and see us at the stadium! We're looking forward to seeing you.' His speech was followed by a round of applause. The interpreter said something to Isaguirre, and he nodded and took the mic from Yurioka. Saying something in Spanish, he pointed to the moose. Then the interpreter translated, 'Congratulations on the opening of the Scandinavia Exhibition. I want to put on the white suit and ride on that reindeer, would that be okay?' Laughter rang out across the audience.

'What do you think?' the interpreter asked the presenter, and he laughed and shook his head. Isaguirre spoke at great speed, then said 'Muchas gracias,' lifted a hand and waved, and gave the mic to the presenter. The interpreter said: 'I'm so happy to be back, please keep supporting Cangrejo Ōbayashi. The hominin is just as great as I remember, thank you very much.'

At this mention of the hominin, I cast a look behind me at Mr Sugai. He was standing stiff as a rod, nodding from time to time, staring intently at Isaguirre and Yurioka as they moved back behind the presenter. As the applause rang out, I let out all the sneezes I'd been holding in while the footballers had been speaking, and felt, as I did so, that I'd reached a decision.

I cut off about a fifth of my Basque-inspired roll cake and moved it onto Ms Eriguchi's plate.

'Okay, then you have some of this,' she said, making to cut off a piece of her blueberry cheesecake, but I shook my head.

'No, no, thank you.'

'Are you sure? You've given me all this!'

'Yes, it's fine. I've got a pollen allergy and if I put raw fruit in my mouth, it might swell up.'

'Oh.' Ms Eriguchi shot me a strange look. I explained that this was one of the symptoms of the alder allergy that had flared up during my time at ODP.

'I didn't know that pollen allergies could affect the inside of your mouth too!' she said, looking almost impressed, and jotted something down in her note-book. It seemed that she was already quite at home in her role of producing the *ODP Magazine*.

'You were at the opening event too, weren't you?' she said. Apparently, she'd been there as a member of the press. The Scandinavia Exhibition had reputedly struggled for visitors at first, but once their PR team began publicising that they'd invited the real Santa Claus from Finland, and were allowing people to take photos with him and the stuffed reindeer, and how they'd also created a pop-up cafe where people could enjoy an afternoon fika – coffee-and-cake break – things had been picking up. As the one who had perforated the tickets, this news made me happy.

'Are you taking the rest of the year off?' Ms Eriguchi asked me, and I nodded. I'd left the park job the previous week. Mr Hakota and the others had vaguely tried to persuade me to stay on, but when I explained my allergy situation and suggested that they employ Mr Sugai in my place, they agreed. They sent me on my way with friendly advice to pay attention to the wind direction as spring drew closer, along with a whole box of breadfruit crisps. Mr Hakota and I may have had the odd difference of opinion, but I still maintained that he and the team were really good sorts.

Mr Sugai took up the job in the hut as my successor, as I suggested. With over six months' experience living in the park, there was no faulting him as a guide, and by all accounts he was a better buggy driver than I was. I'd heard via Miss Kudō that Mr Hakota imagined that if it proved too difficult for Mr Sugai to manage on that kind of hourly wage before he made it onto a permanent contract, he'd probably return to his previous job. Mr Hakota and Mr Sugai travelled home in the same direction, and had been for drinks after work a few times.

'I think it would be good for him to go back,' Mr Hakota had apparently gone on to say. 'The person doing this role before also came to us because something had happened in her previous workplace. If this job makes people realise they can return to their work after all, and they want to, then that's fine by us.'

I went to inform Mrs Masakado that I'd quit, and explained what 'the easy desk job in a hut in a big forest' had been about. 'How fascinating!' she'd said. 'There are so many jobs in this world I still don't know a thing about.' She offered to find me another position, but I said no, I was planning to take the remainder of the year off.

'Is that so?' she said, nodding. 'In that case, if there's anything I think would suit you in our final batch of vacancies this year, I'll pick them out and post them to you.'

Now, speaking about the park job to Ms Eriguchi, I mentioned that I'd felt a bit sorry for my boss, because his bad back prevented him from moving around as he wished to, and Ms Eriguchi told me that her mother also suffered from back problems.

'She had me when she was forty, so she's getting on a bit, although it seems as though it's less the actual work that's the problem and more the commute.'

'Oh, right.'

Adding forty to what I guessed Ms Eriguchi's age to be, I arrived at a figure that was about the age of my own mother. Perhaps in part because she commuted into work by car, my mother didn't really complain about her back – she suffered more with her knees.

'It's quite a way from the station, by the sound of things, and there's a long hill she has to travel up, although it's not that steep. So she's decided to retire at the end of January. She's already over retirement age, so it hardly comes as a surprise.'

'January, right … It's somehow hard to leave a job with the close of the calendar year, isn't it? Although I seemed to manage it … '

'Yes, she was saying she didn't like the idea of disappearing with the start of a new year. Anyway, so here's the thing—' Ms Eriguchi paused to take a sip of tea before continuing. 'My mother's work is looking for someone to take her place, and I was wondering if you'd like me to put you in touch? I remember seeing on your CV that you're a certified social worker, right?'

This unexpected turn in the conversation knocked me for six. I did indeed have my social work certificate. I'd worked as a medical social worker in hospitals and other facilities for fourteen years, and all of that had been detailed on the CV I'd given out to all the companies I'd worked for, including the bus company, but somehow I'd never imagined that Ms Eriguchi would know that – or, even if she had known it at some time, that she would have retained that information all this while.

'When Mr Kazetani filled me in on who was coming to work for us, I remember noting that you worked in the same field as my mother, and it just stuck in my head.'

I nodded, turning my face away a little and sighing. The image of the book stuck in the tree branches flashed through my mind once again, and I recalled the conversation I'd had with Mr Sugai when I had my handover session with him.

'I'm really grateful they're taking me in full knowledge that I ran away from my previous job, but I also feel guilty about it, and a bit scared,' he'd told me. And so I'd confessed. I told him how I'd done the same job as him, and how at some point I'd been unable to take it any more, and had quit – that I'd more or less run away. I told him how after that, I'd flitted between whatever short-term jobs had been offered to me, and how it hadn't been at all bad, but there'd always been the possibility for me that, like Mr Sugai, I'd leave home and stumble into a totally different kind of place, and end up living there instead.

Now, it struck me that this feeling wasn't specific to the profession that Mr Sugai and I shared. Whoever you were, there was a chance that you would end up wanting to run away from a job you had once believed in, that you would stray from the path you were on.

'I think because I'd got so much joy from it, the sense of powerlessness really tortured me, you know?' Mr Sugai said. 'I didn't even need words of thanks, it was enough to see the faces of those people which had been so overtaken by worry break into a smile before they left the building. It was the difficulty of the work which meant we had such a sense of unity, and we had the trust of other sections, but I started to feel so incredibly exhausted I didn't know what to do with myself.

'And then, after all that, the club I supported was relegated. There are pitfalls like that everywhere, lying in wait to trip you up. The more feeling you put into your work or whatever it is you're devoting yourself to, the more of them there are.

'And you know, living by myself in the forest for months, spending all my time either tracking down food or sleeping really wasn't that bad, but there was something missing.'

He had swum his fingers through the air and said, 'Accepting those ups and downs, choosing to take on difficult jobs – that's what life is about. That was the conclusion I came to.' This was clearly a thing of his, to illustrate life's undulations with this wave-like gesture.

'And yet, I still didn't really have the courage to leave, so I'm really glad that you guys found me. I promise to repay the favour in some way,' he'd said. I had no idea whether Mr Sugai would carry on working in the hut, or would end up returning to his previous job, but I guessed it was okay not to know.

Now, I took a long sip from my teacup until there was just a quarter remaining and said to Ms Eriguchi, 'If you tell me the name of your mother's workplace, I'll have a look at the website. Oh, and if you know any of the specific details about the job, will you text them to me?'

'Okay,' she agreed, and told me the name of the hospital. I was playing calm, but I could feel my insides constricting. Really, I wanted to let out an enormous sigh, but I restrained myself.

Ms Eriguchi and I ordered another cup of tea and more cake, and in the end we spent about three and a half hours in the Far East Flamenco Centre cafe. It was a comfortable place to be. Ms Eriguchi said her work had finished the previous day but she'd be tinkering on articles for the next issue during the New Year's holiday. Afterwards we went to eat udon for dinner. Parting ways, we said that we should do this again soon, and wished each other a good new year.

Back at home, my mother informed me that I had post. I looked at the sender on the envelope to discover Mrs Masakado's name. Just as good as her word, she had sent through those jobs from the last batch of the year which she thought might be appropriate for me. I cut open the envelope with scissors, sat on the sofa and removed the contents. Collected together in a clear file were photocopies of several job postings, supplementary papers giving detailed breakdowns of the job contents and information on the kind of people they were looking for, and a handwritten note from Mrs Masakado.

'Well done for all your hard work this year! I'm sending through some new postings, so please take a look,' it read. The name on the uppermost job vacancy was that of Ms Eriguchi's mother's workplace. I sat there looking down at the description, and this time I really did heave a big sigh. Then I swam my fingers through the air, in imitation of Mr Sugai.

The time had come to embrace the ups and downs again. I had no way of knowing what pitfalls might be lying in wait for me, but what I'd discovered by doing five jobs in such a short span of time was this: the same was true of everything. You never knew what was going to happen, whatever you did. You just had to give it your all, and hope for the best. Hope like anything it would turn out alright.

ACKNOWLEDGEMENTS

Kikuko Tsumura would like to thank her mother and her friends.

Polly Barton would like to thank everyone who helped during the translation process, especially Geraint Howells, Motoyuki Shibata, Kimihiro Tomioka and Asa Yoneda, as well as everyone from the translation community at large for their invaluable support at every stage of bringing this book into existence: it truly made a big difference. Huge thanks go to Angelique Tran Van Sang, without whose enthusiasm and general brilliance this translation wouldn't exist, and Saba Ahmed, for her wisest and wonderfullest editorial eyes. Gratitude also to all the lovely people at Bloomsbury. The final thank you goes to Kikuko Tsumura, for bringing this incredible book into the world: it's been an utter joy and a privilege to share part of its journey.

A NOTE ON THE TYPE

The text of this book is set in Bell. Originally cut for John Bell in 1788, this typeface was used in Bell's newspaper, *The Oracle*. It was regarded as the first English Modern typeface. This version was designed by Monotype in 1932.